Censure, politics and criminal justice

Open University Press
New Directions in Criminology series

Series Editor: Colin Sumner, Lecturer in Sociology, Institute of Criminology, and Fellow of Wolfson College, University of Cambridge

Current and forthcoming titles include:

Imperial Policing
Philip Ahire

Lawyers' Work
Maureen Cain and Christine Harrington

Feminist Perspectives in Criminology
Loraine Gelsthorpe and Allison Morris (eds)

The Enemy Without: Policing and Class Consciousness in the miners' strike
Penny Green

Regulating Women in Wartime
Ruth Jamieson

Black Women and Crime
Marcia Rice

Criminal Justice and Underdevelopment in Tanzania
Leonard Shaidi

Censure, Politics and Criminal Justice
Colin Sumner (ed.)

Reading the Riot Act
Richard Vogler

Censure, politics and criminal justice

EDITED BY
Colin Sumner

Open University Press
Milton Keynes • Philadelphia

Open University Press
Celtic Court
22 Ballmoor
Buckingham MK18 1XW

and
1900 Frost Road, Suite 101
Bristol, PA 19007, USA

First Published 1990

Copyright © The Editor and Contributors 1990

All rights reserved. No part of this publication may be
reproduced, stored in a retrieval system or transmitted
in any form or by any means, without written permission
from the publisher.

British Library Cataloguing in Publication Data

Censure, politics and criminal justice – (New directions in
   criminology)
   1. Criminal law. Justice. Administration. Mediation
   I. Sumner, Colin   II. series
   306.2

   ISBN 0-335-15189-2
   ISBN 0-335-15188-4 (pbk)

Library of Congress Cataloging-in-Publication Data

Censure, politics and criminal justice/edited by Colin Sumner.
      p.   cm.
      ISBN 0-335-15189-2. – ISBN 0-335-15188-4 (pbk.)
      1. Criminology. 2.   Social control.   I. Sumner, Colin.
   HV6025.C38   1990
   364--dc20   89-78211CIP

Typeset by Inforum Typesetting, Portsmouth
Printed in Great Britain by Biddles Ltd,
Guildford and Kings Lynn

Contents

	List of contributors	vii
	Acknowledgements	ix
	Series editor's introduction	xi
1	Introduction: contemporary socialist criminology Colin Sumner	1

Renewing sociological theory

2	Rethinking deviance: towards a sociology of censure Colin Sumner	15
3	Reflections on a sociological theory of criminal justice systems Colin Sumner	41

The politics of censure

4	Magistrates' courts and the struggle for local democracy 1886–1986 Richard Vogler	59
5	The censure of 'communism' and the political trial in South Africa Cathi Albertyn and Dennis Davis	93

Media, censure and politics

6 Dramatic power: television, images of crime and law
    enforcement   123
  Richard Sparks
7 Strategies of censure and the suffragette movement   142
  Alison Young
8 The press censure of 'dissident minorities': the ideology of
    parliamentary democracy, Thatcherism and *Policing the Crisis* 163
  Colin Sumner and Simon Sandberg

Index   194

List of contributors

Cathi Albertyn graduated in law from the University of Cape Town, and has a Master's degree in criminology from Cambridge University. She is finishing off a doctorate at the Cambridge Institute on political trials in South Africa. She has lectured in law at the University of Witwatersrand and is currently practising law in Johannesburg.

Dennis Davis is a professor of law in the University of Cape Town and teaches jurisprudence, sociology of law, labour law and income tax. He has co-authored *Detention and Torture in South Africa* (David Philip, 1987) and co-edited *Crime and Power in South Africa* (David Philip, 1985). He has written extensively on jurisprudence and the sociology of the state. He too is currently finishing a doctorate at the Cambridge Institute, on the South African state and the control of the black labour force.

Simon Sandberg is a Research Officer at the Health Education Authority with special responsibility for the study of alcohol abuse and alcohol education. He is now putting the last touches to a Ph.D. thesis on *Schooling, Hegemony and the Social Formation*. His research interests include the current industrialization of education.

Richard Sparks is currently a lecturer in criminology/penology at the Open University. Having written several articles on media issues, and co-edited (with Philip Brown) *Beyond Thatcherism* (Open University Press, 1989), he is now completing a Ph.D. thesis on television viewing and social anxiety about law and order. He has also recently finished fieldwork, and a report (with Will Hay and Tony Bottoms), on the problems of order in long-term prisons.

Colin Sumner is a lecturer in sociology at the Institute of Criminology, and Fellow of Wolfson College, Cambridge. Having published *Reading Ideologies* (Academic Press, 1979), *Crime, Justice and Underdevelopment* (Heinemann, 1982), *Crime, Justice and the Mass Media* (Cambridge Institute of Criminology, 1982), and several articles in the sociology of law, he has been a Visiting Professor in Sociology at Queen's, St Mary's and Simon Fraser Universities in Canada, Visiting Lecturer at the University of Dar es Salaam, Tanzania, and Hamburg University, West Germany, and Visiting Research Fellow at the University of California at Berkeley. He is heavily involved in supervising doctoral research at the Cambridge Institute, and is currently writing a book on *Social Censures*.

Richard Vogler is a solicitor who has practised criminal law since 1977. In 1984, he completed his doctoral research at the Cambridge Institute on the growth of summary jurisdiction in England, and currently teaches law at Sussex University. He has also published work on European criminal justice systems.

Alison Young is a lecturer in law at the University of Manchester. Having completed her Ph.D. in the Cambridge Institute, on the press representation of Greenham Common and women's deviance, she has revised the thesis for publication as *Femininity in Dissent* (Routledge, forthcoming). Her current research deals with categories of femininity in legal discourse.

Acknowledgements

Many thanks to John Skelton of the Open University Press for his confidence in us, and for his patience in supporting this publication; to Pat McNeill, Marian Szymanski and Ben Sumner for their endless assistance and tolerance; and to Rosie Gandolfi and Evi Krinbill for their profound spiritual support when the going got rough.

Series editor's introduction

This series is founded upon the socialist and feminist research carried out in the Institute of Criminology during the 1980s. It is, however, concerned more broadly to publish any work which renews theoretical development or opens up new and important areas in criminology. Particular attention will be paid to the politics and ideology of criminal justice, gender and crime, crimes of state officials, crime and justice in underdeveloped societies, European criminal justice, environmental crime, and the general sociology of censure and regulation. The series will centre upon substantial empirical research informed by contemporary social theory, and will be unusually international in character.

Behind the series is a belief that criminology cannot be limited to policy-oriented studies and must retain its integrity as an area of independent, critical enquiry of interest to scholars from a variety of disciplinary backgrounds. A criminology that wants to remain dynamic and worthy of its complex subject matter must therefore constantly renew theoretical debate, explore current issues, and develop new methods of research. To allow itself to be limited by the often narrowly political interests of government departments or the funding agencies' need for a parochial 'relevance', especially in an age when 'realism' is so often defined by short-run philosophies, is to promote its own destruction as an intellectual enterprise. A criminology which is not intellectually alive is useless to everybody. We live in increasingly international societies which, more than ever, require a broad, non-parochial vision to ensure their viability and health. The various kinds of administrative criminology may be necessary for wise government, but they can only be of general value if they remain closely connected to an independent, intellectually rigorous criminology, which, even now, actually provides them with ideas, topicality, drive, depth and legitimacy. The latter, equally, must retain a close connection with political reality if it is to achieve real insight and sharpness. Both, I believe, must be committed to a general drive towards increased democratization and justice, and the indivisibility of freedom, truth and justice, if they want to avoid a drift into the twin cul-de-sacs of 'police science' and political propaganda.

Some might argue that criminology is an outdated term in that very few people believe any more that a positive science of crime and criminal justice administration is possible. Indeed, some of the studies in this series will look more like studies in the sociology of law, or in political sociology, and their view of science is never positivistic. I have decided to retain the term criminology, however, because I intend this series to contribute to redefining its meaning, so that it clearly includes sociology of law, political sociology, social history, political economy, discourse analysis, and so on. Criminology merely refers to any kind of study concerned with crime and criminal justice. It is an umbrella term covering a multitide of topics and approaches. The task for all of us is to give it a meaningful substance to meet the emerging and exciting challenges of the 1990s. The Cold War is almost over; now, we enter a phase which will demand a new clarity on fundamental social values, and a stronger vision of the substance and form of social censure and regulation necessary to promote peace, health, growth, equity and co-operation on an international scale.

The present volume has taken a long time to come to fruition, and in some respects bears the marks of the middle-1980s, but is nevertheless a better book for having had time to ripen. It is entirely my fault, and the contributors deserve medals for their patience. At one point, the book was beginning to look like a *festschrift* to a dying soul, rather than a platform for future development. However, the powers of regeneration are a wonderful thing, whatever time and strange routes they take. Therefore there is a profound sense in which this book is a testimony to the human and social capacity for regeneration. We dedicate it to the released political prisoners of South Africa and Eastern Europe, whose re-emergence onto the world stage with dignity, strength and purpose proves yet again that the human spirit is indomitable. These people, once-censured as enemies of the state, now take their rightful place as the authentic leadership of their societies. This process will recur and reverberate throughout all aspects of life in the 1990s. Never again should we put others through the torment and pain of unjust censure when we know that our own judgement is perpetually flawed.

1 Introduction: contemporary socialist criminology

Colin Sumner

The essays in this book emerge from the work done by myself and the doctoral students under my supervision at the Institute of Criminology, Cambridge, over the last 10 years. They reflect the continued vitality, and hopefully the development of a socialist criminology which, across the globe, is changing and growing in tune with the times. It is a criminology which draws upon the insights of Gramsci, Althusser, Foucault, Habermas, Poulantzas, Hall and, of course, the feminist movement. It thus bears little resemblance to that of Willem Bonger which, for all its merits, gave little attention to the political and ideological dimensions of crime and justice (see Bonger, 1916, and Buchholtz et al., 1974, for a later variant). That kind of economistic socialism which accepted crime uncritically as the behavioural effect of capitalist economic relations is much too crude, and is effectively dead as a theoretical model in the light of post-1945 social theory and socialist politics in Europe. Equally, ours is a contemporary socialist criminology which rejects the romantic formulations of the 'new criminology' of the late 1960s (see Taylor et al., 1973). Its anarchistic iconoclasm rocked the criminologies of both the capitalist and socialist establishments by proclaiming the political character of social deviants, but it went too far and over-politicized deviant behaviour. As its proponents now themselves recognize, those censured as deviants are not a unitary group economically, politically or ideologically, and what is referred to as a social deviance may often be victimizing, psychologically self-destructive, socially harmful and politically reactionary responses to social contradictions or problems.

The criminology we are advocating also rejects any simplistic analysis of criminal law as an instrument of class rule. Building upon positions developed earlier which emphasize the political and ideological character of law in the hegemonic bloc's direction of social development (see Sumner, 1979: 293–4 and 246–77), it recognizes the complex social power of the criminal justice system as an expression of hegemonic forces of various kinds and therefore its nature as a site of political contestation. Consequently there is no assumption that the criminal justice system will ever be anything but a repressive mode of social regulation employed by inequitable states riven by divisions of class, ethnicity, gender, nationality and region. Modern socialist criminology, however, acknowledges the sociological importance of criminal justice systems, as expressions of some moral-political consensus (however artificial) which attempt to regulate and maintain the dominant social relations within a society while containing and pacifying forces for change or disruption. It ought to be unnecessary to add that any criminology which ignores the social roots and contested character of the criminal justice system, by taking state definitions of crime as adequate definitions of types of behaviour, is not only antediluvian but also discreditable as a dominant-ideological arm of the state. Criminology today, in short, includes the sociology of criminal law.

Criminology now has a developed school of socialist thought, and socialist ideas, issues and policies have irrevocably altered the character of criminology. But it is also true that socialism increasingly embraces criminology, and that questions of morality, criminal justice and democracy can no longer be shelved until after the revolution or relegated to a specialist interest. Socialist politics have moved on. Many now question the concept of socialism as we have known it (see, e.g. Bauman, 1976; Anderson, 1980; Lindsay, 1981; Kitching, 1983; Leftwich, 1983). Perhaps it was a political vision too closely tied to the limited goals of new proletariats, in their attempts to win a position of power within a bourgeois world and then to sustain it against the challenges of both élite and popular forces. Events, first in Stalin's Russia, then in European labourism, and most recently in Deng's China, suggest that socialism is still merely a critique of class domination and is nowhere near realizing its full potential as a vision of global harmony under common ownership and popular democracy. Globally speaking, it probably needs a dose of pluralism in both theory and practice to mature into a politics which can use power flexibly and democratically. In practice, this means that world socialism is still held back by the antiquated politics of the old men of the labour movement, clinging on to dreams of eternal power based on dictatorships, a politics which glosses over the fact that unless those dreams include the democratic aspirations of all sections of the population, one of which is the abolition of all dictatorships and injustice, they are simply recipes for renewed class domination.

In socialist criminology, this means that we can never rest content with a class analysis of criminal law, moral censure, or offensive behaviour, nor can we ever relax the drive to democratization of criminal justice or social administration. Recognition of the historic damage caused by social divisions other than class, of the central role of moral censure and criminal justice in struggles for hegemony, and of the automatic and inherent harm done to the collective spirit and individual soul by managing societies through systematic censure, must produce a growth in socialist criminology – a growth that will make it fit to join the contemporary transformation of socialist politics into a force which can both take power and make progress towards a complete revolution in bourgeois social relations.

Much of the resurgent socialist criminology in Britain has rightly emphasized the importance of research and policy arising out of, or connected with political practice within Labour-led local authorities (see, e.g. Taylor, 1981: 122; J. Young, 1988). Indeed, there has been a lot of value in this connection. But socialist research and policy cannot just be tied to local, immediate needs, nor to particular political parties, whose desire for power often outruns their commitment to progressive change; they must be underpinned by contemporary revolutionary theory and informed by less 'applied' and more 'purist', broad-ranging studies in criminology. Otherwise, there is a grave danger of running into the cul-de-sac of a social democratic, parochial reformism which is not so far away from neo-positivist, administrative criminology. Empirical research, everyday political practice and general theory should continually interpenetrate and inform each other, or else socialist criminology will run into the problem always facing administrative criminology, which is that the political objective and the funding source cripple the possibility of any general truths, any searching questions, or any new insights.

Whatever the epistemological problems involved in defining truth, it is not enough to juxtapose one political bias against another. One of the major democratic demands of modern socialism, and of people everywhere, is that the search for truth should not be restricted by the pursuit of economic growth, political power or cultural purity. Besides, the history of socialism itself suggests that there are no guarantees that political pragmatism will produce anything progressive or unique within criminology, or, indeed, even anything criminological at all.

Science, ethics and politics demand the exposure and criticism of mystifying or oppressive ideology in all its forms, whether it be in the form of law, pornography, or indeed criminology, by discovering more truthful accounts of phenomena. They demand an analysis of the way that such ideologies are combined with partisan or excessive coercion in the construction, practice and justification of criminal justice systems across the globe; systems which protect, and often brutally enforce, the exploitation of international capital, the power of established political élites, bureaucratic and political corruption, male chauvinism and widespread racism. Therefore, we cannot accept the premise of the 'new realists' that 'the major crimes, *as presently defined by criminal law*, are agreed upon by the mass of the population' (Young, 1987: 355).

From our standpoint, such a position seems parochial and superficial. How can it deal with South African pass laws, laws banning major political parties, and emergency powers legislation? How can it deal with contemporary changes in environmental consciousness which reveal to the public the inadequacy of anti-pollution legislation? Moreover, if criminal law here means statutes, the position merely deals with abstract prohibitions and vague approval of them, and not with what is treated as crime in police practice, nor with the ambiguous, changing and even hypocritical, moral substance behind people's formal opinions. It therefore glosses the murky social reality of crime as a practical social censure. What Young calls the 'rational core' of criminal law is therefore for us merely its abstract component, a feature which tends to conceal its practical reality and which therefore can be described as its ideological character. It is not so much 'a realistic basis for a consensus' (Young, 1987), in our view, as an unrealistic obstacle to practical and theoretical insight, an abstraction more likely to yield a superficial shared misunderstanding (see Thompson, 1975: 193–4; Sumner, 1981: 279).

We are not 'new realists', but old realists (see Sim *et al.*, 1987: 39–59, for further criticisms of 'new realism'). Too many 'new realist' statements implicitly accept a notion of crime as a form of behaviour separate from state definitions (e.g. 'It [Left idealist criminology: CS] does not concentrate on why people become criminals but how the state criminalizes people': Young, 1986: 17). Such positions ignore the wisdom of a major tenet of socialist criminology, which is that people become 'criminals' *because* the state criminalizes them; the popularity of a particular law and the social damage of a particular, criminalized practice are separate questions, with historically variable answers. It is very important to study the causes of anti-social practices, but that does not mean we should allow the state, or a media-constructed consensus, or well-founded local fears, or even our desire for political power, to define 'anti-social' for us. To believe that what is anti-social, wrong, wicked, dangerous or a nuisance is a matter of collective, transcendental, normative or moral agreement, and not a question of economic, political and ideological constitution, is contrary to the evidence of history, and therefore a poor basis for a realistic politics of criminal justice. It is, essentially, to abandon sociology altogether, and socialism, in favour of a return to the transcendental idealism of certain old theologies; if it is proposed as a sociological argument, then it is closer to the evolutionary consensualism of Parsons, to Bell's 'end of ideology', or to the pragmatism of Dewey than to the historical materialism of Marx or the moral realism of Habermas and Gramsci.

Understanding the social relations and contexts expressed in, and producing, anti-social practices and the ideologies of crime and punishment is central to socialist criminology. Reading the ideology of both offence and offenders is a major theoretical task. The most important intrinsic character of ideology is that it is a partial sign or sectional representation of the social world, and therefore its partiality can only be analysed accurately in full in relation to the national or international social context that provoked it and which it re-presents in specific historical circumstances (see Sumner, 1979). It is quite insufficient merely to read discourses in texts, however thoroughly. Although, of course, we must attend carefully to the doctrines and nuances of those texts, the ideological character of criminal justice is not to be discovered in legal discourse, but in the relation of that discourse to the economic, political and cultural reality which it translates and represents (its con-text). That context always needs to be sociologically documented and analysed before the specific role of ideologies can be rendered fully comprehensible and assessable. The work recorded in this book does not bracket off the question of ideology; it puts it in the foreground alongside the political dimension in the long march away from economic reductionism.

Consequently, these essays represent a commitment to sociological research which is fundamentally informed by socialist theory and politics but based on extensive empirical enquiry or fieldwork and the anti-positivist, and anti-relativist, principles of epistemological realism (see Keat and Urry, 1975; Hacking, 1983) and historical materialism. What follows in the next two chapters are general statements of some of the ideas and views which underpin much of the work in this volume. We have made no attempt to produce theoretical unity – each contributor has his or her own ideas – but there are some common threads and assumptions.

The essays in this volume

This book was a project devised for a practical purpose; namely, to assist and stimulate the studies that it draws upon. Following various discussions and seminars, while never becoming a fully collective project, its most immediate aim was to counter the alienating and counterproductive individuation that is an acute feature of doctoral research in Cambridge. We will resist commenting further here on its emergence from an Institute not known for its role in the development of socialist criminology. Suffice it to say that we believe the views of Wiles (1976: 12) and Cohen (1981: 237–8) to be greatly mistaken. Against Wiles, socialist criminology *is* possible within an Institute that is fundamentally independent of the Home Office; and, against Cohen, it has been a *struggle* rather than an accommodation.

The sociological theory of censures, as a critique of the sociology of deviance, is important to most of the essays in this book, and has been discussed in postgraduate seminars at the Institute a great deal. Therefore, a revised basic formulation of it is the substance of Chapter 2. It outlines our notion of the ideological character of 'crime' and 'deviance' and gives the reader an idea of where we have come from criminologically. Much more work is needed to develop the concept, but it at least registers several positions which we take as axiomatic, and which we see as the beginnings of a fundamental theoretical break with the sociology of deviant behaviour. Chapter 3 contains some recent reflections on the relationships between criminal justice as a system of social regulation and social censures as fundamental elements of social division. It synthesizes recent socialist thinking on criminal justice, building in some conclusions from research on underdeveloped societies. Again, much of this is exploratory and by no means definitive or complete. However, these two chapters represent an attempt to renew analysis and debate in theoretical sociology, something which many people now regret being sidelined during the Realpolitik of the 1980s.

The relationship of regulation and censure to the processes of economic development is clearly a vital aspect of the theory. This will be reflected more substantially in the contributions from Penny Green (in press), Philip Ahire and Leonard Shaidi (both forthcoming) to the series of books of which this volume is part. Much of our work in this book, and the series as a whole, is moving towards what might be loosely called a crime and development perspective, which attempts to locate the censure of crime and deviance within the historic phases of social development that give rise to key national and international moments. In this sense, it is part of a more general movement away from the ahistorical, ethnocentric, androcentric and thus non-contextual character of most administrative criminology. Serious academic criminology can no longer work with the static behaviourist models, amoral value avoidance and fake apoliticism of so much that has gone before.

The second section of the book, reflecting that developmental perspective, looks at the political character of the censure of crime in two very different areas. The relationship between local power, the state and the ability to censure crime is the reference point for Richard Vogler's essay in Chapter 4 (see also Vogler, forthcoming). It focuses upon the political character of the magistracy, as representatives of economic classes, during the growth of the modern British criminal justice system. Drawing upon Poulantzas' work, Vogler explores the recent re-theorization of the bourgeois state, emphasizing the complex dynamics between (1) state institutions, (2) these institutions and class relations, (3) state and civil society and (4) local and central state. This enquiry informs an original research into the extent to which the composition of the magistracy of England and Wales over the last 100 years has not conformed with democratic principles, indicating the great importance of this for the British constitution. This history, based upon some remarkable new material from Labour Party archives, reveals the political, class character of appointment to the bench. Even on a broad definition of the term 'socialism', socialists and working-class people have been systematically under-represented on the bench in the UK for a long time. Vogler observes that, since 1945, the selection issue has been substantially depoliticized through the efforts of the Magistrates' Association, with its project of a 'professional' image for the bench, and that the desire for politically neutral, scientific skills, to aid the professional magistrate, eventually played a strong part in the establishment of the Cambridge Institute of Criminology. The labourist project of democratizing the bench was thus 'eclipsed' by the conservative bench's demand for a scientific criminology, a demand which did nothing to redress the class-political imbalance on the bench. Thus we see, in a way that is very close to home, how the most basic daily institution of criminal justice is biased politically and how criminology has served to depoliticize the character of criminal justice. The advocacy of an apolitical, professional, scientific criminology is revealed as, in actuality, an extreme political position, justifying the sustenance of bourgeois and Tory domination of the judiciary.

The politicality of censuring is more than matched by the censoriousness of politics. Retaining power has always involved denouncing and censuring the opposition. Arguably, power itself only exists in relation to the strength of other powers, and therefore to weaken the enemy and to validate one's own violence through censorious propaganda is doubly effective politics. Indeed, the expansion of power is even better served if other powers can be successfully portrayed as the enemy of the whole nation, and not simply as political rivals. Chapter 5, by Albertyn and Davis on political trials in South Africa, is a good example of this process. It illustrates the importance of the censure in politics. The formal vote of censure in parliament and the public statement censuring a foreign government ('East Germany censures Hungary', reads this morning's headline) are two well-known forms of this. A third is the political trial, which enables a judicial censure of a whole political movement. Moreover, the essay illustrates the way that political censures draw upon ideological images of deviance to portray opponents as abnormal people or even as inhuman. Politics and morality have thus always been intertwined. The sustenance of power involves the constant invention and reproduction of images of immorality, and the sustenance of morality requires power, whether it be the strength of self-empowerment, exploitation or alliance.

Albertyn and Davis focus on the place of law in authoritarian political systems (see also Albertyn, forthcoming; Davis, 1985, 1987, 1988; Foster *et al.*, 1987). It is interesting that the suppression of black power in South Africa so often involves the deployment of law. The political trial is a classic example: why does the South African state not just use detention without trial, as it does so often, especially under the emergency regulations? Moving beyond Kirchheimer's work, Albertyn and Davis argue that political trial and censure is an important device in the struggle for hegemony within the white population. In this case, the use of the censure of communism to characterize and downgrade resistance to Apartheid is particularly striking. The increased readiness to deploy that censure reflects the crisis on the political terrain and offers a chance of regaining control over the face of political change. As such, the political trial, with its inbuilt censure, reflects and expresses the need for dominant-ideological redirection and clarification in the heat of political struggle. Two major trials are analysed to reveal the political processes in which they are lodged and the role of criminal justice in changing the balance of political struggle. The essay fills a large gap, because political trials have been very neglected within all kinds of criminology.

In the final section of the book, there are three papers which examine mass media expessions of censure. All three bring forward themes developed in the previous section, illustrating the political character of social censure. However, they add to this by showing how social censures are often deeply political in their language and their basic ideological assumptions, even when representing social practices as deviant and strange. As detailed studies of specific narratives of discourses, they exemplify the importance of careful scrutiny of the language of censure in whatever form it takes. Censures are revealed as quite complex compositions of images of personal deviance and images of political propriety. The mass media are by no means the only agency involved in extensive and powerful social censuring, and others must be studied. Informal censure by friends and relatives probably remains as powerful as any other expression of disapproval. However, such informal censure must, in our view, be heavily conditioned by the constant expression of what 'society' thinks is bad in the output of the mass media.

Social censures usually presuppose, or even demand, a typical normative narrative of transgression and retribution. They are tied to a desire to prevent or punish, which is translated in ideology into the inevitability of punishment upon continuation of the offence. Badness always causes the bad some pain, if only in the form of punishment: a moral-political tale of some antiquity which has now been converted into nightly soap opera on television. Television is probably the main medium whereby the dominant morality of our age is disseminated as entertainment on a mass scale. How could criminology proceed for so long without grasping that however scientific and professional it tried to make the criminal justice system, however apolitical it imagined that system to be, television would infuse and surround criminal justice with a powerful set of ideological images of immorality, heroism, evil, efficiency and justice? The political values and interests integral to the censure of crime in television crime drama daily reinforce state definitions of crime, the value of censure and punishment, and the importance of state violence for our comfort and safety.

Richard Sparks, in Chapter 6, begins to rectify British criminology's serious neglect of this vitally important aspect of modernism by presenting an analysis of one month's television crime drama (see also Pratt and Sparks, 1987; Sparks and Taylor, 1989; Sparks, forthcoming). Lodged in an appraisal of the critical aesthetics of writers such as Eco, Bourdieu and Gerbner, his essay describes the way that television drama contains patterns of narrative which tell the moral tale of police heroism successfully solving the crime problem, bringing the villain his or her just deserts and restoring the harmony of social order. He concludes that this tale presents law enforcement as a form of poetic justice, in which due process takes second place to order and retribution, suggesting that such recurrent and well-disseminated imagery might affect public discourses on crime and law enforcement in such a way as to reinforce or precondition any social tendencies towards a more authoritarian 'law-and-order' society.

Crime is often depoliticized before it reaches the courts, through public censure which negates any political content and consigns it to the dustbin categories of badness or madness. Alison Young, in Chapter 7, shows how this happened in the case of the censure of the 'suffragettes' (see also A. Young, 1988). Drawing on Foucauldian inspiration, she locates the censure within the idealization of womanhood predominant at that time, showing how important it is to locate censures within their constitutive ideological formations in particular political conjunctures, and how the negative implications for the 'suffragettes' were thus linked to the routine regulation of women at that time. The term suffragette itself is exposed for what it is: a distinctly derogatory word expressing a censure. Young's analysis of the media discourse reveals a strong ideological emphasis on female hysteria, as well as the familiar criminalization of political militancy. As with so many censures of female deviance, and of political dissenters, the censure of the 'suffragettes' attacked the normality of their sexuality, and subsequently the police assaults upon them often took a sexual character. Once depoliticized ideologically, the protesters felt the full force of the hegemonic masculinity of the law (see also Sumner, in press). Never was there a better example of the importance of a moral censure as a sub-text conditioning a particular kind of punitive, political response using the criminal justice system.

The correspondence between tendencies in the moral-political rhetoric of the media and tendencies within the state-form, more specifically between the emergence of a 'law-and-order' rhetoric in the press and the development of the seeds of Thatcherite authoritarianism within the British state, is the subject of Chapter 8 by myself and Simon Sandberg. Through an analysis of the press censure of political demonstrations in 1973, we examine the correspondence between the ideology contained in the censure and the growing Tory rhetoric for a programme of penal law and a morally aggressive state. The essay critically assesses the analysis in *Policing the Crisis* and the debate around the concept of authoritarian populism, arguing that the restructuring of liberal ideology in the early 1970s was an antecedent causal condition of Thatcherite authoritarian statism and the neo-liberalism of the 1980s.

A major conclusion from our empirical study was that although most demonstrations were censured, a sizeable percentage were not. A close examination of the 'approved' demonstrations suggests strong press support for the Tory-encouraged rise of the moral majority and for subsequent Tory legal strategies, and a small degree of ideological pluralism within the national press. Ideologies of 'law and order' are not necessarily effects of change in state form, but can be vital ingredients in its initial establishment. Public consciousness of the need to censure and 'crack down' upon 'dissident and deviant elements' can be stimulated to support a toughening of the system of criminal justice. The essay thus represents an attempt to illustrate how, under certain conjunctural conditions, state form and political practice can be crucially transformed following the moulding of public opinion by politicians and the media.

Conclusion

Criminology's job is to inform. Unless its theories and studies recognize the significance of politics and ideology in the emergence, operation and effects of moral censures and criminal justice systems, it cannot fulfil that obligation and will become, in effect, an agency of state research. There is no question of glossing over the offender in search of a sociology of the offence; it is simply that the offender is defined by the offence, and therefore the study of moral and legal censures, and the vitally important, stressful social relationships generating them, is a logically prior demand. The essays in this volume are an attempt to uncover the social constitution of censures, focusing particularly upon the political relationships and the ideological interpretations giving rise to censure.

These essays may raise more questions than they answer, but they at least stand up for a socialist criminology which is theoretically informed and well-grounded in empirical research, without regressing into discredited old ideas and methodologies. They represent a call for theoretical renewal in criminology, and an assertion of the value of contemporary socialist analysis for the understanding of moral censures and criminal justice systems.

References

Ahire, P. (forthcoming). *Imperial Policing: The Emergence and Role of the Police in Colonial Nigeria 1860–1960*. Milton Keynes: Open University Press.

Albertyn, C. (forthcoming). *Political Trials in South Africa 1948–1989*. Milton Keynes: Open University Press.

Anderson, P. (1980). *Arguments within English Marxism*. London: Verso.

Bauman, Z. (1976). *Socialism: The Active Utopia*. London: Allen & Unwin.

Bonger, W. (1916). *Criminality and Economic Conditions*. Boston: Little, Brown.

Buchholtz, E., Hartmann, R., Lekschas, J. and Stiller, G. (1974). *Socialist Criminology*. Farnborough: Saxon House.

Cohen, S. (1981). Footprints on the sand. In *Crime and Society* (M. Fitzgerald, G. McLennan and J. Pawson, eds). London: Routledge and the Open University.

Davis, D. (1985). Introduction: Criminology and South Africa, and Political Trials in South Africa. In *Crime and Power in South Africa* (D. Davis and M. Slabbert, eds), Cape Town: David Philip.

Davis, D. (1987). Repression and integration. *International Journal of Sociology of Law*, **15**(1), 61–84.

Davis, D. (1988). Post-apartheid South Africa: What future for a legal system? *South African Law Bulletin*, 219–36.

Foster, D., Davis, D. and Sandler, D. (1987). *Detention and Torture in South Africa*. Cape Town: David Philip.

Green, P. (in press). *The Enemy Without: Policing and Class Consciousness in the Miners' Strike*. Milton Keynes: Open University Press.

Hacking, I. (1983). *Representing and Intervening*. Cambridge: Cambridge University Press.

Keat, R. and Urry, J. (1975). *Social Theory as Science*. London: Routledge.

Kitching, G. (1983). *Rethinking Socialism*. London: Methuen.

Leftwich, A. (1983). *Redefining Politics*. London: Methuen.

Lindsay, J. (1981). *The Crisis in Marxism*. Bradford-on-Avon: Moonraker.

Pratt, J. and Sparks, J.R. (1987). New voices from the ship of fools. *Contemporary Crises*, **11**, 3–23.

Shaidi, L.P. (forthcoming). *Criminal Justice and Underdevelopment in Tanzania*. Milton Keynes: Open University Press.

Sim, J., Scraton, P. and Gordon, P. (1987). Introduction: Crime, the state and critical analysis. In *Law, Order and the Authoritarian State* (P. Scraton, ed.). Milton Keynes: Open University Press.

Sparks, J.R. (forthcoming). *Television and the Drama of Crime*. Milton Keynes: Open University Press.

Sparks, J.R. and Taylor, I.R. (1989). Mass communications. In *Beyond Thatcherism* (P. Brown and J.R. Sparks, eds). Milton Keynes: Open University Press.

Sumner, C.S. (1979). *Reading Ideologies*. London: Academic Press.

Sumner, C.S. (1981). Race, crime and hegemony. *Contemporary Crises*, **5**(3), 277–91.

Sumner, C.S. (in press). Foucault, gender and the censure of deviance. In *Feminist Perspectives in Criminology* (L. Gelsthorpe and A.M. Morris, eds). Milton Keynes: Open University Press.

Taylor, I.R. (1981). *Law and Order*. London: Macmillan.

Taylor, I.R., Walton, P. and Young, J. (1973). *The New Criminology*. London: Routledge.

Thompson, E.P. (1975). *Whigs and Hunters*. London: Allen Lane.

Vogler, R. (forthcoming). *Reading the Riot Act: The Magistracy, Police and Army in Civil Disorder*. Milton Keynes: Open University Press.

Wiles, P. (1976). Introduction. In *The Sociology of Crime and Delinquency. Vol. 2: The New Criminologies* (P. Wiles, ed.). London: Martin Robertson.

Young, A. (1988). 'Wild Women': The censure of the Suffragette Movement. *International Journal of Sociology of Law*, **16**(3), 279–93.

Young, A. (1989). *Dispersing the commonplace*. Ph.D. dissertation, University of Cambridge, Institute of Criminology.

Young, J. (1986). The failure of criminology. In *Confronting Crime* (R. Matthews and J. Young, eds). London: Sage.

Young, J. (1987). The tasks facing a realist criminology. *Contemporary Crises*, **11**, 337–56.

Young, J. (1988). Radical criminology in Britain. *British Journal of Criminology*, **28**(2), 289–313.

Renewing sociological theory

2 Rethinking deviance: towards a sociology of censure

Colin Sumner

Students still ask 'Whatever happened to the theoretical debate about deviance in the early 1970s?' (see Hirst, 1975; Taylor *et al.*, 1973, 1975; Pearson, 1975; Young, 1975; Sumner, 1976). That debate had not only cast doubt upon the value of the concept of deviance, but also the nature and possibility of a Marxist alternative. It is a very good question, because recent Marxist work in this area is clearly outside the old deviancy theory framework, yet there has been little attempt in those studies to reconceptualize 'deviant behaviour' (e.g. Thompson, 1975; Glasgow Media Group, 1976; Hall *et al.*, 1978; Corrigan, 1979; cf. Sumner, 1981a). Perhaps the revulsion for theory and theoretical wrangling, the return of empirical research, the new popularity of historical work and the general air of hard-nosed realism in the late 1970s and early 1980s, have all contributed to the demise of theoretical dynamics in this field. Deviance is certainly no longer at the forefront of debates in sociology: some Leninist comrades would even see it as one of those pre-theoretical discourses that are only of value in teaching undergraduates.

Of course, Marxist scholarship is little concerned to rescue the sociology of deviance and has its own imperatives. It could hardly be expected to display much sympathy to a field which, in the late 1930s in the USA, emerged as an alternative and counter to the political economy of social crisis. On the other hand, it has never been a Marxist view that better concepts will automatically emerge if researchers simply immerse themselves in historiography or practical politics. Facts about the past are no better than contemporary ones at speaking for themselves.

Similarly, immersion in practicalities restricts opportunity for reflection on theoretical matters, and requires the immediate application of existing concepts rather than time-consuming deliberation on their successors.

Theoretical renewal was always integral to the Marxian approach to analysis, and practice, experience and perspective continually interact and successively feed each other's growth. This should therefore be the case for socialist criminology too. It does not mean that we want to return to that impossibly idealist search for a general theory applicable to all times and places. In Marxism, there is always a strong distinction between things in general and their form of existence in a particular period in a particular society. However, there *are* general concepts in Marxist theory and there *is* an abiding concern to develop them, and new ones, in order to provide an analysis of, and practice within, contemporary social conditions. Marxism is a *living* tradition, because it is still the most persuasive account of societal development and must never allow itself to be petrified by the dead hand of its own past.

This essay is thus seen as a minor contribution to the development of a better conception of what used to be called deviance, based on the concepts and methods of contemporary, European, Marxist analysis and social theory. It is premised on the view that empirical research and political experience, however radical their concerns, are not enough on their own, and that theoretical renewal, or re-engagement with social theory, is vital in discovering, reflecting and interpreting good, new information. It represents a refusal to allow Marxist approaches to social policy issues to become bogged down, either by the parochialism of political realism or by the dogmatism of theoretical evangelism.

In developing my earlier observations on the subject of Marxism and deviancy theory (see Sumner, 1976, 1981a, 1982), I shall argue that contemporary socialist criminology regards the categories of deviance (i.e. those moral conceptions which specified what became known in post-1945 sociology as deviance) as new forms of social censure. Whatever the authority of their legal definition, or the pseudo-scientific validity of their use in social work or welfare agencies, these notions are still moral judgements. As descriptive categories they can only be said to have a loose and selective proximity to their supposed empirical referents. Their establishment in the laws, practices and policies of the welfare state, and thus their expression in the apparently neutral language of law, policy and sociology, merely concealed their fundamental character as moral ideology, as partial and partisan judgements of what is truly immoral, useless, dangerous, anti-social and inadequate. Censures such as militants, muggers, extremists, deviants, criminals, thieves, prostitutes, perverts, nutters, slags, delinquents, bastards, villains, the socially inadequate, freaks, rioters, loonies and scroungers (believe it or not) are not adequate behavioural categories.[1]* Indeed, with the demise of welfarism and the rise of the openly capitalist, morally aggressive Right in the 1980s, recent social polarizations have made this even clearer. Now, the ideological and political character of moral censures is so open, and the rulers' fear of their social divisiveness so minimal, that the concept of social deviance is revealed as being, at root, a notion within the politics of social democracy and therefore truly a creature of the post-Depression era, of the 'end of ideology' (Bell, 1952) phase. Ideology is again blatant, and the concept of social deviance stands disrobed, as rude as its forerunners, the concepts of moral degeneracy and social inadequacy.

Apart from being plainly culturally and historically specific, moral censures can be seen as negative notions within dominant ideological formations. They make no sense at all outside the sectional ideologies which constitute them and the economic, political and cultural contexts which generate, sustain and precipitate their use. In short, deviance is not defined by a set of distinguishable behaviours offending collective norms, but by a battery of flexible, interconnected ideological terms and feelings of disapproval which are expressed, in varying strength, regularity and openness, in the practical networks of domination. The censures of deviance are key features of the discourses of the dominant; forces deployed in the policing of what they specify as deviance and dissent. Although often presented in legal, technical or universal forms, as mere descriptions, they are organized slanders in what is essentially a political or moral conflict.[2] Clearly, then, it is vital to study the use, development and sanctification of these censures in the networks of 'discipline' (Foucault, 1977) and 'tutelage' (Donzelot, 1979), their practical application in particular cases by the state's agencies of moral and political hygiene, and, of course, the kinds of social practice to which the censures are applied. Such research must go hand-in-hand with responsible normative debate about the moral censures which would be better in complex, postindustrial societies moving towards full democratization. But first, let us specify the problems with the concept of deviance and look at existing efforts to overhaul it.

The concept of deviance in sociology

Although ultimately rooted in the Durkheimian dream of a social order with fully matching normative consensus and division of labour, and although it emerged during the period of The New Deal in a practical and theoretical attempt to supersede the social disorganization of the 1920s and early 1930s, the concept of deviant behaviour is first manifested as part of a systematic theory of society in Parsons' work (see Parsons, 1951).

---

* Superscript numerals refer to numbered notes at the end of each chapter.

Here deviance was non-conformity with others' expectations in a given social system. Plainly, such a notion does not *of itself* negatively portray the act of deviation, nor demand a focus on behaviour defined as deviant. Logically, it does not even require us to think of deviance as behaviour at all. It surely posits, at root, that deviance is an outcome of a relation between people in conflict. Yet the subsequent history of deviancy sociology has, on the whole, tended to focus on deviant behaviour as though it was a coherent behavioural category, and to portray it negatively.

Non-conformity soon became 'failure to conform' (Bredemeier and Stephenson, 1970: 123), and the search was on for the social strains, personality weaknesses and interactional milieux which supposedly induced that 'failure' and the 'careers' of failure found in the urban and cultural ghettoes of the new welfare states. The 'expectations' of the dominant culture, which in the original formulation are defined as vital constituents of social deviance, were taken for granted as a consensual, natural evolution and forgotten. These 'expectations' could also have been accounted for, logically, as the pathological outcomes of 'social strain', or as the deficiencies of conscience in opinion leaders, or as the effects of the 'moral careers' of politicians. Instead, deviancy sociology soon became the sociology of deviant behaviour. Even today, it is still only partially a sociology of dominant culture; and a sociology of relationships which generate censure is very much embryonic. Its various theoretical possibilities have been very partially developed, which naturally suggests that political and moral ideology have again played their part in the history of a supposed science.

The sociology of deviant behaviour was thus developed within a theory of society as a cybernetic system, and helped in a small way to legitimize the welfare state's deployment of various forms of psychotherapy and its increasing intervention into the life of the working-class family. Bearing in mind Habermas's observations, we can see it as a clear example of the technocratic rationality of 'social engineering'; as instrumentalist reason which detaches its own judgement and others' action from the moral and political contexts constituting their internal meaning, and which reframes them within the behaviouristic categories and systems analysis of supposedly scientific discourse (or science as understood in positivism). Habermas (1971: 42–3) himself commented that:

> The personalization of what is public is thus the cement in the cracks of a relatively well-integrated society, which forces suspended conflicts into areas of social psychology. There they are absorbed in categories of deviant behaviour: as private conflicts, illness and crime. These containers now appear to be overflowing.

Once divorced from the normative and political conjuncture that give it meaning, 'deviant behaviour' was ready as an apparently neutral object of knowledge to serve in the power-laden practices of policing, tutelage and discipline, as an agency in the processes of domination and social regulation: 'Today the psychotechnic manipulation of behaviour can already liquidate the old fashioned detour through norms' (Habermas, 1971: 118). The deviant was now identifiable directly, as an 'inadequate', 'undersocialized', or 'inappropriately' socialized cultural rebel: as a rebel without a cause. Properly fitted up, after an identification parade where only the police and a carefully cultivated public opinion were present, the Deviant, and subsequently a whole rogues' gallery of Deviance, was constructed in a way that took some knocking down. The fact that the concept of deviant behaviour was still used by radicals in the 1970s is testimony to its significance for the age of the welfare state and for social-democratic reformism at any time.

It is my persuasion that the concept of social deviance as behaviour breaching social norms is so inherently problematic, and so dangerous in its consequences, that it should be abandoned once and for all – along with all the theoretical baggage that goes with it. As the Thatcher and Reagan regimes mark the demise and deconstruction of the post-war age of 'welfare consensus' (the age of the 'end of ideology' and the 'one nation'), we should move with the times and finally supersede the sociology of deviant behaviour which this period engendered. It is necessary to follow the implications of recognizing that deviance is simply a developed modern form of a much older censure, and indeed that it is no more than a censure, a moral-political judgement.

Of course, it is not new to question behaviouristic concepts of immorality. Since Durkheim's day, a surprisingly large minority of criminologists have, at least in principle, rejected the reliance on the moral-political categories of crime and deviance in explaining anti-social action, although very rarely have they ventured into the question as to what was truly anti-social.[3] The criticisms made in criminology are parallel and overlapping with those in the sociology of deviance, and therefore it is worth looking at them.

Sometimes, as in Sellin's work, the emphasis was on the extensive normative conflict in society which prevented the presentation of such reliance as a neutral scientific activity: 'The unqualified acceptance of the legal definitions as the basic units or elements of criminological inquiry violates a fundamental criterion of science' (Sellin, 1938: 23). Sometimes, attention was simply drawn to the normative character of the object of enquiry:

> In this respect crime is like all other social phenomena, and the possibility of a science of criminal behavior is similar to the possibility of a science of any other behavior. Social science has no stable unit, as it deals with phenomena involving group evaluations. (Sutherland and Cressey, 1974: 20)

This concern was not peculiar to sociologists either. Criminologists from all disciplines are well aware of the failure of empirical research to establish any intrinsic, distinguishing features of 'criminal behaviour', and therefore, presumably, of the possibility that both the explanation and prevention of 'criminal behaviour' have no real, discernible object. In fact, one of the most remarkable observations was made by the British psychologist, Trasler (1973: 67):

> It is not immediately obvious that criminal behaviour constitutes a viable field of scientific discourse. . . . [R]epeated attempts to show that offenders as a class can be sharply distinguished from the law-abiding in respect to intelligence, emotionality, extraversion, physique, and social origin have generally met with little success. . . . [W]hat is and what is not criminal is defined by the laws of the state presently in force; consequently the meaning of the categories 'criminal' and 'crime' varies substantially between one society and another.

Of course, none of this wisdom prevented criminologists from continuing to use samples of convicted offenders as representative of anti-social personalities. However, it is clear that the twentieth century has seen a growing awareness, albeit an oft-ignored sub-text in criminology, that what is truly criminal is only very partially defined in state codes of criminal law. At last, perhaps, it is no longer seen as radical to echo the sentiments of Pascal (1966: 46):

> Three degrees of latitude upset the whole of jurisprudence and one meridian determines what is true. . . . It is a funny sort of justice whose limits are marked by a river; true on this side of the Pyrenees, false on the other . . .
>
> Larceny, incest, infanticide, parricide, everything has at some time been accounted a virtuous action. Could there be anything more absurd than that a man has the right to kill me because he lives on the other side of the water, and his prince has picked a quarrel with mine, though I have none with him?

What is censured as crime and deviance reflects the political economy and culture of a society. Anthropologists and internationalist scholars have thus tried very hard to spell out the damning implications of this for that legion of criminologists who take the categories of deviance or crime as behavioural descriptors rather than cultural or political expressions (see Schapera, 1972; Robertson and Taylor, 1973; Lopez-Rey, 1970; Sumner, 1982). For example, Lopez-Rey, for many years the UN's voice in criminology, argued that criminology has relied too much on the statistics of government officials and has thus focused on 'juvenile delinquent behaviour' at the expense of the majority of crimes, including the most serious areas of crime such as genocide, international corporate crime, war crime, and the crimes of the state.[4] This recalls Paul Rock's (1977: 392) nice observation that 'the erratic history of criminology has been marked by the organised neglect of many, if not most, of the phenomena that constitute crime'. Lopez-Rey (1970: xii) goes on to condemn the recurrent, crass pretensions and theoretical cretinism of orthodox criminology in the West:

> Criminology still persists in styling itself a natural or naturalistic science by borrowing more and more concepts, methods and techniques from natural sciences. This ignores the fact that natural science is unable to provide the socio-political approach required by the extent of crime . . .
>
> Criminologists have frequently overlooked the fact that the explanation of conventional crime, even if successful, would never be valid for the whole of crime, the greater proportion of which is conveniently ignored not only by most of them but also by the vast majority of governments and agencies as well as political parties and politicians in developed and developing countries.

It is my own view that the methodology of Western criminology is in dire need of a complete revolution if it is to come to terms with the political and cultural character of the censure of crime. A hermeneutics of crime is required, which can explicate its meaning as a practical but ideological censure within an historically and culturally specific political economy.

As Lopez-Rey said, criminology has mistaken the essential character of its central topic:

> Contemporary criminology regards crime as a socio-economic or psycho-psychiatric entity or a combination of both. *Actually, it is primarily a socio-political concept and only secondarily a causal event.*
> (Lopez-Rey, 1970: 234: my emphasis)

Foreshadowing my own argument (see Sumner, 1981b), he implores us to see criminology as the study of the 'socio-political concepts' and as part of the struggle for justice. Naturally, if crime is returned to its normative-political home, the liberal or radical politics that flow from this must be to reform or revolutionize the 'socio-political concepts' and the institutions that apply them. Such conclusions seem not only inevitable but irresistible when we look at crime in the exploited and underdeveloped societies under the yoke of neo-colonialism (see Sumner, 1982). Mushanga (1976: 18) illustrates my point well when he reverses normal usage and writes that the social censures of crime and deviance are selective, interested, and often insulting moral-political categories:

> Mass murders, massacres, genocide and general brutality and terrorism against civilians by those in power may be due to the fact that power is in the hands of vandals, hooligans, nitwits and anomic delinquents.

In short, it is clearly not a recent discovery of radical scholarship that no particular behaviour of personality can be shown to be universally deviant or criminal, and that the censures of crime and deviance are irredeemably suffused with ideology. More orthodox scholars have nevertheless persisted in studying deviant or criminal behaviour separate from their definitive ideological concepts and political practices of application. One can only conclude that this apparently perverse persistence has political, ideological and maybe even financial roots.

In contrast, the hallmark of radical intellectual work in the sociology of crime and deviance has been its constant drive to demystify those categories (see Hall *et al.*, 1978; Sumner, 1981a; Box, 1983). As early as 1943, C. Wright Mills argued that what was defined in the literature of social science as deviant, maladjusted or pathological behaviour, or as a 'social problem', was very much a product of the ideology of the definers. Their definitions were constituted by the yardstick of their own ideals and norms, which were usually those of 'independent middle-class persons verbally living out Protestant ideals in the small towns of America' (Mills, 1943: 180). In effect, he concluded that their definitions of social pathology actually amounted to 'propaganda' for their own distinctive, sectional morality. Edwin Lemert (1951: 1) formulated this same view with great clarity:

> Generally speaking, these late nineteenth and early twentieth century sociologists grouped together under the heading of 'social pathology', those human actions which ran counter to ideals of residential stability, property ownership, sobriety, thrift, habituation to work, small business enterprises, sexual discretion, family solidarity, neighbourliness and discipline of the will. In effect, social problems were considered to be any forms of behaviour violating the mores from which these ideals were projected.

Since Lemert wrote that, however, many sociologists of deviance have persisted in studying the exotic 'subcultures' of 'delinquents', 'nuts, sluts and perverts' (to use Liazos' phrase) to find out what is so nutty, slutty or perverted about these people, as if they (and their behaviours) are quite different from the rest of the human race (see Liazos, 1972). On the other hand, many other sociologists have turned their attention to the labels themselves, and have shown that they are best understood as moral or political categories representing specific moral or political interests (e.g. Becker, 1963; Chambliss, 1964; Gustfield, 1967). This work, commonly known as that of the 'labelling theorists' (a misleading and imprecise label itself), has frequently been criticized for its liberal, pluralist perspective, which is limited to attributing the origin of the moral categories to interest groups active on the political scene. Such a limitation, I would argue, results in superficial analysis of symbolic political in-fighting for legislation, or of merely stated moral beliefs, and a neglect of the more fundamental social structures and institutions of our age (see also Gouldner, 1968). This criticism is more or less true; however, it is equally problematic that the 'labelling theorists' (1) never specified in detail the ideological constitution of the moral and criminal categories, (2) never fully explored the links between these categories and the social structure, and (3) only dealt with the relationships between moral/legal condemnation and 'interest' in an instrumentalist way. That is, the advantages of a moral or legal campaign to its immediate protagonists were observed, but little more than that.

The rise of radical approaches (conflict theory, Marxism and anarchism) to crime and deviance in the late 1960s, and their continued growth in the 1970s, did lead to a more profound analysis of criminal law, which linked the interests and ideologies of legislative groups to the basic structures of economy and politics. Often using historical research, such scholars drew attention to the constancy and armory of established political power and to its roots in economic exploitation (see e.g. Chambliss, 1974; Quinney, 1977). However, this work has focused on criminal law and, like pluralist analysis, has tended to emphasize the material and instrumental functions of that law. Work has been done on the mass-media portrayal of deviance (see Cohen and Young, 1973; Glasgow Media Group, 1976; Hall et al., 1978), but this also has not involved a formal reconceptualization of deviance. The moral roots of the modern penal system in ideological categories of deviance, and the concepts for grasping this, have been relatively neglected. Power and general economic functions have been at the fore; not surprisingly, because these are the areas that radical critics felt were neglected in 'labelling theory' (see Gouldner, 1968; Liazos, 1972; Taylor et al., 1973; Thio, 1973).

In consequence, a common position emerged which is well defined in an essay by Chambliss (1974: 37, 38, 39):

> The criminal law is . . . first and foremost a reflection of the interests and ideologies of the governing class. . . . [T]hose who control the economic and political resources of the society will inevitably see their interests and ideologies more often represented in the law than will others. . . . Nothing is inherently criminal, it is only the response that makes it so. If we are to explain crime, we must first explain the social forces that cause some acts to be defined as criminal while other acts are not.

The danger in this view is that it has a tendency to reduce the origins of criminal law to class conflicts over material resources, and to gloss over the ideological character and composition of such laws: the origins and prehistory of the ideological categories in the law rarely get a look-in. Of course, it is vital that studies be done to illustrate the role of the criminal law as a crucial instrument of class power in the development of economic systems (e.g. Shivji, 1982). But, logically, we also need to understand fully the complexity of the forms of consciousness (or ideologies) which are expressed in apparently general, universalistic legislation in order to comprehend the precise social character, purpose and function of criminal law (see Thompson, 1975, for a study which never glosses over the importance of moral sensibilities and ideological conceptions; and, more abstractly, Sumner, 1979: ch. 8). Forms of moral sensibility, feelings of moral righteousness, codes of law, and ideological concepts are powerful forces in human history. Indeed, in a very real sense, they are definitive – of the crucially important differences in degree and form of oppression; to ignore them is to suppose that there is one single form of exploitation and one single form of domination based upon it.

Habermas's view seems outmoded. He argued that, because of the technological rationality of legislators in advanced capitalist states in crisis, law and morality are now at such a distance that moral ideology is not a key component of modern law (see, e.g. Habermas, 1979). The moral majorities invoked by Thatcher and Reagan were invaluable and integral forces in their administrations. Legislators in even the most technocratic of modern states attempt to formulate their interest according to moral ideas with potential for common assent – when they bother to use the law at all – and their careers are still subject to the threat of sexual or financial scandal. It therefore cannot be precise enough to say that 'it is the existence of structurally induced conflicts between groups in the society that determines the form and the content of the criminal law' (Chambliss, 1974: 8). Such a formulation does not bring out the role of moral ideology in determining the content of the criminal law. Structure, interest and consciousness are conflated to produce an all-too-neat picture: it overlooks the relative autonomy of each of these aspects and their uneven interrelations. The radical criminologists of the early 1970s, I suggest (see also Spitzer 1980), tended to read off criminal law from the social structure as a fairly direct expression in political consciousness of a monolithic 'dominant economic class interest' (with the notable exception of Carson, 1974, 1979, 1982).

This failure to take account of the distinctive and relatively autonomous dialectics of politics and ideology often left radical criminological analysis of law with an economistic and instrumentalist character (see, e.g. Quinney, 1977; Reiman, 1979). The specific ideological character of moral and legal censures was left untheorized. Some writers even turned the clock back by romanticizing deviation as political activity and thus reaffirming that deviants were different kinds of people (for example, Taylor et al., 1973; see the critique in Sumner, 1976). Very few attempted to reformulate the concept of deviance in alternative theoretical terms – the tendency being to say 'Deviance, yeah, right on' (see Pearson, 1975, for an excellent commentary on radical criminology and the cultural revolt of the late 1960s). Even recent perceptive Marxist commentaries presented no clear alternative (see Werkentin et al., 1974; Greenberg, 1981; Hinch, 1985; Melossi, 1985; O'Malley, 1988).

The one outstanding attempt to retheorize deviance, by Spitzer (1975), unfortunately suffers much from this tendency to economism and instrumentalism. For Spitzer (1975: 640), the 'problematic quality' of deviant groups 'ultimately' resides in their challenge to 'class rule'. 'Problem populations' are said to present a threat or cost to capitalist relations of production, although he does include within this category people who challenge socialization practices and revered 'forms of social organization'. Such a formulation reduces problems of deviance to threats to the relations of production. A better formulation would bear in mind that violations of political and cultural rules are socially censured as well as violations of economic rules, and that the former violations are not reducible to the latter. More importantly, Spitzer does not attempt to rethink the meaning of the concept of deviance, being happy to sustain the notion held by some interactionists that it refers to a status. In my view, this is not a tenable position, because it conceals the fact that different censures have different implications for social status, and that only the strongest censures automatically and totally reconstruct the recipient's social status. Therefore, the very conception of deviance as a full social status presupposes the importance of deviance for status and, in effect, takes a consequence of deviance as its essence.

However, Spitzer (1975: 640) does recognize that these deviant statuses are 'social categories' and that

> Most fundamentally, deviance production involves the development of and changes in deviant categories and images. A critical theory must examine where these images and definitions came from, what they reflect about the structure of and priorities in specific class societies, and how they are related to class conflict.

This position is close to the direction which I want to follow, although it implicitly reduces the origins of social censures to class relations. In my view, relations of race and gender (for example) are often co-ordinated with class relations but are not reducible to them. However, on the whole, radical sociology had made little effort to reconceptualize deviance, or crime, despite the fact that in the practice of research (e.g. Hall et al., 1978), or of politics, many on the Left now regularly treat deviance and crime as a matter of moral-political judgement, and therefore as social censures rooted in ideological formations. Therefore, I see what follows as an attempt to articulate something which many people now recognize in practice; a new conception of deviance which has emerged within the intellectual movement of what one might summarize as contemporary socialist criminology.

Social censures

The conception of social censure is simple. Years of research in sociology and criminology have shown that the categories of the criminal law and common morality are hopelessly inadequate as empirical descriptions of specific social behaviours. Whether we take their abstract, discursive definitions or their practical definitions in the course of law enforcement or moral stigmatization, it is clear that the definitions of deviant behaviour, even within a single society, exclude what should be included, include what should be excluded, and generally fail to attain unambiguous, consistent and settled social meanings. To this we can add massive cross-cultural differences in the meaning, enforcement and even existence of categories of deviance, and endless instances of resistance to them involving alternative categories. Clearly, they are highly acculturated terms of moral and political judgement. As Thompson (1975: 193–4) said, they are moral categories which, if relied upon as descriptive, will automatically undermine scientific enquiry; (see also Hall *et al.*, 1978: 189). In an earlier essay, I reached this conclusion:

> These complex, composite cultural forms, containing the ideology of the dominant classes and a selective sprinkling of reality, continue to block clear-headed enquiry. . . . The first step of any intellectually rigorous enquiry into matters of crime and deviance must be to suspend a commonsensical acceptance of these categories and to investigate the social relationships, ideologies and contexts which combine to form them and give specific historical meaning. (Sumner, 1981a: 279)

Given the impossibility of using the social categories of crime and deviance as scientific categories or observational terms with definable, constant and consistent behavioural referents, it makes most sense to treat them as elements of highly contextualized moral and political discourses, i.e. as negative ideological categories with specific, historical applications. These negative categories of moral ideology are social censures. The sociology of crime and deviance must therefore become a sociology of social censures; their structural roots, institutional forms, discursive and practical meanings, systems and policies of enforcement, hegemonic functions, effects and significance for 'offenders', and normative validity.

Censures are used for a variety of purposes and in a variety of contexts. They are practical; that is, they are invoked or exist within the course of historically specific social practices. Their meaning is therefore usually fairly flexible; although some may have fundamental and strong roots in the human psyche, given the course of human history, and may almost be archetypal in Jung's sense and therefore recurrent in essence if not form.[5] However deep-rooted they are in history, their current meaning and effect is primarily governed by their expression in a contemporary social practice, which is of course structured, motivated and contextualized. Their general function is to signify, denounce and regulate, not to explain. Their typical consequence is not an adequate account of a social conflict but rather the distinguishing of 'offenders' from 'non-offenders', the creation of resentment in their targets, or the cessation of the offensive matter. They mark off the deviant, the pathological, the dangerous and the criminal from the normal and the good. They say 'stop', and are tied to a desire to control, prevent or punish.

As such, they are clearly moral and political in character. Because they signify worth and correctness against wrong and danger, they simultaneously form a justification for repressive action against the offender and for attempts to educate the recipient into the desired habits or way of life. Their frequent appeal to general moral principles gives them inherent political potential in the constant struggle for hegemony. Nuts, sluts, perverts, prostitutes, slags, murderers, psychopaths, villains, freaks, wreckers, troublemakers, militants, muggers, rioters, squatters and scroungers are all social censures with the potential to mobilize the forces of law, order and moral purity against targeted sections of the population.

In societies which are substantially divided by class in terms of wealth, power and ideology, it is inevitable that the class bloc which dominates the economy, owns the means of mass communication and controls the reins of political power, will have the greatest capacity to assert its censures in the legal and moral discourses of the day. But this will also be true of the dominant gender and the dominant race. Enunciated in the mass media, enforced in the courts and other policing institutions, and materially rooted in the dominant social relations of the epoch, such censures must soon take on a more generalized character as other people internalize them. Therefore, the sectional censures applied by the white, male, bourgeoisie tend to become the social censures of capitalist society. They tend to be the ones that are institutionalized in the discourses and practices of the state and the ideological apparatuses. Such censures are only ever formed in practical conflict with opposing groups and therefore are always subject to continual resentment, resistance and redefinition by these oppositions. They are essentially unstable forms. The perpetuity of contestation of social censures in divided societies means that there are always oppositional, alternative or negotiated forms of censure existing within subordinate group milieux, opposition parties, and political or cultural movements. These groups and movements frequently clash with the hegemonic forces in parliament, the courts, the streets, and in film or literature. Thus the formal motion of censure emerged in politics; alongside the judicial homily and sentence, the editorial harangue, the police assault, and other censorious procedures. If the subordinate groups do not 'learn', history has taught us to expect the dominant regulatory agencies to try to destroy, colonize or police their cultures, until the censure is overthrown or falls into disuse.

Moreover, and here my thoughts are very tentative, the social censure in itself, as a distinct form of response to conflict, may well be an historically specific phenomenon, not at all universal or inevitable. It may be an outcome of the formation of class divisions, growing alongside courts, police, judges and armies. But this may not be a sufficient account. Perhaps we should also consider that it is a particularly masculine response (see Sumner, in press), that it implies a fractured community disinclined towards more discursive processes of mediation and persuasion, and that it supposes a high degree of fear of others' freedom. It is probably also true that the emergence of negative moral categories from repetitive social process, their hardening into systems of law, and, later, the proliferation of moral and legal censures, all seem to be milestones in the history of social individuation; a history which accelerates dramatically with the emergence of industrial capitalism. We are yet to begin the study of the processes, following industrialization, whereby the plurality of diffuse censures becomes the object of hegemonic struggle, whereby most censures are adopted and transformed by hegemonic ideology in its work of collectivization of the public morality, and whereby older, often more subversive, meanings are lost.[6]

On a more basic level, it is important to recognize that social censures intrinsically contain two elements which enable their plausibility and legitimacy:

1 Because they are formed or invoked within the rich texture of social practice, they relate to real, and therefore two-sided and generalizable, issues; to real, therefore rarely angelic, often hurt and resentful, people; and to real, therefore rarely harmonious or simple, relationships; albeit superficially, selectively and partially.
2 Because it is rarely morally acceptable to use raw self-interest as a clinching argument, they usually invoke the widely accepted, general moral principles of an epoch (e.g. condemning violence, exploitation, and idleness), albeit superficially, selectively and partially.

Therefore, censures are not *just* labels, or mere words uttered in the heat of the moment, but categories of denunciation or abuse lodged within very complex, historically loaded practical conflicts and moral debates.

Social censures have a profound existence: at the heart of intense emotional patterns, in the centre of politically and economically significant moral-ideological formations, and in the struggles and self-justifications that make history. They are part and parcel of the very processes which constitute the social fabric itself. Deeply imbricated in human practice, within its reflexive and self-justifying character, social censures express, construct and contain, in varying degrees in different instances, the whole historic weight of economic contradictions, social divisions of all kinds, levels of moral development, the struggle for democratization, and the limits of human reflexivity. As such, they are vital forces in the constitution of societies.[7] In short, they are one eye on the world, one key to the door of human history, and thus one dynamic entrée into the sociology of any social relationship. Social censures are not just a vital element within the developing sociology of social regulation, but also a major dimension of sociological analysis in general.

In contrast, the concept of the label, so vital to the labelling perspective of symbolic interactionism, connotes voluntarism and arbitrary, self-interested, external application, implies no real reference point or justifiability, and suggests the philosophies of pragmatism and nominalism. This is hardly surprising, given the roots of symbolic interactionism in those philosophical traditions (see Rock, 1979). Social censures, in contrast, contain and express interpretations of real phenomena, models of human nature, principles of moral self-justification, and the weight of self-interest. They are rarely arbitrarily applied, and are rarely just external to their targets, whose capacity for reflexive action means that they were probably already aware of their discreditability (see also Goffman, 1963). They are sometimes quite justifiable to a wide audience, both normatively and in terms of having empirical evidence, however selective and partial this justification. Moreover, when they are 'knee-jerk' reactions, social censures are not always easily understood as 'voluntary' responses, or as practical or sensible moves.

Thus conceived, we cannot begin to understand social censures without reference to (1) the ideological formations, social relations and human fears which support and constitute them, (2) the phenomena they interpret and signify, and (3) the historical conjuncture within which they are applied.

In this way, the concept of social censures breaks sharply from the interactionists' tendency to detach deviant labels from the wider social structures of wealth, power and meaning, while retaining the interactionists' sense of the importance of subjective reflexivity, the dynamism of praxis, and the role of specific agencies in mobilizing particular campaigns. This break has been primarily achieved through the application of a contemporary Marxist *theory of ideology*, which sees ideologies as both sectional reflections of social structure *and* as active, creative, integral components of reflexive social practice, not simply as the systematic, intellectualized, false consciousness of group interest (see Sumner, 1979, for an extended critique of both liberal and orthodox Marxist theories of ideology; see also the critique of the interactionists' conception of labels in Werkentin *et al.*, 1974).

The development of the theory of social censures obviously owes much to, and is partly dependent upon, the value of this theory of ideology. It has taken the argument beyond instrumentalist (conflict theory or Marxist) approaches, because this analysis of ideology, influenced by European phenomenology, hermeneutics and cultural studies, posits many qualifications to the orthodoxy of economism and class reductionism, as well as to the Marxist concept of ideology itself (see Hall *et al.*, 1978; Laclau, 1977; Johnson, 1979; Sumner, 1979: 10–56, 207–38, 286–97). A brief sketch of the associated social-theoretical positions is probably helpful to a broad readership.

While it tries to avoid lapsing into 'culturalism' (see Johnson, 1979), this analysis insists that the state is a site of considerable struggle; that capitalist social relations and ideologies can involve complex overlaps of, and divisions between class, race, gender, age and nationality; that ideologies (as reflections of these social relations) can thus be extremely complex forms; that in advanced capitalism the high development of the industries and institutions of ideological practice can institutionalize ideologies to the point where they become major, relatively autonomous forces of social development; and, finally, that all formulations about the contemporary role of dominant ideology should be historically specific. In terms of the concept of ideology itself, broadly speaking, the analysis holds, on the negative side, that it is not to be equated necessarily with the false, the bourgeois, the political, the systematic or the economic reflex, but rather that, on the positive side, it can be enlightening, revolutionary, practical, and sustained in sites of oppositional culture. In short, while the dominant symbols of an epoch will still stand for its fundamental structural features and will mobilize support for them, the modern analysis of ideology recognizes that most symbols or signs can be mobilized in many ways and that most aspects of social life have acquired surplus significance, after being rendered significant in one political discourse or another. What makes this a distinctively Marxist position is the retention of the insistence that the dialectics of the various social ideologies remain dominated by the dynamics of class formation, struggle, alliance and demise which reflect the development of the dominant mode of production, the societal motor-force. It is consonant with the Foucauldian emphasis on the practical and powerful character of knowledge, but finds his non-use of the term ideology ill-justified (see Foucault, 1980: 118).[8]

In this theory of ideology, the content of new ideological formations, with diverse elements from diverse roots, finds its unity in the target of the ideological discourse or practice: a thesis drawn from Laclau's broader formulations (1977: 92–111). The targeted character of ideological discourses and practices brings together various symbolic components into an ideological formation, despite their occasional inconsistency and disparate historical origins. Social censures, as negative ideological formations, are thus highly targeted, despite the universality or indeterminateness of their form in language, especially legal language.

Generally, therefore, they are characterized by their expression in the vernacular of ideological discourses involved in, and generated by, the historic struggles between classes, genders, nations and other social groups. These languages have their own relatively autonomous existence and dialectics, and must in consequence be analysed in their own discrete specificity. There is no question of this analysis of social censures glossing over the internal logic and evolution of moral languages (e.g. the language of the law). Indeed, the analysis suggests that a sociological etymology of the language of censure, examining the historic meanings and moments of formation of terms like prostitution, vandalism, 'nicking', 'perks', militancy and drug abuse would be an invaluable new tool in the explication of forms of censure and social regulation. Moreover, the whole approach demands much closer connections between sociology and literary analysis; it requires sociologists to use literary sources far more than at present. However, there is equally no question of succumbing to discourse determinism. Moral language is formed and developed in social practice; its expression of unified ideological formations in censures is enabled, primarily, by that unity, which is itself forged in the targeting process. The practical processes involved in targeting social censures are extremely important, especially with bureaucratically enforced censures, and need urgent study.

In conclusion, our main objective in research must be to unearth the social relations and contexts material to the genesis of the conflicts of interest and mores which are the cradle of social censures and the censorious ideological discourses. The starting point will often be a reading of moral discourses, an historical hermeneutics, to discover the full meaning of the censure in a particular historical and structural context. This historical-sociological etymology should reveal the target of the censure, the agencies and procedures of targeting, and the shifts in its meaning and contexts of use. Such research will often begin with the questions: What does the censure (e.g. vandalism) mean? When was it first used? And against whom? Who was behind it and who enforced it? What ideological concepts give it such a meaning? What was the political and structural context of its application? Of course, there are many other associated researches which need be done; some are exemplified in this volume, others in later books in this series. This perspective, in my view, generates many questions, many research projects, many theoretical developments, and many policy implications. Too many to summarize here: but then, that is a good sign.

Some examples

Maggie Sumner's research (1980) on the censure of prostitution in Victorian England provides a good illustration of the value and character of the concept of censure. Her analysis demonstrates that prostitution refers to what women defined as prostitutes represent, rather than to a specific social practice. These women were observed and dealt with as signs; as signs of various awful social possibilities concerning work, public order and sexuality. Various texts by doctors, priests and legislators reveal that the Victorian middle class had nothing like a precise definition of prostitution. Their writings refer to delivering herself up 'to a life of impurity and licentiousness', being 'indiscriminate in the selection of her lovers', 'using his person other than for procreation', 'illicit intercourse' (meaning 'the voluntary surrender of her virtue'), existing professionally 'by the fruits of her lewd conduct', and being 'a kept woman' (see M. Sumner, 1980: ch. 3). Whatever it was in the abstract, prostitution as far as the police were concerned was a way of earning a living; in the practice of enforcing the censure, clandestines (part-timers) did not count (M. Sumner, 1980: 117–18). The clearest, and probably the most philosophically accurate, definition came from one Mr Thomas, secretary of the London Female Preventive and Reformatory Institution, who submitted to the 1871 Royal Commission on the Administration and Operation of the Contagious Diseases Act that 'prostitution is prostitution'.

The kind of woman referred to as a prostitute is characterized by Lord Acton:

> What is a prostitute? She is a woman who gives for money that which she ought to give only for love, who ministers to passion and lust alone, to the exclusion and extinction of all the higher qualities derived from the intercourse of the sexes. She is a woman with half the woman gone, and that half containing all that elevates her nature, leaving her a mere instrument of impurity. (Quoted in M. Sumner, 1980: 129)

This 'sad burlesque of a woman' (prostitutes are nearly always defined as female) was usually identified or stereotyped in middle-class discourse (i.e. *targeted*, in the sense defined above) as follows: she was working class, either a labourer's daughter or servant, and had distinct 'mannerisms'; her appearance was shameless, being dirty and dressed in scruffy, tawdry garments; she cursed, was ignorant of religion, drank heavily and was frequently seen in public houses or in the streets of poor districts; she was a bad parent, lacked maternal instincts and was often infertile; she was a nymphomaniac, tending to abort during her third month of pregnancy and having a completely different menstrual cycle to other women.

Prostitution was what she represented. She was the living symbol: the material proof and target of the ideological censure of prostitution. And she was fruitfully employed: as the symbolic opposite of the hegemonic ideology of bourgeois-Protestant sexuality. Maggie Sumner (1980: 277–8) concluded that:

The examination of the nineteenth century material . . . makes it abundantly clear that 'prostitution' is not just a simple observational category referring to the sale of sexuality; such a sale is only prostitution when it is conducted publicly in the streets, when vendors actively seek purchasers with whom they may have no other relationship, are dressed in particular types of clothing, have no other jobs, and so forth.

Although the content of the censure was clearly in part mythical, it also clearly contains references to many real aspects of working-class culture. However, equally plainly, this was no neutral moral symbol, free of class prejudice or gender stereotypes. Nor was it free of political interest. It was a censure that reflected the desire and the need to keep 'public order' in the urban areas (see also Bujra, 1982), i.e. to control and prevent the emergence of working-class resistance to the developing bourgeois society. Maggie Sumner argues that the censure (and the interests behind it) was expressed at the intersection of three Victorian discourses. The prostitute was represented as (1) a fallen woman, (2) a fallen worker and (3) a dangerous citizen. She offended the ideal image of bourgeois womanhood, the ideology of the industrious worker, and the ideal of the law-abiding, privatized, subordinate citizen. As such, she offended three ideological conceptions which were direct and active reflections of the dominant social relations of British capitalism, during a particular phase of industrialization.

Prostitution is quite simply *not* the exchange of sex for consideration (in the legal sense). If that were true, most people are guilty, yet rarely charged. We cannot understand why a particular, small group of women are targeted for surveillance, harassment and prosecution as prostitutes, nor why the law has been so unfairly interpreted and enforced, unless we study and comprehend the historic social meaning of prostitution as a censure. To study the women censured, or even self-defined in terms of the censure, as prostitutes, in order to tell us something about why they are in trouble with the law, is absolutely useless if we think that their behaviour is the sole cause of their arrest. It is certainly valuable to talk to those women censured as prostitutes to discover the patterns and effects of censure enforcement, and thereby to obtain clues about the targeting and purposes of the selective censure. However, to study the behaviour or personalities of those women, as a representative sample of prostitutes, to find out why people prostitute themselves is as absurd and as dangerous as studying the directors of multinational corporations to discover why people work for a living.

The ideological character of censures is nowhere clearer than in the history of colonialism. After independence, Zimbabwe's landless poor tried to reclaim their land often by simply repossessing it, only to find white settler-farmers denouncing them as squatters and calling for the enforcement of the law. Of course, as many have pointed out, the white farmers in fact are the squatters. Similarly, the violence of colonial military conquests could be legitimized as part of the 'civilizing mission', yet the violence of nationalist revolt is censured as 'terrorism'. Refusal to leave the land, to move from subsistence farming to wage labour in the colonists' mines and plantations, was met with the violence of a militaristic police and the persuasiveness of penal tax legislation (see Van Onselen, 1976; Fitzpatrick, 1980; Shivji, 1982). Even tax evasion can be censured with the full weight of the criminal law in some historical circumstances. Once converted to the horrors of wage slavery in brutal, unhygienic and ill-paid working conditions, workers often did not work well – only to find themselves heavily censured as loafers and deserters (Shivji, 1982). Those who were beaten to death by the mine-owners' police were not said to be murdered: these were defined as accidental deaths probably caused by the enlarged spleen of the worker. This illustrates well how even the serious crimes are fully subject to the theory of social censures. Murder is not a behaviour but a censure, applied to certain killings, whose pattern of application is thoroughly ideological. Traditional mores suffered no better than the economy supporting them in the drive to capitalist agriculture: indigenous farmers found their land tenure practices and agricultural techniques censured as criminal offences against the Western colonial ideology of appropriate agriculture (see Sweet, 1982). Even the breach of agricultural regulations, and other such, apparently administrative, legal instruments, can be the subject of heavy censure; as it was in colonial days, and as it is in many 'socialist' societies (see Shaidi, forthcoming). When the local people resisted the colonists, through secret societies, cults, syncretic religions, trade unions and nationalist movements, they were further censured and suppressed in the name of Western civilization, the Christian religion, the principles of natural justice and, of course, ethnic superiority. The class-political interest in a censure has never been so piously justified.

What the colonial episodes reveal with particular clarity are the sectional and often amoral character of moral censures, and their class connections with the practical dynamics of economic life. They compel us to begin the political economy of morality. Colonial censures may be stark examples, but their parallels in our own history are not hard to find.

Corrigan's study (1979) showed that, in a period of high unemployment, schoolteachers' censures of pupils as lazy, slow or rebellious look strikingly ideological, in the service of keeping order in the school and appropriately filtering and certificating the future labour force (see also Pollard, 1979). *Policing the Crisis* (Hall *et al.*, 1978) suggests that the press and police censure of 'the mugging wave' of 1972–3 looks highly ideological in the light of the lack of evidence for it, the variety of acts brought under the censure, the political conjuncture of the day, and the continual police pressure on blacks in the inner cities. *Bad News* (Glasgow Media Group, 1976) documents the way the intensive censure of industrial militancy is constructed by television news out of evidence which could indicate that the real militancy is that of industrialists and government, in adopting policies of severe wage restraint, masked of course in ideology as 'the social contract'. Several other recent studies in the sociology of crime and deviance implicitly employ the conception developed here, without naming it, and provide further empirical evidence for a thorough going reconceptualization of the field. The time is right for more.

Conclusion

> Delinquency, with the secret agents that it procures, but also with the generalised policing that it authorises, constitutes a means of perpetual surveillance of the population: an apparatus that makes it possible to supervise, through the delinquents themselves, the whole social field. Delinquency functions as a political observatory. . . . This production of delinquency and its investment by the penal apparatus must be taken for what they are; not results acquired once and for all, but tactics that shift according to how closely they reach their target. (Foucault, 1977: 271, 285)

For 'delinquency' substitute 'social censures' and Foucault's comment becomes applicable to the whole field. Social censures combine with forms of power and economy to provide distinct and important features of practices of domination and social regulation. These ideological categories of morality and politics help both to explain and to mystify the routine targeting of the practices of surveillance and regulation: explain, because their surrounding, constitutive discourse tells us something about the specific offence; and mystify, because censures are often expressed in universalistic language which appeals to general moral principles. Targeted law enforcement practices have been described by interactionists and ethnomethodologists in their studies of the informal norms of practical policing, but their theoretical approach left them as unexplained biases: it presented them as merely incidental or organizational. Such accounts never came to terms with the fact that these informal prejudices and targets are lodged in broader ideological formations and discourses related to dominant interests and social structures.

The concept of social censure registers several key features of modern practices of social regulation: their political character, their reliance on value judgements, and their formal, bureaucratic character. It also clearly conveys the sense of regulation from above – unlike 'deviance', which implies abnormal individual psychology and behaviour. Deviance in itself is a concept silent on the political activity involved in regulation. It suggests that a norm has been broken, but little more. As a description of a whole branch of sociology, however, it is more dangerous, in suggesting that there is a set of definable behaviours in breach of a normative consensus. On the other hand, a sociology of social censures, almost by definition, throws its emphasis on the social relationships which generate opposing ideas and interests, and on the political conflicts which precipitate their condensation, and subsequent implementation in practices of penalty and tutelage. Therefore, its immediate, strategic political implications relate to the struggles for justice and rights.

The normative and political critique of social censures must now be developed and advanced at a pace. Hopefully, the labour movement will join feminism and black consciousness in this development, so that the critique and ensuing reconstruction will be fully in accordance with the moral and political principles of contemporary, revolutionary socialism. This will necessitate the revival of normative debate within jurisprudence and sociology. For too long, jurisprudence, sociology and criminology have been merely analytic and empirical, taking for granted the moral and legal fabric of modern bourgeois societies. The normative and political critique of social censures, in the short run, demands protection against their arbitrary and unreasonable application, and in the long run their transformation in line with the ideas of another political force. The full recognition of the political and ideological character of 'deviance' must lead to a politics of defensive and prefigurative rights struggles (see Sumner, 1981b), and to a moral politics which challenges the immorality of many social censures and their selective application. This is roughly the direction in which socialist-feminist and anti-racist criminology in contemporary Britain is already going. What is needed now is the full reconsideration of the censure and punishment of anti-social practices, not just in the light of class politics, but also in view of the politics of gender, race, age, environment and region, with a view to immediate, and future, radical changes in the moral fabric and legislative contours of this society. The old moral order, highlighted at its worst by the many evils of Thatcherism, needs a revolutionary overhaul.

Acknowledgements

This is a revised version of the 'Rethinking deviance' essay (Sumner, 1983), which in turn was based on a paper called 'Abandoning deviancy theory' given to the American Society of Criminology conference on 'The Future of Criminology' in Washington, D.C., in November 1981 (in Spanish: Sumner, 1985). John Clarke, Caryn Horwitz, Steven Spitzer and Alan Hunt gave me several useful comments and much encouragement at that conference; Karen Lubarr gave detailed comments on the 1983 article; and the enthusiasm of successive generations of students at Cambridge University has persuaded me to persist with my ideas. I am also very grateful to John Lowman and his doctoral students at Simon Fraser University, and Fritz Sack and the postgraduate group in criminology at Hamburg University, for their recent strong support. This revision improves the clarity and precision of the 1983 article considerably, with the benefit of its continued use in teaching, and thus supersedes it.

Notes

1 Of course, this is stupendously obvious, but why does criminology around the world still proceed as if legal categories were scientific? Indeed, why does popular opinion still often see them that way? In a nutshell, to describe the categories of crime and deviance as ideological is not simply to denounce them, or to explain them away, but to say something important about their nature and functioning. Their partiality is one thing, the capacity of people, in the course of motivated social practice, to elevate them to the status of custom, or to conceal their character as judgements, is another.

2 That this is so is amusingly evidenced by the American thesaurus I am using as part of the Microsoft Word 4 software. It defines deviant thus: 'deviate, debaucher, pervert, weirdo'. How could American sociology imagine that deviance was anything more than an abusive denunciation? A term that is synonymous with weirdo or pervert is hardly the value-free concept so desired by the 'end of ideology' brigade in American sociology.

3 This question, with all its ecological as well as political implications, must, and I think will, become one of the most important issues for sociology and society in the 1990s. In this specific sense, we must advocate the 'greening' of criminology. To tease the terminology of the 1920s, the time is ripe for an ecology of the anti-social.

4 An exact example of this occurred at the UN's conference on crime and development in Costa Rica in 1984. In the final plenary session, I had disturbed the calm of sunny bonhomie by arguing that international cooperation on research into crime and development in Latin America would simply reproduce dominant North American criminological concerns with the 'subcultures of violence' of the urban poor, if the steering committee did not contain some brown/black faces and some women. By the end of the proceedings, I found that most of the male, North American criminologists were saying nothing to me, and that most of the Latin Americans were enthusiastically endorsing my demand for the study of police violence, vigilantism, corruption, the crimes of the CIA, and practices of the multinational corporations. Never has the enduring class character of the censure of crime, and of criminology itself, been more starkly exposed as white-coated, local waiters served tray after tray of cuba libres.

5 Future research might usefully spend some time examining what seem to be archetypal censures, and their corresponding narratives or moral tales, in order to develop a proper social psychology of censure.

6 Thus, for example, the censure of vandalism changed from being a critique of industrial and architectural ruination of the environment to a rebuke of working-class assaults upon the public monuments erected by those self-same

industrialists and architects (see Stone, 1982). It is no doubt time we reversed this historic process. Also, we should consider that the extensive vocabulary of censure during early industrialization (e.g. the many different words for thief) seems to be reduced and simplified in the repackaging work of the era of criminal law codification.

7 These formulations can be seen as similar to those in Giddens' theory of structuration (1984: 30–3). But they give censure and sanction a more creative role in the constitution of social forms, just as I want to give more weight to the sectional deployment of power and therefore to ideology, than he does (see Giddens, 1984: 14–16).

8 Foucault's later work increasingly reintroduces the Marxist concepts of ideology and hegemony into his analysis (see Foucault, 1978). Besides, even before that, he had, in my view, merely dropped the use of the term, and not the concept. His initial objections to the concept (1980: 118) are pre-Althusserian, aim at a very old Marxist notion of ideology, and were agreeable to most Marxist social theorists at the time of their publication in French.

References

Becker, H. (1963). *Outsiders*. New York: Free Press.
Bell, D. (1952). *The End of Ideology*. New York: Free Press.
Box, S. (1983). *Power, Crime and Mystification*. London: Tavistock.
Bredemeier, H. and Stephenson, R.M. (1970). *The Analysis of Social Systems*. London: Holt, Rinehart and Winston.
Bujra, J. (1982). Women 'entrepreneurs' of early Nairobi. In *Crime, Justice and Underdevelopment* (C. Sumner, ed.). London: Heinemann.
Carson, W.G. (1974). Symbolic and instrumental dimensions of early factory legislation. In *Crime, Criminology and Public Policy* (R. Hood, ed.). London: Heinemann.
Carson, W.G. (1979). The conventionalization of early factory crime. *International Journal of Sociology of Law*, 7, 37–60.
Carson, W.G. (1982). *The Other Price of Britain's Oil*. Oxford: Martin Robertson.
Chambliss, W.J. (1964). A sociological analysis of the law of vagrancy. *Social Problems*, 12, 67–77.
Chambliss, W.J. (1974). The state, the law and the definition of behaviour as criminal or delinquent. In *Handbook of Criminology* (D. Glaser, ed.). Chicago: Rand McNally.
Cohen, S. and Young, J. (eds) (1973). *The Manufacture of News*. London: Constable.
Corrigan, P. (1979). *Schooling the Smash Street Kids*. London: Macmillan.
Donzelot, J. (1979). *The Policing of Families*. London: Hutchinson.
Fitzpatrick, P. (1980). *Law and State in Papua New Guinea*. London: Academic Press.
Foucault, M. (1977). *Discipline and Punish*. London: Allen Lane.
Foucault, M. (1978). *The History of Sexuality*, Vol. 1. New York: Vintage.
Foucault, M. (1980). Truth and power. In *Power/Knowledge* (C. Gordon, ed.). New York: Pantheon.
Giddens, A. (1984). *The Constitution of Society*. Cambridge: Polity.
Glasgow Media Group (1976). *Bad News*. London: Routledge.

Goffman, E. (1963). *Stigma*. Englewood Cliffs, N.J.: Prentice-Hall.
Gouldner, A.W. (1968). The sociologist as partisan. *The American Sociologist*, May, 103–16.
Greenberg, D. (ed.) (1981). *Crime and Capitalism*. Palo Alto Calif.: Mayfield.
Gusfield, J. (1967). Moral passage. *Social Problems*, **15**, 175–88.
Habermas, J. (1971). *Toward a Rational Society*. London: Heinemann.
Habermas, J. (1979). *Communication and the Evolution of Society*. London: Heinemann.
Hall, S., Critcher, C., Jefferson, T., Clarke, J. and Roberts, B. (1978). *Policing the Crisis*, London: Macmillan.
Hinch, R. (1985). Marxist criminology in the 1970s. In *The New Criminologies in Canada* (T. Fleming, ed.). Toronto: Oxford University Press.
Hirst, P.Q. (1975). Marx and Engels on law, crime and morality. In *Critical Criminology* (I. Taylor, P. Walton and J. Young, eds). London: Routledge.
Johnson, R. (1979). Histories of culture/theories of ideology. In *Ideology and Cultural Production* (M. Barrett, P. Corrigan, A. Kuhn and J. Wolff, eds). London: Croom Helm.
Laclau, E. (1977). *Politics and Ideology in Marxist Theory*. London: New Left Books.
Lemert, E. (1951). *Social Pathology*. London: McGraw-Hill.
Liazos, A. (1972). Nuts, sluts and perverts. *Social Problems*, **20**, 103–20.
Lopez-Rey, M. (1970). *Crime*. London: Routledge.
Melossi, D. (1985). Overcoming the crisis in critical criminology: Toward a grounded labeling theory. *Criminology*, **23**(2), 193–208.
Mills, C.W. (1943). The professional ideology of social pathologists. *American Journal of Sociology*, **49**(2), 165–80.
Mushanga, T.M. (1976). *Crime and Deviance*. Kampala: E. Africa Lit. Bureau.
O'Malley, P. (1988). The purpose of knowledge: Pragmatism and the praxis of marxist criminology. *Contemporary Crisis*, **12**, 65–79.
Parsons, T. (1951). *The Social System*. London: Routledge.
Pascal, B. (1966). *Pensées*. Harmondsworth: Penguin.
Pearson, G. (1975). *The Deviant Imagination*. London: Macmillan.
Pollard, A. (1979). Negotiating deviance and 'getting done' in primary school classrooms. In *Schools, Pupils and Deviance* (L. Barton and R. Meighan, eds). Driffield: Nafferton.
Quinney, R. (1977). *Class, State and Crime*. New York: David and McKay.
Reiman, G. (1979). *The Rich Get Richer and the Poor Get Prison*. New York: John Wiley.
Robertson, R. and Taylor, L. (1973). *Deviance and Socio-legal Control*. London: Martin Robertson.
Rock, P. (1977). Review symposium. *British Journal of Criminology*, **17**(4), 390–4.
Rock, P. (1979). *The Making of Symbolic Interactionism*. London: Macmillan.
Schapera, I. (1972). Some anthropological concepts of 'crime'. *British Journal of Sociology*, **23**(4), 381–94.
Sellin, T. (1938). *Culture, Conflict and Crime*. New York: SSRC.
Shaidi, L.P. (forthcoming). *Criminal Justice and Underdevelopment in Tanzania*. Milton Keynes: Open University Press.

Shivji, I. (1982). Semi-proletarian labour and the use of penal sanctions in the labour law of colonial Tanganyika (1920–38). In *Crime, Justice and Underdevelopment* (C. Sumner, ed.). London: Heinemann.
Spitzer, S. (1975). Toward a Marxian theory of deviance. *Social Problems*, 22, 638–51.
Spitzer, S. (1980). 'Left-wing' criminology – an infantile disorder? In *Radical Criminology* (J.A. Inciardi, ed.). Beverly Hills Calif.: Sage.
Stone, C. (1982). Vandalism: Property, gentility and the rhetoric of crime in New York City 1890–1920. *Radical History Review*, 26, 13–34.
Sumner, C.S. (1976). Marxism and deviancy theory. In *Sociology of Crime and Delinquency in Britain. Vol. 2: The New Criminologies* (P. Wiles, ed.) London: Martin Robertson.
Sumner, C.S. (1979). *Reading Ideologies*. London: Academic Press.
Sumner, C.S. (1981a). Race, crime and hegemony. *Contemporary Crises*, 5(3), 277–91.
Sumner, C.S. (1981b). The rule of law and civil rights in contemporary Marxist theory. *Kapitalistate*, 9, 63–91.
Sumner, C.S. (ed.) (1982). *Crime, Justice and Underdevelopment*. London: Heinemann.
Sumner, C.S. (1983). Rethinking deviance. In *Research in Law, Deviance and Social Control*, Vol. 5 (S. Spitzer, ed.). Greenwich: JAI Press.
Sumner, C.S. (1985). El abandano de la teoria de la desviacion. *Revista Cenipec*, 7, 45–66.
Sumner, C.S. (in press). Foucault, gender and the censure of deviance. In *Feminist Perspectives in Criminology* (L. Gelsthorpe and A.M. Morris, eds). Milton Keynes: Open University Press.
Sumner, M. (1980). *Prostitution and images of women: A critique of the Victorian censure of prostitution*. M.Sc. thesis. University College of Wales, Aberystwyth.
Sutherland, E.H. and Cressey, D.R. (1974). *Criminology*. Philadelphia: Lippincott.
Sweet, L. (1982). Inventing crime: British colonial land policy in Tanganyika. In *Crime, Justice and Underdevelopment* (C. Sumner, ed.). London: Heinemann.
Taylor, I.R., Walton, P. and Young, J. (1973). *The New Criminology*. London: Routledge.
Taylor, I., Walton, P. and Young, J. (eds) (1975). *Critical Criminology*. London: Routledge.
Thio, A. (1973). Class bias in the sociology of deviance. *American Sociologist*, 8, 1–12.
Thompson, E.P. (1975). *Whigs and Hunters*. London: Allen Lane.
Trasler, G. (1973). Criminal behaviour. In *Handbook of Abnormal Psychology* (H.J. Eysenck, ed.). London: Pitman.
Van Onselen, C. (1976). *Chibaro*. London: Pluto Press.
Werkentin, F., Hofferkert, M. and Baurmann, M. (1974). Criminology as police science: Or how old is the new criminology? *Crime and Social Justice*, 2, 24–40.
Young, J. (1975). Working class criminology. In *Critical Criminology* (I. Taylor, P. Walton and J. Young, eds). London: Routledge and Kegan Paul.

3 Reflections on a sociological theory of criminal justice systems

Colin Sumner

It is not only the concept of deviance that is overdue for a theoretical overhaul. The Marxist approach to criminal justice is also. The most systematic statements on the subject from a Marxist point of view are still too instrumentalist and too economic-reductionist for modern taste. Social theory and politics have moved on a long way in the 1980s. So many new pieces of a revised jigsaw are now on the board, it is time we started to put them together to see what the new picture looks like. This essay is a first effort in that direction. It draws upon the real and valuable changes in the Left's approach to criminal justice over the last 15 years to offer a synthesis of some of the new ideas which must now be explored in empirical research and political practice (see also Ratner and McMullan, 1987: chs. 1, 5, 8, 10 and 11). Even if it only reinforces present directions and stimulates further reflection within socialist criminology, it will be of some value.

Criminal justice and the polity

One of our major concerns in this volume, and in this series as a whole, is with the political and ideological dimensions of criminal justice, and their connections with particular phases of societal development. Criminal justice is not just an effect of economic development, nor a mere index of social morality, nor simply a harsh and cumbersome expression of state power. Such formulations imply that it is just an effect of other causes. Yet it is, in itself, a very active and effective political and ideological force with profound consequences. It conditions our whole experience of sex, growth and death. It helps to define and support relations and regimes of production, and therefore to build and protect an economy. It reinforces a distinction between public and private morals; thus creating a public world, a polity, with formal standards of behaviour, and a private world where anything goes if you can afford it. Its masculinity and ethnocentrism work towards preserving male domination, imperial culture and a militaristic, paranoid state. Its language and procedure constantly announce to us that this is the form our collective, natural reason should take. It is, of course, also the most legitimate way in a modern society of levying violence against the disruptive, the dangerous, the inconvenient and the dissident.

Criminal justice, in these ways, is an important, relatively autonomous force in defining public and private morality, and in conditioning the culture of the whole society. This role is not reducible to its immediate, and often illusory, effects. Just as the most important consequences of the mass media are not in effecting direct imitations, but in conditioning, and participating in, the meanings we give to things, so, too, the most important outcome of the operation of criminal justice is not the number of prison inmates, nor even its deterrence value, but in the role it has in structuring social practice and popular morality. In this sense, it is a very *public* institution. Its essential theoretical, practical and historical foundations prioritize the preservation of *public* order and establish the ideological value of *publicity* in the practice of social regulation. Consequently, its public image and its practice in public are integral to its historic task. The criminal justice system will always be right at the centre of the definition of the public. That breaks both ways: it means that the system defines and represents the public realm, its integrity, value and role, but also that the public defines and regulates the criminal justice system. Criminal justice is therefore central to the integrity of the modern state; its creature and creator, a barometer of the balance of social power.

But criminal justice is not just active as an external determinant of social practice and morality, it is effective also in that it is internal to the members of the body politic, in partially constituting their sense of order, safety, morality and unity as members of a collective unit. It is integral to our ideas about the way that the modern state works and, more profoundly, to our sense of the ultimate morality of the universe. We are thus deeply interested in its operations, dramas and effects. When it is unjust, inefficient, authoritarian and corrupt, our commitment to the public realm, and even to the nation itself, is seriously reduced. It therefore plays an important role within the subjectivity of the modern citizen.

In that their task is to sustain, reinforce and restore power relations, and to articulate the dominant societal ideologies amidst a field of social contradictions, chaos and struggles, the criminal law and the criminal justice system are institutions lodged within the realm of political practice. They are not thereby purely class weapons, or 'organised class terror' (Pashukanis, 1978: 173), and in no way do they resemble any simple 'will of the people' (see Chambliss, 1974). They are too embroiled in the world of the public to be the former, and too much in the hands of the powerful to be the latter. Their very existence is an integral part of the development of the state, and of a public political world separate from what came to be known as civil society. As such, the criminal law and the criminal justice system are expressions of, and participants in, an historically variable and constantly changing field of conflicting political forces.

Their historical roots are still not adequately documented or theorized, but we know that even in Roman law what we today understand as the major functions of criminal law were discharged by the law of delict, a form of private-restitutive law with a punitive component (see Nicholas, 1962: 207–11).'A rapid expansion of the criminal law' only occurred 'in the disturbed conditions of the late Republic' (ibid., p. 209). Indeed, going further back into the earliest phases of social development, a reading of anthropology (see, e.g. Malinowski, 1926) and ancient history suggests that the criminal law develops later than the delictal (Nicholas, 1962: 208; cf. Durkheim, 1901, and see Lukes and Scull, 1983), and that 'the provision of sanctions for private wrongs remains the chief activity of the law throughout the primitive era' (Diamond, 1971: 62). It seems clear that the earliest forms of criminal justice were direct protections of the status and wealth of the rulers; containing overt censures of any challenge to the representatives of public or collective power. In this way, they protected the embryonic state form. Lodged in conflicts within the polity, they slowly develop to become the most legitimate and public form of modern social regulation, gradually embracing a whole range of moral censures which are only tangentially connected to the preservation of state power. This form in time became thoroughly bureaucratic, nationalized, centralized and penetrative. But for a long time 'after the primitive age', the 'trial and punishment of crime remains . . . a matter for rough and ready methods of trial and arbitrary vengeance by king and mob, smacking in some degree of political action' (Diamond, 1971: 63). Indeed, there are still parts of the underdeveloped world where the whims of the dictator and the rough justice of the 'hue and cry' are not unfamiliar features of criminal justice.

Therefore, while probably nobody, except the dictators of this world, wishes to see criminal justice swallowed up by the narrow imperatives of petty politics, it is naïve and ingenuous to hope that criminal justice can remain free of political concerns and influences, when, as I have shown, it is fundamentally and irredeemably lodged in the heart of the constitution of the polity. Indeed, on this argument, anyone who tries to keep politics out of criminal justice altogether must be automatically suspected of having a narrowly political axe to grind, because to exclude politics is to prevent the criminal justice system being receptive to the opinions and interests of anyone other than the managers and practitioners of criminal justice. To the extent that criminal justice does not reflect the opinions and interests of all sectors of the polity, it becomes an instrument of sectional violence.

Criminal justice systems and capitalism

The exact relation between criminal justice and capitalism is a complex question. Despite qualifications which could be made concerning Eastern bloc countries, it does seem that only with the development of capitalist social relations across an integrated national territory is there an accelerated development of modern criminal justice systems, both within themselves and across the whole field of social relations. Perhaps this is the formulation which unites Foucault with Marx. It is wrong to attribute the rise of criminal law to capitalism (cf. Quinney, 1980: 53). Criminal law came earlier. It is important to distinguish between the criminal law, as a form of law, from the developed modern system of criminal justice, as an integrated network of state institutions within a field of social regulation.

It is true, as Foucault (1978: 77–102) argues, that the juridical form of regulation has been subsumed within a wider complex of policy-oriented, regulatory mechanisms and, therefore, dethroned (or at least socialized) as the queen of the regulatory institutions. But it is equally true, following Marx, that it is only with the development of modern capitalism, as a system of generalized exchange relations (including the exchange of labour-power), that the juridical form of regulation penetrates the whole field of social relations and every nook and cranny of the national territory. Witness the lack of penetration of the juridical form of regulation, and the importance of pre-juridical forms and the penality of terror in underdeveloped societies, such as Tanzania. In passing, I acknowledge that this amounts to a rejection of Pashukanis's commodity-fetishist theory of criminal justice, which totally failed to see the significance of the commoditification of labour-power (see Sumner, 1981, for a detailed analysis). Indeed, I would add that it is also the case that only with the advance of modern capitalism, and the formation of the social, did the juridical system of regulation adopt social policy objectives and social-administrative procedures. Foucault assumes that the law had remained static and glosses over its modern social policy-linked form. Finally, it seems evident that only with the full internationalization of capitalist economic relations, following the growth of advanced monopoly capitalism, did the juridical form of regulation penetrate the field of international social relations.

The modern system of criminal justice, like its predecessors, is still an arena of contestation between unequal forces. It is one of the social realms where the inequities of social stratification, with all their variety and overlap, are fought out. To paraphrase a famous statement by Marx, structural contradictions are not just fought out or mediated within the economic structure itself, but also within the institutions of the superstructure. The criminal justice system is one of the regulatory institutions of modern society charged with the tasks of pacifying, rephrasing, defining, defusing and treating the products of social tension. Its role, at any point in time, is structured throughout by the society's need for public order and private peace (i.e. in order to sustain the realm of the social). But ruling groups' ideological perception of what is peace, safety, health and order dominate the public articulation of legal and moral censures, and the specification of target populations for those censures. In return, subordinate forces continually contest consciously, or threaten unconsciously, the validity, purpose and morality of hegemonic censures. Such dominance and contestation are vital features of the normal legal procedure and practical pattern of criminal justice systems.

Contestation is central and normal. But when there is a complete domination by ruling forces and ideologies, for example under conditions of acute societal stress or armed conflict, the usual procedure and pattern of criminal justice is drastically changed by emergency legislation, as in South Africa or Northern Ireland. The permission of a civic realm of liberties, a supposed key dimension of the rule of law, is much restricted or withdrawn in such 'emergencies' and there is a return to a more primitive form of punitive regulation, namely military or militaristic pacification, which is sanctified by still being legal and by ideologies of the national interest (see, e.g. Boyle *et al.*, 1975; Thompson, 1975; Mahabir, 1985). Other examples would include periods where there is complete domination by patriarchal or colonial forces, and we see the denial of normal legal rights or liberties, enjoyed by men or colonialists, to women and the colonized (see, e.g. Sachs and Wilson, 1978; Fitzpatrick, 1980). The important lesson to be learned is that the legal and practical reality of the rule of law varies considerably depending on the balance of power between different groups or nations: it has little consistency across social strata, types of society or historical periods.

It also follows from this analysis that it is quite insufficient to say either that criminal justice is an instrument of class domination or that it is a site of struggle between competing class forces. To a limited, and varying, extent, it is both these things. But a better formulation is that, because criminal justice is always an effect of, and participant in, fractured social relations of all kinds, and because social relations of all kinds overlap in practice, the class character of criminal justice, in all modes of production, is thoroughly intertwined with, and overdetermined by, its other social features; the exact picture varying with national, cultural and historic context. Therefore, while – and indeed because – capitalist criminal justice systems will, in the long run, tend to reflect the political and ideological needs of the hegemonic class bloc, as well as their economic interests, they will also be responsive to a multiplicity of opinions and needs (to the extent necessary to sustain some legitimacy within the polity), of an ethnic, gender, age, environment or regional character; or else they would not command any assent and, therefore, be useless in the hegemonic struggle.

Criminal justice, ideology and symbolic ritual

The practices of offenders also reflect social tensions, and express particular political and ideological interpretations of those tensions. As Engels made clear in 1844, these responses are not necessarily any more or less progressive than those of the legislators or police (Engels, 1975). We may, indeed, all agree, in some cases, that they are instances of practices that we thoroughly deplore. But this does not alter the fact that the criminal justice system is part of the social space where the enforcers of the hegemonic ideologies of order and peace clash with those who appear to the enforcers to ignore, breach or challenge that order and peace. Therefore, the practices of censured offenders may be popularly censured, yet amount to a small, highly selective sample of that offence. Equally, they may receive popular approval yet be comprehensively criminalized by the state. In the abstract, there is no relation of logical or rational necessity between what is popularly morally censured and what is practically censured in the criminal justice system; it is a political relationship, and therefore the degree of correspondence between the two will reflect the level and type of democracy within the state and its apparatuses of social regulation.

Given that the modern, social-democratic state tends to need legitimation to work effectively, popular censures are often selectively drawn upon and remoulded as a sub-text of the criminal justice system: an active, practical process of ideological incorporation which occurs at both legislative and enforcement stages, and which is subject to much historical variability and contestation. As experience shows, however, the abstract meaning of the law in legislative discourse can be quite different from its practical meaning on the streets, or in the boardrooms, or indeed from region to region. Popular opinion plays a part in defining the meaning and practice of the criminal law, but with different degrees of effectivity at different levels of the criminal justice system, and within different regions of the social formation. Any state that ignores it completely loses the value of criminal justice as a hegemonic force, and converts it into a simple instrument of repression. Historically, such states are backward or retrogressive, and eventually, one way or another, are superseded by democracies, one of whose major driving forces, or nation-building elements, is the reform of the criminal justice system in a more social and democratic direction.

Criminal justice, as a mode of modern social regulation, is therefore a thoroughly social space, interpenetrating with a whole range of moral sentiments and social practices contained within a social formation. As such, it is a profoundly social form, which can never be reduced analytically to the logic of capital, the whims of the state, or the demands of popular opinion. It is too deeply rooted in the very structure, culture and politics of modern society for that; and that is why it will sometimes trouble the powerful as well as the poor, and will sometimes serve the majority as well as the élite. However, given the deep inequities of modern societies, it is a space where the prestigious, the powerful or the affluent rarely appear as offenders. It is a social space, not one that is primarily defined by law. It therefore rarely rises far above fundamental social inequalities. As Bittner (1976) argued, criminal law is merely a resource for keeping the peace, and, as the Greenham Common struggle has so tellingly illustrated (see A. Young, 1989), what is peace is very much a question of politics and ideology.

The criminal justice system is, however, not just an arena of contestation between unequal forces. It is also the setting for one of the most powerful symbolic rituals in any society, where good is marked off from evil; or, rather, where the trusted and respectable agents of the state ritually and magisterially identify and condemn the practices of 'the lower orders' (in capitalist societies), or the 'politically backward elements' (in socialist societies), as 'crime' and thereby celebrate their noble protection of the nation's moral health as 'justice'. Thus, the daily legal censure of crime, generally, reiterates and reinforces the dominant ideological definitions of acceptable behaviour, both public and private, at the expense of the subordinate and competing definitions. Power thus recharges its moral batteries. This ritual defeat of the Forces of Evil by the Forces of Good must stand as the criminal law's most important ideological function, in comforting and reassuring the population (see also Hay, 1975). The daily trial in the magistrates' court, and the nightly 'cops and robbers' shows on television, soothe the existential fears of many, however irrationally, through a stream of conveyor-belt convictions and efficient, if somewhat violent, detections.

That ritual is now highly modernized in the West. What was a ramshackle, secretive, parochial and very matey game between the local bobby and the villains on his patch, a dark struggle of attrition between representatives of the old classes, no one able to break the deadlock – like a slow duel from a film on feudalism by Kurosawa or Bresson – has been very creatively transformed into a shiny, high-tech advertisement for the post-welfare state. It remains a macho man's game at the grass roots. But now the police are more open and the old struggle has become Crime Wars; a fully publicized, semi-participatory, computer game, complete with guns, radios, plastic bullets, fast cars, an infinite number of small-time villains to catch, a whole range of accompanying children's miniatures, a vast collection of ever-more realistic plots and narratives available as scripts from television (well-advised by former policemen), a huge range of videos, comics and novels, and of course regular news bulletins on the state of play. It is now mass marketed, just like a Hollywood movie or television series, with all the saleable accoutrements.

Crime Wars are like Reagan's Star Wars, distinctly modern in style and ritual: their moral basis is threadbare, they are superficially conceived, they don't work, but they are fully computerized and cost a fortune. They are the late twentieth-century, home defence strategy of affluent states in pursuit of business-as-usual.

This strategic defence initiative is interestingly executed. Essentially, the population is bombarded with stories of 'orrible murders and 'eroic policing for several hours every day; the stone-age character of most of this popular criminology being hidden under the veneer of the latest technology, much salaciousness, and a lot of very rapid, unexplained action (see Altick, 1970 and De Vries, 1971, for evidence of the longevity of this practice). Then, the populace are encouraged to leap up and start arresting each other, under the name of Neighbourhood Watch, Crimewatch, Crimestoppers or something like that, thus assisting the police with their major problem of how to jack up a hopelessly low, real detection rate. How far it succeeds is really debatable. It probably does work to legitimate 'efficient' (i.e. tough) policing outside of 'due process' and on the fringe of 'the rule of law'. Contemporary academic opinion tends to the view that the mass media do stoke the fires of punitiveness and reinforce crude stereotypes of crime and justice (see, e.g. Chibnall, 1977; Hall *et al.*, 1978; Cohen and Young, 1973; the discussion sections of Sumner, 1982; Carlson, 1985; cf. Graber, 1980); and the harsh reality of life in the inner cities does undoubtedly generate some well-founded fears for the media to feed upon (see Jones *et al.*, 1986; Kinsey *et al.*, 1986; Matthews and Young, 1986).

Media ideologies of crime and justice certainly permeate popular consciousness, and even the criminal justice system itself. Indeed, the more the latter happens, the more the reality of policing comes to resemble crime and justice in media output. The relationship between media discourses and reality is increasingly one of dialectical interpenetration. The rituals of denunciation may have had divine authority in Hay's (1975) tale of the eighteenth century, but today nothing is sacred in a world where fierce fantasy is rapidly colonizing a disintegrating reality. Ironically, a resurgent, more realistic, socialist criminology is confronted with the prospect of trying to discover the empirical reality of a world increasingly conditioned by, and permeated with, the media ideologies of crime and justice it once dissected as mere fiction. A thoroughgoing epistemological realism must recognize that it is being undermined daily by the mass reproduction of fantasies in an ever-more fragmented world. Realism must struggle at a time when lies and fantasy are becoming the dominant mode of discourse; nevertheless, struggle it must. The rest of criminology is part of the fantasy.

Crime and national unity

The daily censure of crime in modern times attempts to unify and publicize the hegemonic bloc's vision of the nation and its morality (see Opolot, 1976; Hall *et al.*, 1978; Fitzpatrick, 1980; Paliwala, 1982; Mahabir, 1985). It thus has a propensity to represent what are mostly either personal difficulties or political differences, both intimately related to the social structure and therefore essentially structured and sociological in character, as signs of moral degeneration, as 'behaviours' that are deeply unstructured, merely psychological, and a serious threat to the national health.

In this sense, the construction and defence of a strong system of criminal justice is historically a vital step in the establishment of the hegemonic bloc's vision of nationality and nationhood as the national identity and interest of the whole population. The mechanism of selective censure, and/or criminalization, is a key part of the building of the nation and the nation state, and, recently, of international and multinational political blocs. Arguably, in its wake, it brings the notions of crime control, the crime wave, the crime zone, crime as a social problem, and the breakdown of law and order, as signs of a moral malaise threatening the constitutional integrity of the state. These are the ideologies inevitably interconnected with the co-ordination of social practices of criminalization as a national criminal justice system, during the period of 'modernization', or industrialization, of the capitalist economy. The rise and rapid diffusion of the social censure of crime, and later on the censure of moral deviance, is thus intimately linked with the construction and defence of the nation, the sense of nationality, the nationalist spirit, and the integrated expansion of state power.

This representation of crime as a moral malaise within the body politic is a translation of the modern state's practical interventions into public morality, which utilize and construct a field of associated moral and political censures, sanctified in the criminal law, with the often successful effect of dividing the population into (for example) troublemakers and moderates, madonnas and whores, hooligans and quiet boys, communists and conservatives, thieves and non-thieves, blacks and whites, men and women. With each of these exemplary instances, it is predictable whose practices are seen as 'deeply unstructured', 'psychological' or irrational behaviours: the censured side of the dialectic. The discourses on crime, whether from magistrates or journalists, never suppose that these censured groups could act spontaneously in the national interest; the censured, in these dominant ideological conceptions, are all to some degree seen as subversive of national unity.

These moral divisions are targeted at the population at large, often with collusion from the population itself (see Lees, 1985, for a nice example), and are daily reinforced, in both their content and targeting, by the courts, politicians, police, prison officers, psychiatrists, social workers, probation officers, welfare officials, housing officers, unemployment and social security officials, accredited moral spokespersons, and the mass media. Divide and rule probably works. Foucault's (1980: 15) formulation is, however, too crude and functionalistic, in assuming too much intent and too much success, but it imports a similar idea:

> The third role of the penal system: to make the proletariat see the non-proletarianised people as marginal, dangerous, immoral, a menace to society as a whole, the dregs of the population, trash, the 'mob'. For the bourgeoisie it is a matter of imposing on the proletariat, by means of penal legislation, of prisons, but also of newspapers, of 'literature', certain allegedly universal moral categories which function as an ideological barrier between them and the non-proletarianised people.

If we also include the counter-censures of the population at large, and the alternative censures of counter-hegemonic groups which, for example, might define businessmen as 'hard cases', lawyers as crooks, and politicians as hypocrites, then, arguably, the full result is a politically disintegrative tendency in modern life towards everyone seeing everyone else as morally degenerate, and thus towards national disunity.

None of this, if correct, suggests support for any kind of simplistic functional analysis, such as Matza's (1969: 196–7), which supposes a collective consensus on censures and a state always successful in legitimating itself through the criminal justice system. Rather, it points to the disintegrative functions of an integrative strategy, whose very strength turns out to be its greatest weakness, given the ubiquity of division and conflict. The censure of crime produces the censure of authority, and the proliferation of the former accelerates the growth of the latter, just as the censure of ego by alter stimulates ego to return the compliment. Ultimately, from the point of view of the social system, until the practice of censure as a means of social regulation is thoroughly democratically regulated, and kept in balance with practices of approval, it will, on this analysis, tend to dissolve social organizations into mutually suspicious and hostile camps. Blaming practices are inherently unstable as means of integration. The continual censure of folk devils does not create social unity, as Durkheim-inspired sociologies suggest, but rather a temporary stemming of the tide of structurally induced 'deviance' and an explosive store of resentment and disunity. Louis Wirth's (1940: 481 and 478) wartime comment is apposite:

> Propaganda has become the chief means for enlarging the scope of the consensus and the number of persons sharing it, and the consensus we get as a result is often an unstable and spurious one ... such consensus as does exist in modern western society when it is not at war is extremely limited in the sense that those who participate in the consensus constitute only a small proportion of the total society.

The decisive point against any kind of structural functionalism is that, while a fundamentally divided and increasingly individualistic nation needs a state system of social regulation, like criminal justice, for its very survival let alone development, and while the criminal justice system can be partially legitimated as a natural, moral and national necessity, that system from its moment of formation is enmeshed within the interests and ideologies involved in the various, conflictual power regimes of class, gender, race and nation. Criminal justice is thus, from birth and pending the arrival of a utopia, an irredeemably political and ideological field of social practice.

The problem then, in our analysis, is not that ideological values and prejudices keep distorting the impartiality of the criminal justice process, but that the ideology of the neutrality and consensuality of the criminal justice system keeps masking the truth of the predominance of the interests and ideologies of the hegemonic bloc, and the degree of conflict between this bloc and the various counter-hegemonic progressive forces. Enlightenment values of reason, equity and accountability, the foundations of what Habermas called post-conventional culture, can work to conceal, as well as to emancipate us from, unwanted state power. In short, legal rationality on its own does not deliver a nation from conflicts of economic, political and cultural interest, but merely expresses them in another form.

That 'law and order' is an ideological and political issue, a bone of contention and disunity, has become very clear to the public eye in recent years. The cross-party consensus in various Western societies has given way to the open militancy of the new Right on the law-and-order question (see Hall *et al.*, 1978; Hall, 1979; Taylor, 1981, 1983; Lea and Young, 1984; Scheingold, 1984; Fairchild and Webb, 1985; Ratner and McMullan, 1987; Scraton, 1987). Whereas in the past crime and justice issues have not been regarded as party-political, it is obvious now that punitiveness, increased police resources, and tougher criminal laws are the policies of

Conservative parties and lobbies, whereas parties and lobbies on the Left lean towards policies to increase police accountability, to protect civil liberties, to protect groups like women and blacks from attacks, and to increase the communal character of criminal justice (see e.g. Taylor, 1981; Baldwin and Kinsey, 1982; Hewitt, 1982; Lea and Young, 1984; Jefferson and Grimshaw, 1984; Scraton, 1985). Not only do Right and Left differ sharply on policies, they have increasingly different definitions of the problems to be resolved. However, criminal justice is, always has been, and always will be an intrinsically ideological and political field, even during periods of greater national unity when law and order is not so high on the political agenda. It has never been intrinsically a technical question of scientific administration.

As Habermas (1974) argued, the modern, post-Enlightenment, bourgeois conception of the art of good government, as rational-legal administration advised by science, can never found a neutral or natural political order because its very nature (1) provokes a debate about the definition of the good life, reason and legality, (2) demands a close relationship to an ultimately not totally manipulable public opinion, and (3) forces the emergence of democratic procedures and discourses (see Sumner, 1983, for a fuller exposition of Habermas's observations on law). Indeed, I would argue that scientistic conceptions of socialism provoke the same issues, albeit in different ways, and therefore are equally problematic. Modern criminal justice systems contain within themselves, at all points, the dimensions of ethics, justice, representativeness and publicity, which means that, in deeply divided societies, their problems can never be successfully resolved by merely technical, administrative discourses, strategies and disciplines.

In other words, there is a fundamental contradiction within modern criminal justice systems that will not disappear without proper political resolution: their role as state protection agencies, to put it crudely, is in direct opposition to their potential as instruments of good government. It is essential that criminology recognizes and reflects this, and halts its relentless expansion into the dangerous cul-de-sac of administrative scientism.

Criminal justice and the civilizing mission

From its nineteenth-century beginnings, the British criminal justice system was coloured by the ideology of the white, imperial patriarchy which dominated the British state, and later half the world. Its conditions of existence as a national, public system, not a loose rag-bag of private institutions, were the militaristic pacification of the reluctant new proletariat, and then the reduction in the role of the military and the corresponding rise of civil policing (see Ahire, forthcoming; Geary, 1985; see also Brogden, 1982; Vogler, forthcoming). Its inner constitution is not simply a matter of physical coercion and political interest: it also involves the diffusion of the codes of civil policing and the diverse categories of criminal censure deep into the hearts and minds of resistant human territories. These ideologies of the required civic behaviour of both police and citizens helped to stabilize and legitimize the emergent criminal justice system, and indeed were a prelude to the later development of the system, along the lines of welfare state ideology (see Garland, 1985, for a thorough discussion of that period).

Civil policing and the expansion of the range of moral censures represent the Victorian ruling class's long-term strategic response to the political instabilities and social problems arising from the maelstrom of full proletarianization. One strategy among many, criminal justice was part of a network of institutions of social regulation geared to the moral and political education of the new working class. In fact, the accelerated development of the criminal justice system in most countries can best be understood as the major political and ideological expression in modern times of the hegemonic bloc's efforts to secure continued proletarianization on a stable basis; as a key feature of the processes of civilization.

From this perspective, criminal justice was a key institution in the formation of civil society, as an ideologically defined sphere of moral action free from militaristic state interference and regulated only from within – by the self-control of the people themselves and by a civil police force which was to be at least formally subject to local customs, civic ethics and local authorities. Governor Cameron of Tanganyika saw this point very clearly in 1927:

> A system of indirect native administration has been instituted in Tanganyika during the last two years to which I attach the greatest possible importance as I believe that we shall secure, as far as it is humanly possible to foresee now, the political and social future of the natives in a manner which will afford them a permanent share in the administration of the country on lines which they themselves can understand and can appreciate, building up at the same time a bulwark against political agitation and averting the social chaos of which signs have already manifested themselves in other countries similarly situated. (Quoted in Morris and Read, 1972: 3)

As such, the criminal justice system was a vital force in the construction of the basic moral and political fabric of what we know as modern society. As such, it developed a major significance within bourgeois ideological discourse, linking the concept of civilization with state-sanctioned freedom, self-control, regulated policing, and the demilitarization of social regulation. Indeed, it is arguable that it is the core political-ideological conception contained in the meaning of the phrase 'civilized society'.

That is perhaps why British imperialists found it so suitable during the age of the second imperialism after 1885 (see Worsley, 1967). They were soon to justify their repressive and devastating interference into the everyday lives of colonized peoples on the alleged grounds that their criminal justice worked to 'civilize' populations who, if left to their own devices, would allegedly dissolve into bloody internecine feuds, or would never learn the merits of modern economic practice (see Pritt, 1971; Fitzpatrick, 1980; Paliwala, 1982; Sweet, 1982; Shaidi, forthcoming). Nowhere is it clearer than in the colonies that the so-called culture of civility was intimately linked to the regulation of proletarianization in a capitalist economy, via the interventions of a criminal justice system containing a substantial element of 'indirect rule' and 'customary law' (as the colonists called them), backed in times of 'emergency' by special police forces using rival 'tribesmen', the army and 'emergency' powers legislation; all of which were a lot less than civil.

The links between this criminal justice system, the civilizing mission and the complex networks of social regulation developed as part of the rise of the interventionist welfare state (or, in relation to the underdeveloped societies, the rise of the international state: see the special issue of the *International Journal of the Sociology of Law*, 1983) now need to be theoretically analysed as the most significant feature of the period between 1885 and 1979 (marking the onset of Thatcherism). Criminal justice is intimately connected with the state's education of the working class, with its constant waves of immigrant recruits from rural economies, into the mores, attitudes and skills required for the civil society of advanced capitalism. The latter developed its own sophisticated methods of 'indirect rule' and 'customized' criminal justice.

But we also need to examine urgently the recent reversal of these historic trends: because a return to militaristic policing, military pacification, direct state rule and reduced local power seem to be the growing partners of deproletarianization in the age of multinational capital, computer technology, deindustrialization and the dismantling of the welfare state. The conflict of the two different modes of criminal justice, the militaristic-repressive and the social-democratic, in a period of increasing internationalization and awareness of the political ecology of economic growth, could be one of the major issues of the 1990s.

References

Ahire, P. (forthcoming). *Imperial Policing: The Emergence and Role of the Police in Colonial Nigeria 1860–1960*. Milton Keynes: Open University Press.
Altick, R.D. (1970). *Victorian Studies in Scarlet*. London: Dent.
Baldwin, R. and Kinsey, R. (1982). *Police Powers and Politics*. London: Quartet.

Bittner, E. (1967). The police on skid-row. *American Sociological Review*, **32**(5), 699–715.
Boyle, K., Hadden, T. and Hillyard, P. (1975). *Law and State: The Case of Northern Ireland*. Oxford: Martin Robertson.
Brogden, M. (1982). *The Police: Autonomy and Consent*. London: Academic Press.
Carlson, J.M. (1985). *Prime-time Law Enforcement*. New York: Praeger.
Chambliss, W.J. (1974). The state, the law and the definition of behavior as criminal or delinquent. In *Handbook of Criminology* (D. Glaser, ed.). Chicago: Rand McNally.
Chibnall, S. (1977). *Law-and-Order News*. London: Tavistock.
Cohen, S. and Young, J. (eds) (1973). *The Manufacture of News*. London: Constable.
De Vries, L. (1971). *'Orrible Murder*. London: Macdonald and Jane.
Diamond, A.S. (1971). *Primitive Law Past and Present*. London: Methuen.
Durkheim, E. (1901). Two laws of penal evolution. *Année Sociologique*, **4**, 65–95.
Engels, F. (1975). The condition of the working class in England. In Marx, K. and Engels, F., *Collected Works*, Vol. 4. London: Lawrence and Wishart.
Fairchild, E.S. and Webb, V.J. (1985). *The Politics of Crime and Justice*. Beverly Hills Calif.: Sage.
Fitzpatrick, P. (1980). *Law and State in Papua New Guinea*. London: Academic Press.
Foucault, M. (1978). *The History of Sexuality*, Vol. 1. New York: Vintage.
Foucault, M. (1980). On popular justice. In *Power/Knowledge* (C. Gordon, ed.). New York: Pantheon.
Garland, D. (1985). *Punishment and Welfare*. Aldershot: Gower.
Geary, R. (1985). *Policing Industrial Disputes*. Cambridge: Cambridge University Press.
Graber, D.A. (1980). *Crime News and the Public*. New York: Praeger.
Habermas, J. (1974). *Theory and Practice*. London: Heinemann.
Hall, S. (1979). *Drifting into a Law and Order Society*. London: Cobden Trust.
Hall, S., Critcher, C., Jefferson, T., Clarke, J. and Roberts, B. (1978). *Policing the Crisis*. London: Macmillan.
Hay, D. (1975). Property, authority and the criminal law. In *Albion's Fatal Tree* (D. Hay *et al.*, eds). London: Allen Lane.
Hewitt, P. (1982). *The Abuse of Power*. Oxford: Martin Robertson.
Jefferson, T. and Grimshaw, R. (1984). *Controlling the Constable*. London: Muller.
Jones, T., MacLean, B. and Young, J. (1986). *The Islington Crime Survey*. Aldershot: Gower.
Kinsey, R., Lea, J. and Young, J. (1986). *Losing the Fight against Crime*. Oxford: Blackwell.
Lea, J. and Young, J. (1984). *What is to be done about Law and Order?* Harmondsworth: Penguin.
Lees, S. (1985). *Losing Out*. London: Hutchinson.
Lukes, S. and Scull, A. (eds) (1983). *Durkheim and the Law*. Oxford: Martin Robertson.
Mahabir, C. (1985). *Crime and Nation-building in the Caribbean*. Cambridge, Mass.: Schenkman.
Malinowski, B. (1926). *Crime and Custom in Savage Society*. London: Routledge and Kegan Paul.
Matthews, R. and Young, J. (1986). *Confronting Crime*. London: Sage.

Matza, D. (1969). *Becoming Deviant*. Englewood Cliffs N.J.: Prentice-Hall.
Morris, H.F. and Read, J.S. (1972). *Indirect Rule and the Search for Justice*. Oxford: Clarendon.
Nicholas, B. (1962). *An Introduction to Roman Law*. Oxford: Oxford University Press.
Opolot, J.S.E. (1976). *Criminal Justice and Nation-building in Africa*. Washington, D.C.: Universities Press of America.
Paliwala, A. (1982). Law and order in the village. In *Crime, Justice and Underdevelopment* (C. Sumner, ed.). London: Heinemann.
Pashukanis, E.B. (1978). *Law and Marxism*. London: Ink Links.
Pritt, D.N. (1971). *Law, Class and Society*. London: Lawrence and Wishart.
Quinney, R. (1980). *Class, State and Crime*. New York: Longman.
Ratner, R.S. and McMullan, J.L. (eds) (1987). *State Control: Criminal Justice Politics in Canada*. Vancouver: University of British Columbia Press.
Sachs, A. and Wilson, J.H. (1978). *Sexism and the Law*. Oxford: Martin Robertson.
Scheingold, S.A. (1984). *The Politics of Law and Order*. New York: Longman.
Scraton, P. (1985). *The State of the Police*. London: Pluto.
Scraton, P. (ed.) (1987). *Law, Order and the Authoritarian State*. Milton Keynes: Open University Press.
Shaidi, L.P. (forthcoming). *Criminal Justice and Underdevelopment in Tanzania*. Milton Keynes: Open University Press.
Sumner, C.S. (1981). Pashukanis and the 'jurisprudence of terror'. *Insurgent Sociologist*, special issue **x**(4) and **xi**(1), 99–106.
Sumner, C.S. (ed.) (1982). *Crime, Justice and the Mass Media*. Cropwood Series no. 14. Cambridge: Institute of Criminology.
Sumner, C.S. (1983). Law and legitimation in the advanced capitalist state: The jurisprudence and social theory of Jurgen Habermas. In *Legality, Ideology and the State* (D. Sugarman, ed.). London: Academic Press.
Sweet, L. (1982). Inventing crime: British colonial land policy in Tanganyika. In *Crime, Justice and Underdevelopment* (C. Sumner, ed.). London: Heinemann.
Taylor, I.R. (1981). *Law and Order*. London: Macmillan.
Taylor, I.R. (1983). *Crime, Capitalism and Community*. Toronto: Butterworth.
Thompson, E.P. (1975). *Whigs and Hunters*. London: Allen Lane.
Vogler, R. (forthcoming). *Reading the Riot Act: The Magistracy, Police and Army in Civil Disorder*. Milton Keynes: Open University Press.
Wirth, K. (1940). Ideological aspects of social disorganization. *American Sociological Review*, **5**, 472–82.
Worsley, P. (1967). *The Third World*. London: Weidenfeld and Nicolson.
Young, A. (1989). *Dispersing the commonplace*. Ph.D. dissertation. University of Cambridge. Institute of Criminology.

The politics of censure

4 Magistrates' courts and the struggle for local democracy 1886–1986

Richard Vogler

Introduction

This short study will examine in outline the rise and fall of the idea of a democratic magistracy in England and Wales. The present system of selection, based on the feudal principle of secret nomination by the Lords Lieutenant and the Lord Chancellor, has survived the democratic reforms of the past 150 years almost untouched. It is hoped here to throw some light on this curious and tenacious system and the long campaign by organized labour to open it up. It is a history with important implications. The magistracy intrudes sharply into the lives of working men and women and is deeply involved in the repression of political dissent and trade union activity (see, e.g. Christian, 1985; Percy-Smith and Hillyard, 1985; Vogler, 1982, 1986), and yet its political development (in contrast to that of the judiciary) remains obscure.

The problems of democratic participation in a state system of justice dominated by professional élites have been discussed elsewhere (see, e.g. Taylor, 1981: 164–80; Cotterrell, 1984: 323–31), and it is not argued here that such restricted popular involvement would lead to radical change. On the other hand, a more democratic bench of magistrates would provide a powerful strategic base for the 'practical use', as Taylor (1981: 180) puts it, 'of the various interest groups which constitute civil society'. Its influence on legal professionals would be salutary.

The study is based on a view of the state and social class which was developed in the course of a much more extensive project (Vogler, 1984).

As a starting point for work of this nature, the otherwise helpful and pertinent debates which have accompanied the recent growth of interest in Marxist theories of the state did not seem to provide much guidance (see, e.g. Jessop, 1982; McLennan *et al.*, 1984). First, they have not, in general, addressed themselves to an analysis of component institutions within the national state. Secondly, there is no readily available working basis for examining the dynamic character of the state over a period of time under the impact of class and other forces. Finally, there has been no sustained account of the spatial characteristics of the modern state and the dispersal of its institutional structure over a geographical territory. Such problems, although not always central to the more wide-ranging debate, are very relevant to any consideration of a locally based institution such as the magistrates' courts, with a constantly changing class character and jurisdiction. To meet these defects, reference was made initially to the work of Nicos Poulantzas.

There are several reasons for this approach. While Poulantzas' work extends across theoretical terrain associated with all the major traditions of Marxist state analysis,[1] he has managed in his later writing to escape the endless polarities of much of the existing theory. As Hall (1980: 67) puts it, some parts of his 1978 work:

> . . . begin to break the knot in marxist theory which has retarded the development of an adequate conception of the state for so long, best represented in terms of the opposed poles of the state as functional to the needs/logic of capital, and the state as 'nothing but a product of class struggle'.

Three of Poulantzas' major theoretical departures will be discussed briefly here in terms of their usefulness in resolving the special problems outlined above.

The first of these innovations is concerned with what Poulantzas called the 'institutional materiality' of the state. He begins by asking why it is that certain *particular* forms of state correspond to bourgeois political domination (Poulantzas, 1978: 53). His answer implies that class divisions are redrawn within the state itself and thus the state is seen as a complex institutional ensemble of agencies acting in relation to each other. In this way, Poulantzas indicates the broad outline of a Marxist theory which answers to the complexity and differentiation of activities characteristic of the bourgeois state. The materiality of the state, he argues, is not exhausted by the apparatus necessary for the organization of coercion or intervention on behalf of individual or collective capitals.

Here we must pause to consider the obvious parallels with the 'institutional differentiation' school of non-Marxist theorists such as Smelser and Durkheim, who argued that structural arrangements were elaborated in an evolutionary process (Poggi, 1978: 13–15). This should sound a first warning of the tendency of this approach to slide into pluralism. However, provided the primacy of productive relations is accepted, there is no reason why the concept of institutional materiality may not provide a valuable tool of analysis of state power and practice. In particular, it opens up to scrutiny specific sub-units of the state which have been regarded hitherto only in functionalist terms. The magistracy appears in this study not as a mere channel for class or state authority, but as a material institution with a distinctive ideological character sustaining complex relationships with other such institutions and class groupings.

The second major area of advance is the stress upon the dynamic quality of state composition. Poulantzas regarded the state as the site of 'the political condensation of class struggle', so neither class division nor class struggle can be regarded as logically prior to its formation. State and economy cannot be separated either in chronology or in causality.

Poulantzas' model of class relations is considerably more complex than those of his predecessors. Because the state is grounded in such class relations, Poulantzas opens up the possibility of a more sophisticated 'relational' analysis which may take account of the 'fissured, contradictory nature of the capitalist state' (Jessop, 1982: 157). Under the hegemony of the leading bourgeois fractions, the power block is unified and organized politically through the state apparatus. The flexibility of the state structure is such that shifts in the relation of forces between dominant classes and dominating fractions can be accommodated by institutional reorganization and changes within the location of power within the state. In his earlier work, Poulantzas had illustrated the relation between class struggle and both the 'exceptional' forms of state (1969) and those characteristic of monopoly capitalism (1974). In *State, Power, Socialism*, he goes on to demonstrate the potential of internal state dissension for popular struggles as the state moves deeper into intervention (1978: 140–4).

The struggle for class authority within such an institution as the magistracy is seen here as one important aspect of a wider confrontation. It scarcely matters at which point the boundary between state and civil society is drawn, for as Poulantzas (1978: 37) remarks:

> ... the state spreads out into the tiniest vein and – what here concerns us most – tends to circumscribe power sectors and every class power. ... All the same, class powers – and not just economic ones – still stretch beyond the state. For instance, even if we take into account its ideological apparatuses, the state's discourse does not exhaust all political discourse; and yet it includes a class power in its structure. Similarly ideological power is never exhausted by the state and its ideological apparatuses.

As this study demonstrates, the struggle to appropriate the judicial authority and the institutions of the crown has taken place primarily at the level of ideology. In the post-1945 period, above all, the conflict between democratic and professionalist views of the bench has been decisive.

The third innovation considered here concerns the spatial and territorial aspects of the materiality of the state. The need for historical periodization is well established (see, e.g. Mandel, 1975: 108–46; Poulantzas, 1974: 14–20 and 107–15). What has not yet become sufficiently clear, despite the proliferation of analyses which depend on the internationalization of productive relations, is the geographical specificity of particular state forms. As Poulantzas (1978: 104) puts it: '. . . the modern state materialises this spatial matrix in its various apparatuses . . . patterning in turn the subjects over whom it exercises power'.

Although this insistence on the importance of the spatial matrix clearly owes much (through Foucault) to liberal theories of political authority (the importance of the distinction between town and country was, of course, also of great significance to Marx and Engels), nevertheless, the self-definition of the bourgeois state, i.e. its ability to control and organize physical space within fixed boundaries, cannot be ignored.

For Poulantzas, national divisions play an important role in the dual movement of disorganization/unification which is central to his theory of hegemony. However, if we are to provide an adequate account of a particular fragment of the larger institution, we must move beyond the concept of the state as a simple geographical unity. It is at this stage that we must introduce the idea of an organic relationship between the central state (within the national area) and the local state (within the local area).

Although the concept of local state has been current in Marxist theory for some considerable time, there has only recently been any sustained attempt at explanation (honourable exceptions here might include Cockburn, 1977; Broadbent, 1977; Dear and Clarke, 1978; Saunders, 1979; Duncan and Goodwin, 1988). Indeed, the obsession with the central state has led to a certain historical myopia with regard to local courts and policing arrangements. The field of study has, in short, been determined by the self-image of the bourgeois state, the legacy from which Marxist theory is only now beginning to escape. Thus while, on the one hand, the local state has been conceptualized as merely a scaled-down version of the central state (Dearlove, 1973: 11; Cockburn, 1977: 46), on the other, the central state has been displaced entirely in favour of the micro-structures of authority (Foucault, 1977). It is important to ask, for example, whether the local state represents merely the projection of state authority into the localities (see Griffith, 1966; Broadbent, 1977: 128), or whether it enjoys autonomy. Do the local state and central state stand in differing relations with the economy and the relations of production (see Broadbent, 1977; Dear and Clarke, 1978: 80; Nairn, 1977: 306–28; Saunders, 1979, 1986). And does the centre represent more than the sum of the peripheral authorities?

These questions are crucial and can be answered only by a consideration of particular political and economic relations within a historical dimension (see Duncan and Goodwin, 1988: 32–44). As Hogg (1979: 7) and Sugarman (1983: 242) argue, the dichotomy local/centre within the state structure supplies the principle axis along which conflicts over law, state and society are to be understood. For the major part of the period 1785–1888, the local state in England and Wales (as Hogg and others point out) may be regarded as consisting chiefly of the justices of the peace sitting in Quarter and Petty Sessions.[2]

We are now in a position to consider the development of the magistracy throughout the past century during changing conditions of capital accumulation. It will be argued that their class composition has not remained stable and that control of the local bench has been determined to some extent by the ability of class groups to organize at the national level and to exert pressure through the central state. We will then consider the long rearguard action fought up to 1945 to inhibit working-class entry, and the more radical reconstitution of the bench thereafter as a national institution with a characteristic ideology and structure.

An agency of ruling-class alliance: The magistracy to 1886

The importance of the local magistracy in the Georgian state cannot be over-emphasized. The central organization (such as it was) depended upon local benches of landowners to an extent that it became customary to circulate legislation to the Quarter Sessions for vetting before consideration in Parliament (Osborne, 1960: 210). The Webbs have gone so far as to assert that, in respect of legislation which affected the localities, the House of Commons was no more than 'a clearing house for the several courts of Quarter Session' (Webb and Webb, 1963: 554).

Because both the county jurisdictions (in the rural areas) and the borough jurisdictions (in the urban areas) were dominated by the landowning classes, it is not surprising that the question of magisterial selection should become a crucial aspect of class authority. Indeed, the competition in the mid-nineteenth century between landed capitals and newer industrial interests often took the form of a contest for control of these strategic positions. In 1835, the reforming Liberal ministry headed by Russell undertook a complete overhaul of the administration of the industrial urban boroughs,[3] enabling the appointment of magistrates directly by the Lord Chancellor (instead of the Lords Lieutenant, who were usually local landowners or military men of substance in the county). At a stroke, therefore, the county élites lost not only the right of appointment in these areas but also the safeguard of the property qualification. The borough benches were thus opened to new class interests and, according to the *Quarterly Review* of 1842, the Russell administration then embarked on a 'flagrant and extensive prostitution of magisterial appointments for mere party purposes' (lxxi, p. 249). Available figures do seem to confirm this view.[4] What is worth noting here is the extent to which central political pressure was able to subvert local structures of power.

By as early as 1837, the Commissions had become deeply polarized. According to Sir Charles Napier (1857: 8):

> The magistrates are divided into Whigs and Tories and personal enmities; and every mother's son of them is prepared to go to any length for his sect and creed. The town magistrates are Liberal for fear of the populace; the county bucks are too old and too far gone Tories.

In the more buoyant conditions of 1850, however, the magistracy was no longer in the front line of political and street-level confrontation. By this period, the rigid, class-exclusive structure of the provincial Georgian magistracy had been altered almost beyond recognition. The Commission of the Peace now represented a local framework within which the various dominant classes of early Victorian society could be assimilated and their power concerted. It had become, in short, a major mechanism of ruling-class alliance. Two factors favoured this process:

1 The patchwork of county and municipal jurisdictions which, in a period of locally centred capital, permitted the bench to reflect the class structure of dominant groups involved in particular types of production in a rapidly developing economy. The entry into the Commission of sections of the industrial bourgeoisie in the municipal boroughs after 1835 successfully stabilized the urban magistracy, whereas in the agricultural counties the Lords Lieutenant and chairmen of Quarter Sessions continued to be recruited almost exclusively from the landed aristocracy (Zangerl, 1971: 116; Quinault, 1974: 186).

2 The effective combination of the principles of financial eligibility and nomination. Wealthy radicals could be excluded, whereas the institutional mechanism allowed the co-option of professionals and representatives from other classes to strengthen the bench in particular areas without abandoning control (Lee, 1963: 30). Zangerl (1971: 123) asserts that: 'The circle of landed allies on the County bench merely expanded to include bourgeois individuals as well as (professionals).'

The effect of this union during the period 1835–88 was a magnification of their collective social authority (Zangerl, 1971: 116; Harries-Jenkins, 1977: 252; Steedman, 1984: 2) and as Keith-Lucas (1977: 8) puts it, the magistracy in this period 'constituted in a very real sense a ruling class'. *Blackwoods Magazine* (1888: 70) summed up their power thus: 'In short [they] superintended and set in motion, either in whole, or in part, the entire administrative machinery established in the English Counties.'

The Conservative ascendancy 1886–1911

This remarkable agency of ruling-class alliance was not immune however to the social realignments of the 1880s. The agricultural depression of this period critically weakened the authority of the land-owning classes, and in 1888 the county benches were deprived of their remaining executive powers by the Local Government Act, which constituted new, elected local authorities in the counties. However, it was the crisis of imperial policy in Ireland which was to have the most devastating affect.

In 1886, the fall of Gladstone's ministry over the issue of Irish Home Rule destroyed the power base of the Liberals in the counties. Almost overnight the major Whig land-owning families shifted their allegiances to the Unionists, taking with them the Lord Lieutenantships and senior magisterial offices. Under the pre-1911 arrangements, appointments to the County bench were made by the Lord Chancellor on the advice of the Lords Lieutenant who screened nominations. The Lord Lieutenantships were political appointments and hence the impact of the 1886 crisis upon them was marked:

> At the beginning of 1886, of the forty-two English Lords Lieutenant, twenty-six were Liberals and sixteen Conservative. By the end of 1886 at least fourteen of the Liberal Lieutenants had become active Unionists – and only three Lieutenants remained to support Gladstone's fourth ministry in the Upper House in 1892. (Lee, 1959: 88)

As a result, the Conservative stranglehold upon the County bench between 1886 and the return of a strong Liberal administration in 1906 was almost total. Lord Halsbury, the Conservative Lord Chancellor, regarded the power of appointment of justices as a political instrument, admitting candidly that he gave the Lords Lieutenant a free rein in their nominations.[5] As the *Tribune* (10 December 1906, p. 10) put it: '. . . whole army corps of Conservatives were elevated to the local Benches [which] . . . can if they so desire, at any moment, convert themselves into a Tory Committee'.

With the brief return of the Liberals in 1892, the new Lord Chancellor, Lord Herschell, was faced with a dilemma. A deputation of 200 Liberal M.P.s demanded that he ignore the recommendations of Lords Lieutenant and make selections himself. Their Commons Resolution to this effect[6] was bitterly contested by the Conservatives, and in particular Balfour, who argued: 'You wish to turn the patronage of the Bench of Magistrates in England into a wheel in your General Electioneering machine'. Asquith, the Liberal Home Secretary, responded in kind:

> I would say that it does not lie with those who have packed the County and Borough Benches with political partisans to hold up

their hands in holy horror and argue as against their opponents, that politics should have nothing to do with judicial appointments.[7]

However, Herschell was unwilling to precipitate a crisis which might prove fatal to the ailing Liberal administration and bring reprisals in later years. He opted instead for a 'moderate additional appointment of Liberals',[8] increasing the percentage on the Bench, as he claimed, from 22 to 36 per cent.[9] The Liberal activists understandably felt betrayed[10] and Herschell wrote to Gladstone: 'I have been working to an extent almost beyond endurance in these matters. I have done my best – I cannot endure the situation much longer' (quoted in Heuston, 1964: 115). In the event, he endured it until the fall of the Liberals in 1895, whereupon the returning Halsbury embarked on a further round of Conservative appointments.

By 1906, Tory domination on the Bench was almost complete. Figures published by the Liberals in December (see Tables 4.1–4.4) indicated an average percentage of Conservatives in the County Benches of 83 per cent and 65 per cent in the Boroughs. County Benches in Rutland, Nottinghamshire and Shropshire were composed almost exclusively of Tories. Many Liberals, it was claimed, could not find Liberal magistrates to administer oaths at election time. Even some of the Conservative Lords Lieutenant were shocked at the figures. The Staffordshire Lord Lieutenant found the account for his County 'almost grotesque'.[11]

What had happened since 1886 was in many respects a reversal of the class amalgamation of 1835–86. At a time when the land-owning classes were suffering the severe disorganizing affects of agricultural depression, the control of the County benches was pressed more firmly into their hands. To the railway companies, the industrial joint-stock companies and the other agencies of nationally centred capital, a magistracy which was confined to narrow local jurisdictions was increasingly irrelevant. Resistance to changes in the organizational structure thus became less fierce.

One of the first reforms of the Liberal administration returned in 1906, the Justice of the Peace Act, was to abolish entirely the property qualification for magistrates. It was hoped that the change would '[free] the County magistracy for the first time in history from the ascendancy of the landed interest',[12] but the Act was slow in operation and did not impair the discretion of the Lords Lieutenant.

Lord Loreburn acted cautiously. To a deputation of 88 Liberal and Labour members in December 1906, he replied that he was 'not prepared to flood the benches'[13] and went on to complain privately:

> From this little group I received offensive letters and a scarcely concealed demand that I should act as their Registrar and put on whomever they nominate which I will never do . . . those who

Table 4.1 Political allegiances of magistrates in English counties, December 1905

County	Liberal	Conservative	Total	Lord Lieutenant[a]	Percentage Conservative
1 Bedfordshire	21	78	99	C	77
2 Buckinghamshire	29	165	194	C	85
3 Cambridgeshire	52	91	143	L	63
4 Cheshire	93	317	410	C	77
5 Cornwall	32	180	212	C	85
6 Cumberland	42	154	196	C	78
7 Derbyshire	34	171	205	C	83
8 Devon	69	316	385	C	82
9 Dorset	21	165	186	L	88
10 Durham	17	63	80	L	78
11 Essex	47	237	284	C	83
12 Gloucestershire	26	100	126	C	79
13 Hampshire	28	266	294	C	90
14 Herefordshire[b]				C	
15 Hertfordshire	21	164	185	C	89
16 Huntingdonshire	12	47	448	C	84
17 Kent	73	375	448	C	84
18 Lancashire (N)	29	93	122	C	76
19 Lancashire (S.E.)	74	111	185	C	60
20 Lancashire (S.W.)	68	131	199	C	65
21 Leicestershire	24	142	166	C	85
22 Lincolnshire	21	303	324	C	93
23 Middlesex	39	153	192	C	80
24 Norfolk	17	145	162	C	90
25 Northamptonshire	16	64	80	L	80
26 Northumberland	17	71	80	C	81
27 Nottinghamshire	6	72	78	C	92
28 Oxfordshire	30	119	149	C	80
29 Rutland	–	25	25	C	100
30 Shropshire	18	227	245	C	92
31 Somerset	50	193	243	C	80
32 Isle of Wight	4	31	35	C	88
33 Staffordshire	25	199	224	C	89
34 Suffolk	31	299	330	C	91
35 Surrey	49	196	245	C	80
36 Sussex	30	249	279	C	89
37 Warwickshire	22	62	84	C	74
38 Wiltshire	33	159	192	C	82
39 Worcestershire	28	230	258	C	89
40 Yorkshire (E.R.)	14	113	127	C	89
41 Yorkshire (N.R.)	64	237	301	L	79
42 Yorkshire (W.R.)	108	342	450	C	76

[a] C, Conservative; L, Liberal.
[b] Not known.

68 *Richard Vogler*

Table 4.2 Political allegiances of magistrates in Welsh counties, December 1905

County	Liberal	Conservative	Total	Lord Lieutenant[a]	Percentage Conservative
1 Anglesey	26	32	58	C	55
2 Breconshire	14	101	115		87
3 Cardiganshire	24	60	84		71
4 Carmarthenshire	6	38	44		86
5 Carnarvonshire	12	35	47		74
6 Denbighshire[b]					
7 Flintshire	15	98	113	C	87
8 Glamorgan[b]					
9 Merionethshire[b]					
10 Monmouthshire	30	184	214		86
11 Montgomeryshire	19	73	92	C	79
12 Pembrokeshire	28	110	138	C	80
13 Radnorshire	8	67	75	C	89
Total	182	798	980		81

[a] C, Conservative; L, Liberal.
[b] Not known.

Table 4.3 Summary of political allegiances of county magistrates, 1905

	Liberal	Conservative	Total	Percentage Conservative
England	1434	6855	8289	83
Wales	182	798	980	81
Total	1616	7653	9269	82

complain make it difficult by sending me names, not of the best men, but of the snobs and the hacks whom they wish to reward. (Quoted in Heuston, 1964: 154–5)

Lords Lieutenant received extensive lists of Liberal nominees,[14] often 'reckless and ill-considered'. The Marquis of Bath described the local pressure as 'a torrent of lava'.[15] When George Whitely, the Liberal Chief Whip, wrote to the Prime Minister complaining of the serious damage to the party caused by Loreburn's intransigence, the latter merely restated his refusal to 'job the bench' and offered to resign (see Heuston, 1964: 155–6).

Table 4.4 Political allegiances of magistrates in boroughs, December 1905

	Liberal	Conservative	Total	Percentage Conservative
English boroughs				
1 Birmingham	17	81	98	82
2 Bolton	28	37	65	57
3 Bristol	38	48	86	56
4 Cambridge	7	15	22	68
5 Carlisle	13	11	24	45
6 Leicester	21	34	55	61
7 Lincoln	9	18	27	67
8 Liverpool	42	118	160	73
9 Manchester	61	115	176	65
10 Nottingham	25	39	64	61
11 Oxford	7	14	21	67
12 Plymouth	12	26	38	68
13 Stockport	18	28	46	61
14 Sunderland	19	25	44	57
15 Walsall	8	18	26	69
16 Warwick	14	21	35	60
17 Wigan	16	26	42	62
18 Worcester	11	19	30	63
Total	366	693	1059	65
Welsh boroughs				
1 Cardiff	19	33	52	63
2 Carmarthen	7	6	13	46
3 Swansea	17	20	37	54
4 Merthyr Tydfil	5	8	13	61
5 Monmouth	17	18	35	51
Total	65	85	150	56

Source of Tables 4.1–4.4: *Tribune*, December 1906 (various editions).

According to Asquith, between 1906 and 1909, Loreburn appointed a total of 2785 Liberals, 864 Conservatives and 1733 persons of indeterminate politics (whom Asquith accepted were 'mainly Conservatives').[16] Thus although Loreburn was implementing the 1893 Resolution and occasionally overruling the Lords Lieutenant,[17] he was still appointing even-handedly.[18] The *Tribune* had calculated that a ratio of 6:1 in favour of the Liberals over a number of years would be necessary to restore parity.

By 1909, Loreburn's attempts to placate the party managers and Lords

70 *Richard Vogler*

Lieutenant had nearly broken down. Adopting a time-honoured expedient, on 21 July 1909, the government announced a Royal Commission. After a year's deliberation, under the leadership of Lord James, the Commission took up the suggestion made previously by Lord Herschell[19] for bi-party advisory committees in direct communication with the Lord Chancellor.[20] Unfortunately, the degree of control remaining to the Lords Lieutenant was not defined. Moreover, the new committees were exhorted to ensure that 'all shades of creed and political opinion' were represented on the bench while at the same time ensuring that 'political opinion . . . should not be regarded as in any way controlling or influencing the appointment of justices'.[21] How the committees were to achieve political balance without allowing political factors to influence them was not indicated.

Loreburn and Asquith decided at once to set up a system of committees. Because it was widely anticipated that 'the composition of the selection committees will give rise to discussions as acrimonious as [did] the composition of the magistracy . . .',[22] they proceeded without reference to Parliament (Heuston, 1964: 157), ensuring at the same time a preponderance of Liberals on the committees. The committees were limited to five or six members and in the Counties usually included the Lords Lieutenant.

The Liberal campaign was of course not satisfied. Primrose and Agar Robartes released a new set of figures to the *Daily Chronicle* in July 1911[23] and set down a motion in the House of Commons asserting that the new scheme would not '. . . remove the cause of dissatisfaction'.[24] They demanded to know why the proposals had been adopted in such an unconstitutional manner and what instructions had been given to the new committees about the appointment of working men. No such details were forthcoming.

What Asquith and Loreburn had achieved was to break the local chains of patronage which linked the magistracy directly to the Lords Lieutenant. They had achieved a degree of central control while concealing the political aspects of appointment under a cloak of secrecy. As a result, the political initiative of 1911 opened the magistracy up not only to the Liberals but also to the Labour Party, and as working-class representatives began to seek appointment, so the political authority of the magistracy was yet further dismantled.

Working-class magistrates: The struggle for local democracy

No working man was to sit on a magistrates' bench until the last quarter of the nineteenth century. Indeed, although the Municipal Corporations Act of 1835 had enabled mayors and ex-mayors to act as justices *ex officio*,[25] it was not until the extension of the Borough franchise in 1882 that appointment was even theoretically possible. Eventually, the Tory Lord Chancellor Halsbury, after constant pressure, was obliged to concede: '. . . I believe I have the credit, or discredit – I do not know what it is – of having appointed the only working-class magistrate'.[26] The refusal to select working men in any numbers was attributed variously to the restrictions of the property qualification,[27] the lack of free time for working men to attend Sessions,[28] and the absence of any personal knowledge among Lords Lieutenant of the characters of working-class nominees.[29]

Local campaigns on behalf of working men, such as that conducted in 1888 by the *Pall Mall Gazette* against the West Bromwich Commission,[30] were not uncommon. However, it was the widespread industrial disorders of the 1880s and 1890s which translated the political question from the local to the national state level. In 1893, during the Federated Areas National Coal Strike, Asquith pointed to the substantial issues involved in 'the large, increasing and most delicate class of questions connected with labour which are constantly coming before the benches'.[31] In such a case as the recent strike in Hull, he asked, was it right that the employer class should be able to enlist the military aid of the state? Nevertheless, it was not until labour had begun to organize successfully at a national level that any impression was made upon the existing class character of the benches.

The formation of the Labour Party in 1906[32] coincided almost exactly with the abolition of the property qualification for magistrates. As a result, the new party found itself bombarded by nominations from local Trades Councils and Unions. James Sexton of the Liverpool Dock Labourers addressed a typical complaint in February 1906:

> We have practically no Labour representation on the bench here . . . our poor chaps here a considerable number of them . . . going to jail six months out of twelve for arrears of industrial school fees, the present bench having no sympathy or no knowledge of the condition of the men. Thus they become chronic jail-birds and miserable hunted creatuers [sic] having continually to hide from the authorities and shunned by employers who will not employ them as they are taken from their work by police.[33]

By 1907, the overburdened Assistant Secretary of the new Labour Party, J.S. Middleton, confessed that his office was 'inundated' with applications for the bench. So serious was the situation that the Executive Committee was obliged to pass a resolution regretting that they could no longer deal with any magisterial nominations.[34] As the Secretary, Ramsey MacDonald, put it: 'We can really do very little here and no-one knows anything about Justices of the Peace in any constituency but his own'.[35] However, the savage repression of the Syndicalist strikes of 1909–1911 soon convinced the Labour leadership that this policy was a mistake. As John Clynes, a Labour M.P., explained in 1911:

In these days of labour unrest and industrial turmoil conflicts between capital and labour, struggles between employer and workmen are brought before justices and it is essential that men of our point of view should have their share of representation on the magistracy.[36]

It was at such times that exclusion was felt most sharply. Each major labour dispute of the twentieth century was to bring a perceptible intensification of the struggle for entry into the local magistracy. However, labour disputes were not the only area in which class authority in the local state was being exercised by justices. The signature of a magistrate was required for an ex-serviceman's pension[37] and for means test certificates,[38] as well as numerous other bureaucratic transactions.[39] Because magistrates were rarely resident in working-class areas, these signatures usually required a long walk and a display of deference.

Middleton was aware by this period that intervention from the central party would be of immense importance to the working-class community in the local areas. The same political compromise that gave the Liberals access to the Lord Chancellor's office opened the way for the youthful Labour Party too. By 1917, the organization was strong enough to conduct a 'sizeable correspondence' directly with the Lord Chancellor on the subject of appointments and to inaugurate a 30-year campaign to establish the rights of working men to sit on the bench.

From the beginning it was believed that the role of the advisory committees would be crucial. The demand for *one* Labour representative on every committee was adopted as policy by the 1922 Conference[40] and later communicated to Lord Cave, the Lord Chancellor, by a deputation headed by Sidney Webb.[41] However, the effect of the initiative, even when bolstered by electoral success, was slow. A questionnaire completed by Conference delegates in 1923 indicated that only 140 out of 809 advisory committees and only 719 out of 9621 magistrates in the survey were Labour supporters.[42] If these figures may be generalized, they tend to indicate that the party had in 1923 achieved representation on the bench approaching 8.3 per cent at a time when they were polling 30 per cent of the electorate.

In July 1924, the new Labour Lord Chancellor, Lord Haldane, receiving a deputation which included Herbert Morrison, was able to promise only an examination of the composition of the advisory committees with a view to securing a fair proportion of Labour members.[43] Efforts by Haldane to obtain details of the political allegiances of appointees met resistance from the Lords Lieutenant, and he was obliged to undertake to the Magistrates' Association that he would on no account appoint communists.[44] Lord Haldane's period of office was, in any event, short-lived.

The 'grave disproportion'[45] of Labour magistrates was blamed on obstruction by the 'millionaires and aristocrats'[46] who dominated the advisory committees and the Lord Lieutenancy.[47] This took several forms. It was common, first of all, for appointments in the 'Labour interest' to be made without reference to the party from Labour rebels or even active Liberals or Conservatives.[48] Vetting for political activism was common. John Bromley M.P. reported that one of his comrades had been nominated and subsequently approached:

> ... and asked if he took part in the strike of 1926. He said 'of course I did. My organisation was out and I came out.' Then he was asked if he came out during the strike of 1919 and he replied 'of course, when my fellow men are on strike I do not make a practice of going to work'.

The man was, of course, not appointed.[49]

The central problem was that working men could demonstrate their abilities *only* through the party and nominations could be drawn from almost no other source. Throughout the inter-war years, therefore, elevation to the bench became a reward for the political services of 'strong party men' (Barrister, 1938: 12–16). As one observer put it in 1932:

> For the past twenty years ... the party organisations have fought hard to get their representatives on the advisory committees ... the scheming and wire-pulling that goes on in connection with the advisory committees can only be comprehended by those who have served on these bodies or worked to get a nominee appointed.
> (*Solicitor*, 1932: 20)

This state of affairs enabled the enemies of working-class representation to characterize all such appointments as political, in contrast to the 'non-political' appointments of Tory allies in the county élites.

These frustrating tactics prompted the reawakening of demands which had been current in working-class movements since the early nineteenth century. The whole system of secret nomination, it was argued, was essentially anti-democratic and could never serve the interests of working-class communities. Again and again the local parties (particularly in Yorkshire and the North) were to call for a complete reorganization. Popular election to the bench, or, at the very least, appointment by elected council representatives (Tracey, 1925: 38–9), was considered the only answer.[50] Such modest proposals for democratic procedures had been too much, however, for the party in its first precarious tenure of government. After Haldane's cautious initiative, no major review was to take place until the General Strike had convinced labour leaders beyond doubt of the threat posed to the movement by an intransigent and repressive Tory magistracy. The conviction and imprisonment of trade union leaders during the strike,[51] and subsequently under the 1927 Trades Disputes and Trades Union legislation, produced a vigorous response. For the first time the industrial (as opposed to the political) wing of the movement confronted the issue in a concerted manner,[52] with debates at the 1931 and 1932 Conferences of the Trades Union Congress.

The campaign in the Labour movement reached its climax in 1929. In that year, the National Joint Council organized another deputation to the Labour Lord Chancellor, Lord Sankey, who in July announced a completely fresh policy with regard to the advisory committees. After discussions with Middleton, he set about a complete and methodical review.[53] Between June 1930 and June 1931, 85 committees were examined and Labour representation increased on 79 of them. In 1932, the National Joint Council could report that 273 advisory committees had been reconstituted since 1924, and 236 justices of known Labour sympathies appointed.[54] Sankey's 'deliberate and energetic' policy[55] clearly had a significant impact. Although progress was too slow for the satisfaction of many local parties,[56] and preference was perhaps given to the political rather than the industrial section,[57] there was undoubtedly a 'marked improvement from the Labour point of view since 1929'.[58]

The collapse of the Labour administration in 1931 ended Sankey's initiative. For the next 13 years, Middleton worked on almost alone in his thankless work of harassing the Lord Chancellor's office with nominations and coaxing dispirited local parties to produce suitable candidates. In 1937 he complained: 'It took me a good many years to secure adequate Labour membership of the Advisory Committees and the slackness during the last four years has been very marked'.[59]

J.S. Middleton was the grand strategist of Labour representation on the magisterial benches and fully recognized its importance to the democratic Labour movement. On his retirement in 1944, the then Secretary of the Commissions at the Lord Chancellor's office was moved to tell him:

> I know how near to your heart this matter of Labour representation on the magisterial Benches has come and . . . I know perfectly well how hard you have worked for many years to see your dreams come true. If they have not been realised as fully as you would have wished you can at least take into account the comforting knowledge that you have gone a long way down the road you wished to travel.[60]

Middleton was the first to recognize the importance of central pressure in establishing the institutional presence of the Labour Party in the selection process. He had repeatedly attacked the 'chaos' produced by different channels for working men's nominations through union, party and private sponsorship[61] and welcomed the growth of the County Federations and the:

> . . . growing tendency to curtail such sectional representations and to ensure a more comprehensive and more representative machinery such as the County Federations afford to deal with the question.[62]

The importance of concerted central pressure is well illustrated by the Lord Chancellor's refusal to release the details of the composition of advisory committees to local parties. The names were supplied without demur, however, to Middleton at the central office, who duly passed them back to his local parties.

In three respects, however, Middleton's approach was to prepare the way for the collapse of the working-class advance in this area after 1945. First of all, Middleton agreed with Walter Citrine that, provided the advisory committees could be balanced, all would be well. As a result, the central party failed to co-ordinate – and to some extent stifled – pressure from below for a more equitable arrangement, a 'sensible, dignified and democratic system for the appointment of magistrates' which would not depend upon collusion with the county élites and wire-pulling. As one member expressed it, '. . . it should be done openly, without any secrecy, and appointment should be claimed *as a right* not *as a favour*'.[63] Middleton's efforts, however important for the status of the Labour movement, merely served to incorporate party members within an existing undemocratic and, indeed, quasi-feudal structure.

Secondly, Middleton took the view that once working men were represented on the advisory committees, direct central intervention would no longer be necessary. The whole process could be dealt with by the new County Federations: 'I am hoping before long it will become unnecessary for the National Council of Labour and the Head Office to intervene in these matters at all'.[64] This view seems to reflect the earlier misunderstanding of the national/local dynamic inherent in selections. Middleton's third error, which was widely shared in the party,[65] was a belief that the appointment of more Stipendiary Magistrates would undermine the class bias of the benches and end the struggles over the advisory committees.[66] The flaws in this notion were well demonstrated by a trade union delegate in 1931, who pointed out that:

> the class from which Stipendiaries come will generally be found to be not that represented by the Trade Union movement or having any connection with the Labour Party.[67]

The 1939 emergency and the departure of party members for military service seemed likely to damage Labour's case still further, but Middleton promised to keep up the pressure 'war or no war'.[68] In the event, the electoral truce of the 1939–45 period was to produce an unexpected result. Deprived of the usual outlet for energy, the local parties began to focus their attention more and more on the competition for justiceships.

Complaints began to pour in from around the country. In January, Newcastle LP renewed its campaign against its local advisory committee which, it claimed, never met and had arbitrarily expelled Labour members.[69] A Leicestershire agent reported that 'My party is seething with discontent about the matter and I think the same could be said for other Labour parties in the County of Leicestershire',[70] while Banbury reported that it was 'one of the live issues of our policy'.[71] In June 1942, the Yorkshire Region expressed 'grave concern at the failure of the present machinery'.[72]

Middleton returned at once to his offensive, drawing up a list of 'bad cases' and seeking an interview with the Chancellor, Lord Simon.[73] No doubt conscious of rising pressure, Lord Simon decided to adopt more radical means of obstruction. In a speech at the Mansion House on 9 October 1942, he announced his intention of selecting 'people of probity . . . who, as far as the public knows *have not got any politics at all*'.[74] As his audience well knew, this indicated a return to selections from the Tory county élites. Middleton was privately horrified by Simon's speech, knowing that nominations would no longer be sought from Transport House, but contented himself with writing:

> . . . it has been rather disconcerting to find Viscount Simon giving a lead at this time . . . to non-political magistrates . . . it would seem necessary that he should be reminded of the [1910 Royal] Commission recommendations and also that he and his staff should have some fuller idea of the widespead nature of our movement that has grown up in intervening years.[75]

He decided that a collective response was necessary and drafted a lengthy *Memorandum* for the National Council of Labour calling for a speedy examination of advisory committee personnel and for fresh regulations.[76]

In the meantime, Yorkshire Regional Council (RC) was preparing its own report regarding the whole position of the advisory committees.[77] The Northern RC sent a deputation to the Lords Lieutenant of Northumberland and the North Riding.[78] As if to underline the futility of such local action, the latter promised 'sympathetic consideration', but went ahead to appoint a largely non-Labour list.[79] In October 1943, Rotherham LP moved a protest at the 'present methods' of selecting magistrates.[80] A group from the West Midlands RC went to the Lord Chancellor,[81] while Midlands RC called a gathering of all Labour advisory committee members.[82]

In the midst of this upsurge of local feeling, Middleton finally managed to get his *Memorandum* before the National Council of Labour, which agreed to send a joint delegation on behalf of the whole movement.[83] Although there was, as he said, 'a good deal of new direction going on',[84] he was not able to profit from this state of affairs. The proposed delegation was delayed and, towards the end of 1944, the Chancellor announced that, due to war conditions, no fresh appointments of justices would be made.[85] It was at this unfortunate moment that Middleton retired, reflecting sadly to Page:

For something like 30 years I have been interested in securing working class members on advisory committees and on magisterial benches, largely inspired by the knowledge I acquired of the class prejudice that dominated this section of our public life. . . . Thirty years is a long time and it is a matter of regret that I am ceasing this activity with the task still unaccomplished.[86]

The task, indeed, remained enormous. A census conducted in 1946 revealed that a mere 12 per cent of the magistracy were wage-earners, compared with 16 per cent who were of independent means and 56 per cent of the professional and employer classes (see Table 4.6). Between 1930 and 1945, 46 per cent of appointments to the County benches had been Tories, while only 23 per cent were Socialists and 14 per cent Liberals.[87]

New ideologies and the demise of the democratic bench 1945–86

The crisis of 1945, like those of 1835, 1886 and 1906, was precipitated by a dramatic change in the political composition of Parliament. After the massive swing to the Labour Party in the post-war election, socialist under-representation on the bench became as apparent as that of the Liberals in 1906 and radical reform seemed more than a possibility. Calls for the abolition of the lay magistracy were heard from a variety of sources.[88] As R.S.T. Chorley (1945: 17) noted: 'That there is widespread dissatisfaction with it [the magistracy] is obvious and in order to prevent its remaining a social irritant there must be thoroughgoing reform.' Hermann Mannheim (1946: 238) spoke of a 'contemporary crisis of values' which made it imperative to remodel large sections of the criminal law to make 'criminal justice more democratic'. Both he and the Conservative ex-Home Secretary and Chairman of the Magistrates' Association, Lord Templewood, agreed that the ability of the criminal courts to command consent had been shattered,[89] and that they had to be abandoned as part of the 'machinery of the governing class' in favour of a series of democratic 'Treatment Tribunals' (see Fry, 1944; Mannheim, 1946, 1948b).

The post-war Labour Lord Chancellor, Lord Jowitt, like Loreburn before him, temporized, embarking on a modest adjustment, appointing 30 per cent socialists in his first year.[90] When confronted with a deputation from his own party headed by three ministers, he replied:

Look here, what you fellows don't seem to understand is that I am now Lord Chancellor of Great Britain and . . . when it comes to the administration of justice I don't give a damn about politics. (Quoted in Skyrme, 1979: 53)

Because this attitude was encouraging considerable friction in the party, in October 1945 Jowitt tried a complete change of direction. At a meeting of the Magistrates' Association, he proposed, with studied provocation, that the 'ideal' bench should be composed of balanced political partisans: '... a chairman with some legal experience ... sitting with two magistrates drawn from the Right and two drawn from the Left. You would have a perfect microcosm of the nation'.[91]

Correspondents to *The Times* found his words '... breathtaking. He wipes out progress in a sentence',[92] while the Tories initiated a parliamentary debate to demand that the government 'explain to the House what exactly the Lord Chancellor meant'.[93] In fact, Jowitt neatly avoided the difficulties of his predecessors by at once announcing a Royal Commission on the magistracy, which effectively embargoed the whole issue throughout the greater part of the Labour ministry.

The composition of the Royal Commission aroused considerable controversy. As Sidney Silverman pointed out, there was no parliamentary representation:

> In view of the great feeling that has been expressed on all sides of the House on this matter, would it not have been advisable not to limit it to people who are already connected with the operation of the present system.[94]

This was to be an 'in-house' enquiry. After hearing evidence from a variety of sources over 3 years, the Commission, under Baron Du Parcq, reported in May 1948. What is remarkable about this Report is that it made no significant attempt to resolve the issue which gave rise to its establishment.[95] It proposed no changes in the mode of selection and the Chancellor was merely exhorted to appoint fewer politicians to advisory committees,[96] which in turn were to select magistrates from 'various sections of the community'.[97] The Justice of the Peace Act 1949 which implemented the other proposals [98] was also silent on the subject.[99]

In the event, the passage of the Justices of the Peace Bill was an entirely non-political event, Chuter Ede fearing that the Bill had so much support that it would be 'smothered by it'.[100] Viscount Templewood pointed out:

> My Lords there was a time when a debate upon the Lay Magistracy would have involved this House or another place in a bitter controversy. ... It is satisfactory to think that today there are no party issues between us.[101]

While it is certainly true that this period witnessed a significant shift to the left by the Conservative Party (see Taylor, 1981: 38-9), the depoliticization of the selection issue owed a great deal to Templewood and the Magistrates' Association. Central to this intervention was the self-conscious creation for the first time of a 'professional' image for the bench. In order to assess the significance of this departure, it is necessary first to consider the origins of the Association itself, because the new ideology depended critically on the establishment of a national organization and structure.

The Magistrates' Association was formed in 1921 (shortly after the first appointment of women justices) under the auspices of the Howard League for Penal Reform, which had been established only a few months earlier. The Association owed much to the activity of Margery Fry, the first Honorary Secretary of both societies.[102] Funds, premises, part-time staff and committee members were shared between the two organizations,[103] and their aims and ideological positions must be regarded as closely aligned.

The expressed purposes of the Association were two-fold. First, to provide a national cohesion to the magistracy which, as late as 1920, still lacked any organized central policy-making body. As the first edition of *The Magistrate* put it:

> To-day . . . the problems confronting the local bench are often but part of national problems, to solve which a settled policy and a degree of uniformity are necessary between Bench and Bench. . . . [The Magistrates' Association] gives to Magistrates an opportunity of pooling their experience for national purposes and, irrespective of political or other bias, of bringing their collective opinion before the government of the country.[104]

Thus we hear for the first time in 1921 a suggestion that the lay magistracy could become an autonomous national institution which could break out of the 'water-tight compartments' of the petty sessional divisions.[105] The second object was the creation of a 'specific body of knowledge' as Lord Haldane put it, which would be exclusive to the magistracy.[106] The central article of the constitution stated that the primary intention of the Association was 'To collect and publish information upon all aspects of the work of the magistrates'.[107] The character of this information, as it developed in the 1940s, was to have a crucial impact on criminal justice policy.

Despite support from successive Lord Chancellors, the early progress of the Association was slow and it attracted only the small minority of Howard sympathizers on the bench. Thus for the first 20 years it was 'little more than a club for the magisterial elite'[108] holding annual conferences and producing a bulletin. It was not until 1945, as Fig. 4.1 shows, that the Association began to win widespread acceptance. Its growth from this period onwards is remarkable. On 22 October 1948, Viscount Templewood called for a 'more comprehensive organisation' with extra full-time staff to enable the existing membership to be doubled. In 1955, provincial branches were established. In 1962, a Royal Charter was

[Graph showing membership of the Magistrates' Association and growth of the bench from 1920 to 1980, with y-axis from 0 to 25000 and an arrow marking "Royal Commission" around 1948.]

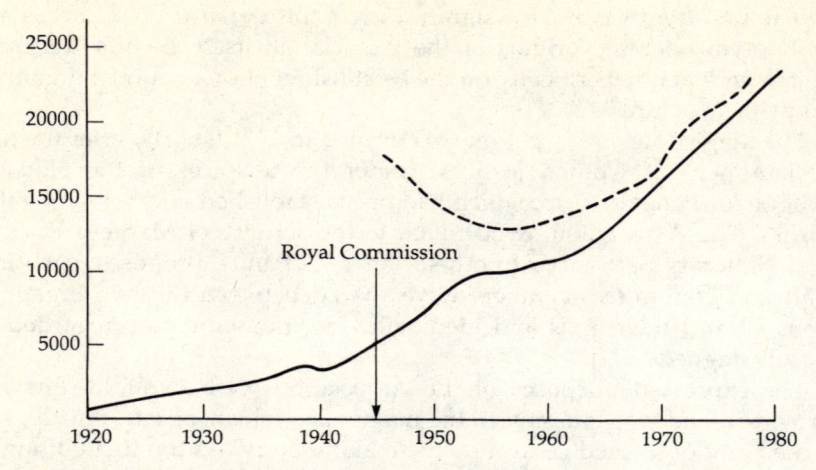

Fig. 4.1 Membership of the Magistrates' Association and the growth of the bench.
– – – = Total number of magistrates in England and Wales; ——— = total membership of the Magistrates' Association.
Source: *The Magistrate* (various editions).

granted, and in the following year Templewood's target was met. During the massive expansion of magisterial numbers in the 1960s and 1970s (see Fig. 4.1) membership of the Association became an almost inevitable consequence of justiceship.

How may we account for the meteoric post-war rise in the fortunes of the Magistrates' Association and what effect did it have upon the equally dramatic re-establishment of the magistracy? Until the post-war period, justiceship was regarded as an honour accorded to the successful politician and businessman; in many ways an inferior knighthood and a reward for services. The Magistrates' Association, under Fry, Templewood and Merthyr, adopted and championed an entirely new image of the magistracy which was based upon scientific skill. They located a type of expertise which could be sharply differentiated from proficiency in law (an area already occupied by other professional groups) and thus outside the entrenched authority of the legal profession.

The rallying call of the Magistrates' Association and the Howard League throughout this period was the word 'Training'.[109] In a growing body of academic literature, magistrates were indicted for their 'woeful ignorance' of new developments in penology (see Chorley, 1945: 13; Mullins, 1948a, b, 1949, 1950). No-one, argued W.H. Sprott (1942: 98–103) in the *Howard Journal*, had any business to deal with delinquents or to 'prescribe treatment' for them unless he were a psychologically (as opposed to legally) trained investigator. Mannheim (1946: 240), adopting Frank's well-known dictum, asked 'Who would be willing to entrust a difficult surgical operation to a medical layman?' Although Mannheim was proposing a professional 'treatment' service (composed of his graduates) to replace the courts, the argument struck a chord with Fabian Socialists (as early as 1920, the Webbs (1920: 124) had envisaged the replacement of punishment with 'curative' treatment in hospitals). It was taken up enthusiastically by advocates of a trained but voluntary magistracy.

By 1946, the Association was organizing correspondence courses and attempts were made to arrange lectures and discussions in the provinces. The campaign reached its climax with the Criminal Justice Act 1948 (for much of which Templewood was responsible), which greatly expanded the range of sentencing options. Templewood at once called on magistrates to 'make full use of the wide opportunities that are expanding before them',[110] and on 22 October 1948, he delivered a major speech to the Magistrates' Association outlining the importance of a scientific understanding of treatment strategies in sentencing, adding: 'The central and local organisation of the Magistrates' Association is expanding to make knowledge accessible to members.'[111] Chuter Ede, introducing the Justices of the Peace Bill the next year, saw the contemporary period as opening a new chapter in the history of the magistracy.[112] Much faith was placed in S.17, which adopted the suggestion made in paras 88–93 of the Report of the Royal Commission with regard to training.[113]

The Magistrates' Association and the Howard League were also active in promoting the study of 'criminal science' in the universities. In 1935, Mannheim had been appointed to lecture in criminology at the London School of Economics and, right up to the fall of the Labour administration, his influence on government action regarding the criminal law was considered crucial (Taylor, 1981: 81n). In 1940, however, Radzinowicz and his colleagues from the Cambridge Law Faculty had formed a committee to promote research and training on the subject. The Magistrates' Association was enthusiastic:

> The members of the Magistrates' Association . . . should take a lively interest in the new departure. We shall not fail from time to time to communicate through the columns of this bulletin such results of the Committee's activities as we consider to be useful to them.[114]

'The long-cherished dream' of the Howard League was about to be realized with the establishment in 1957 of the Home Office Research Unit and, in 1959, the Cambridge Institute of Criminology.[115]

The crucial point here is that, despite the rhetoric, despite Mannheim's 'crisis of values', Templewood's 'climax of history' and Chuter Ede's 'new era for the magistracy' which had contributed to the Labour victory of 1945, the result in terms of the organizational structure and political composition of the bench was almost imperceptible. Indeed, the prospect of a democratic magistracy vanished with the collapse of the radical dynamic of the Attlee administration after only 3 years in office (Anderson, 1964: 46). By 1950, the democratic element in the proposed reforms had been eclipsed by the concept of the expert and by scientific criminology. It was therefore only in exceptional cases, such as the Bournemouth[116] and Rossendale[117] scandals of 1966, and in respect of the notorious Inner London bench (see Skyrme, 1979: 41–2; Burney, 1979: 62–3), that political domination by one party was 'found to pass the bounds of decency' (Burney, 1979: 60) and the matter returned to the political agenda.

In 1966, Lord Gardiner, the Labour Chancellor, began a fresh campaign to appoint more wage-earning justices, but his efforts made little impact on the advisory committees. In an attempt to apply more pressure, committees were required to submit statistical breakdowns of the political composition of their benches, and in 1972 the county committees were divided into district sub-committees. Further efforts were made in the mid-1970s by Lord Elwyn Jones, who approached the Secretaries of the Trades Union Congress and the Labour Party directly for lists of names. Again the initiative foundered on the resistance of the committees (Skyrme, 1979: 56; Burney, 1979: 61).

Since the suppression of the party-political issue in the 1940s, the major expressed aim of successive Lord Chancellors has been, as Lord Gardiner put it, to create a bench which was 'representative of all social classes'[118] and a 'microcosm of the local community in which it operates' (Skyrme, 1979: 62). In 1968, Lord Gardiner claimed that 'a great deal had been achieved'[119] in this respect, and in 1970 Lord Hailsham reported that the magistracy was now a 'representative body'[120] and that it 'came straight from the grass roots of society'.[121] Eleven years later, the President of the Justices' Clerks' Society felt able to announce that the expression 'trial by peers' could 'in these days of enlightened and broadly-based appointments to the bench, include trial by magistrates'.[122] The Society added:

> A major revolution in the selection of Justices was started by Lord Gardiner when Lord Chancellor in 1966 and continued determinedly by each of his successors. Too many changes have taken place for them to be enumerated here, but the outcome is that the quality of appointments to the bench has increased out of all recognition.

To what extent are these claims substantiated? In view of the jealously guarded statistics on the social composition of the benches, it is extremely hard to form a judgement. No study is available until 1966 when Roger Hood (1972: 50) concluded, on the basis of a sample of 538 magistrates, that '. . . there seems to be no evidence of any significant changes in the social class backgrounds from which magistrates came in the years between 1946 and the second half of the 1960s'. These findings, however, related to a period before the Gardiner reforms could be said to have taken effect. Nevertheless, a study by John Baldwin of new appointments in 1971–2 showed that the percentage of wage-earning justices had actually *declined* from 15 per cent in 1947 to 13.1 per cent in 1971–2, while the percentage of professional men had increased from 21.3 to 34.5 per cent and of professional women from 29.6 to 44.8 per cent (see Tables 4.5 and 4.6). He added:

> ... newly appointed magistrates were not drawn from a wider social spectrum than magistrates appointed in the inter-war years: indeed in some respects they appear to have been drawn from a narrower one. (Baldwin, 1976: 171)

These views have been confirmed by Skyrme (1979: 60), Burney (1979: 65) and Mungroo (1980: 10–11). Figures released in 1977, in respect of the Lichfield and Tamworth benches, give similar results (Table 4.6), and in 1979 Sir Thomas Skyrme published statistics from the Lord Chancellor's files which showed that manual workers represented only 8.2 per cent of justices. On the other hand, 10.5 per cent of all magistrates were company directors, 10.6 per cent were managers, 12.5 per cent were educationalists and 10 per cent were members of the medical profession (Skyrme, 1979: 59–61). In short the magistracy is massively and increasingly top-heavy in respect of the managerial and professional classes and cannot fairly be said to resemble in any respect a microcosm of society.

The situation with regard to the selection of black justices was even worse. No appointments at all were made until 1962, and 17 years later the total of sitting black justices had reached only 68 among a population of 23,483 magistrates (Skyrme, 1979: 62). The recent study by King and May (1985) indicates clearly that the situation had not improved significantly, although by 1986 the figures had risen to 455.[123]

An important development of this period has been the consolidation of the existing status of the benches by the creation of large supporting bureaucracies. Increases in the number of magistrates which followed the Gardiner initiative of 1966, and attempts to anticipate the effects of the Courts Act 1972, produced a corresponding expansion in the size of the Lord Chancellor's Department:

> In the early 1970s a great population explosion occurred. . . . The Lord Chancellor's Department has changed from a small staff of personal assistants and advisors into a medium-sized government department fulfilling many of the functions of a Ministry of Justice. (Skyrme, 1979: 24)

This rapid growth in the institutional presence of the magistracy at the level of the central state has been mirrored by a corresponding process in the local areas. Many metropolitan courts in 1981, such as Liverpool and

Table 4.5 Changes in the occupational composition of the magistracy in England and Wales, 1947–77

	Royal Commission (1947) % Male	Royal Commission (1947) % Female	Hood (1966) % Male	Baldwin (1971–2) % Male	Baldwin (1971–2) % Female
Independent means	3.5	16.7	0.8	0.6	3.5
Professionals	21.3	29.6	30.8	34.5	44.8
Employers of 10 or more	30.0	13.4	21.8	18.5	10.3
Employers of 9 or less	16.5	11.2	14.6	12.5	13.8
Salaried employees	13.7	10.5	11.4	17.2	19.5
Wage earners	15.0	7.7	15.9	13.1	3.5
Not known		10.9	4.3	3.6	4.6

Source: Baldwin (1976: 173, table 2).

Table 4.6 Occupational composition of the Lichfield and Tamworth benches in 1977

Profession	Lichfield (%)	Tamworth (%)
Professional	29	7
Farmers	2	10
Company directors	22	10
Trade and Industry (excluding wage-earners)	20	31
Weekly wage-earners	7	7
Housewives	20	35
	100	100
Numerical total of bench	45	29

Source: 5 Pltry. Debs., 925, 3 February 1977, 434.

Manchester, had staffs in excess of 135,[124] and the total number of court employees in 1979 was 3500 (Skyrme, 1979: 18). The promotion of the justices' clerks to commanding positions within these bureaucracies has been of great significance, especially since their professional body (the Justices' Clerks' Society) has now become a pressure group of considerable importance in the central state.

The amalgamation of smaller petty-sessional divisions in 1966, and the reduction in the number of part-time clerks, helped to foster the concept of the professional clerk. Since this period the Society has gone from strength to strength, and in 1981 Lord Hailsham confided:

> . . . there is scarcely a subject connected with magisterial law and practice, law and order, or the administration of justice generally in which your society has not given the government valuable, constructive and responsible advice based upon the wide experience of your members.[125]

In 1966, proposals for complete amalgamation within a central state bureaucracy were put forward by the Society,[126] but they were successfully resisted by the local councils who, as 'paying and providing' authorities (80 per cent of costs are nevertheless met by central funds), still supplied the clerks to the Magistrates' Courts Committees and exercised considerable influence. In 1972, these clerkships were taken over by the justices' clerks themselves and, as a result, the whole situation was to change. Having secured their position in the local structure, the justices' clerks at once abandoned their support for centralization (Skyrme, 1979: 180–1). Indeed, their policy now was to distance the courts (in which they enjoyed exclusive administrative ascendancy) from both the local authority[127] and the central government.[128]

As a result of these developments, the existing selection processes have come under the protection of a bureaucratic agency able to command considerable authority within the central state. The 'self-perpetuating oligarchies' (Burney, 1979: 73) created by the advisory committees are therefore no longer vulnerable to democratic pressure from outside. As the Secretary of the Newcastle Advisory Committee has put it, with obvious approval:

> There's no democratic process by which an individual citizen can become a member. It's an arbitrary decision on the part of the Lord Chancellor. . . . It isn't a democratic business any more than the appointment of judges is a democratic business.[129]

It is beyond the scope of this essay to consider why this 'amazing system' of selections (Pritt, 1971: 72) is permitted to continue. Renewed campaigns for the recruitment of magistrates drawn from among 'manual workers and ethnic minority groups', such as that announced by the Lord

Chancellor, Lord Mackay, in April 1988,[130] will no doubt lead to further token appointments (Pearson, 1980: 81–2), although the institution is now clearly less permeable than it was in Middleton's day.

Conclusion

The intention of this study has been to demonstrate that the magistracy is *not* an institution with a fixed and unchanging class character. No more is it simply an agent or component of the central state. It has been suggested that the geographical jurisdiction is a crucial determinant of authority and status. The potential for change remains. In a period in which the decline of 'treatment' ideologies has thrown into question the whole basis of the post-war expansion, it is important that democratic ideas of popular involvement are available to replace them.

Notes

1 At various stages in his career, Poulantzas has been identified as an Althusserian (Petras and Gundle, 1982), a Gramscian (Jessop, 1982), a disciple of Foucault (Hall, 1980), and even as a proponent of 'stamocap' theory (Jessop, 1982: 189–90).
2 Before the major reform of local administration in 1888, the Justices exercised almost all the powers now vested in local authorities. These included the maintenance of roads, bridges and public buildings, the administration of the Poor Law, local taxes and the militia.
3 5 & 6 Will. IV, c. 76.
4 3 Pltry. Debs., lxii, 5 May 1842, 116–91.
5 Royal Commission on the Selection of Justices of the Peace (Minutes), P.P. 1910 (cd. 5250), xxxvii, 1133.
6 See *The Times*, 23 March 1893, p. 11.
7 4 Pltry. Debs., xii, 5 May 1893, 295.
8 Ibid., p. 173; see also P.P. 1910, xxxvii, 120.
9 See *The Times*, 23 March 1893, p. 11.
10 5 Pltry. Debs., xii (Lords), 2, 21 July 1909, 665.
11 Earl of Dartmouth, P.P. 1910, xxxvii, paras 955–63.
12 *Tribune*, 10 December 1906, p. 7.
13 P.P. 1901, xxxvii, Appendix II, p. 238.
14 For the 4394 appointments made by Loreburn between 1906 and 1908, he received 20,000 nominations (5 Pltry. Debs. (Lords), 2, 21 July 1909, 672).
15 4 Pltry. Debs. (Lords), 172, 22 April 1907, 345–7.
16 5 Pltry. Debs., 32, 15 December 1911, 2724.
17 Lord Loreburn, P.P. 1910, xxxvii, para. 298.
18 Loreburn's assertion in 1910 that he was appointing a ratio of 3:1 Liberals (P.P. 1910, xxxvii, para. 296) ignores the 1733 appointments of indeterminate views.
19 See *The Times*, 23 March 1893, p. 11.

20 P.P. 1910, xxxvii, 12.
21 P.P. 1910, xxxvii, 10.
22 *Justice of the Peace*, **lxxiv**, 23 July 1910, p. 350.
23 *Daily Chronicle*, 5 July 1911.
24 5 Pltry. Debs., 32, 15 December 1911, 2708.
25 The same privilege was extended in 1888 to County Council chairmen, and in 1894 to District Council chairmen.
26 Lord Halsbury, P.P. 1910, xxxvii, para. 1189.
27 Duke of Devonshire, ibid., para. 797.
28 Lord Halsbury, 5 Pltry. Debs. (Lords), 2, 21 July 1909, 676.
29 Duke of Devonshire, 4 Pltry. Debs. (Lords), xiii, 5 June 1893, 65.
30 *Pall Mall Gazette*, 22 September 1888, p. 11.
31 4 Pltry. Debs., xii, 5 May 1893, 290.
32 Formerly the Labour Representation Committee.
33 J. Sexton to J.R. MacDonald, 28 February 1906, LP/GC/1/116.
34 J.S. Middleton, 22 October 1907, LP/GC/20/247.
35 J.R. MacDonald to Whitely, 26 August 1907, LP/GC/18/252.
36 5 Pltry. Debs., 32, 15 December 1911, 2777.
37 T. Rowland Hill, Labour Party Annual Report (LPAR), June 1932, p. 260.
38 Ann Munro, LPAR, June 1932, p. 260.
39 See J. Bromley M.P. (LPAR, June 1930, p. 171) and A. Creech-Jones M.P. to J.S. Middleton, 9 December 1941, LP/MAG/591.
40 LPAR, June 1922, p. 238.
41 LPAR, June 1923, p. 86.
42 LPAR, October 1924, p. 48.
43 Ibid., p. 49.
44 Lord Haldane, *The Times*, 24 October 1925, p. 9.
45 LPAR, October 1924, p. 48.
46 T. Rowland Hill, LPAR, October 1924, p. 119.
47 As late as 1943, there was only one Labour Lord Lieutenant in the entire country. See J.S. Middleton to M. Gibby, 6 November 1943, LP/MAG/578.
48 See, e.g. LPAR, June 1924, p. 119; LPAR, June 1930, p. 171; J.S. Middleton, *Memorandum* 1943, p. 5.
49 LPAR, June 1930, p. 170.
50 A view revived in the unsuccessful Magistrates (Democratic Selection) Bill of 1977 (5 Pltry. Debs., 934, 29 June 1977, 459–62).
51 1610 defendants were charged with acts of disorder and 150 arrests were made for incitement, in all, 632 people were imprisoned (5 Pltry. Debs., 196, 10 June 1926, 16). For the fierce partiality of the Police Courts in favour of the police, see *Solicitor*, 1932: 73–4.
52 See letter of J.S. Middleton, 7 July 1941, LP/MAG/482.
53 J.S. Middleton, *Memorandum* 1943, p. 3.
54 LPAR, October 1932, p. 69.
55 J.S. Middleton to Leo Page, 4 December 1944, LP/MAG/436.
56 See, e.g. complaint of J. Gribble, LPAR, October 1930, p. 172.
57 A. Conley, Report of Proceedings at the Annual Trades Union Congress (RPATUC), September 1931, p. 320.

58 RPATUC, September 1933, p. 218.
59 J.S. Middleton to A.G. Rainbird, 13 September 1937, LP/MAG/91.
60 Leo Page to J.S. Middleton, 7 December 1944, LP/MAG/437.
61 See, e.g. J.S. Middleton to L.P. Hull, 10 August 1943, LP/MAG/488, and J.S. Middleton, *Memorandum* 1943.
62 J.S. Middleton, *Memorandum* 1943, p. 4.
63 G.L. Deacon to J.S. Middleton, 27 November 1943, LP/MAG/388.
64 J.S. Middleton to Councillor Skyvers, 9 August 1943, LP/MAG/523.
65 See, e.g. Jack Jones M.P., LPAR, June 1930, p. 171.
66 See, e.g. J.S. Middleton to L.P. York, 3 November 1943, LP/MAG/552.
67 F.C. Williams, RPATUC, September 1931, p. 319.
68 J.S. Middleton to W.E. Clarke, 19 September 1939, LP/MAG/334.
69 See LP/MAG/182, 188, 194 and 208.
70 W.R. Bonner to J.S. Middleton, 22 June 1942, LP/MAG/9.
71 E. Lacon to J.S. Middleton, 17 January 1942, LP/MAG/239.
72 *Yorkshire Evening News*, 19 January 1942.
73 J.S. Middleton to G. Holland, 2 January 1941, LP/MAG/186.
74 Speech to the Magistrates' Association, 9 October 1942.
75 J.S. Middleton to Sir William Cartwright, 10 February 1944, LP/MAG/616.
76 J.S. Middleton, *Memorandum* 1943.
77 Report of Yorkshire RC to NCL, 28 February 1943, p. 26, NCL/8.
78 Report of Northern RC to NCL, ibid.
79 Northern RC to J.S. Middleton, 4 November 1943, LP/MAG/578.
80 *Sheffield Telegraph*, 27 October 1943, LP/MAG/53.
81 Report of West Midlands RC to NCL, 26 October 1943, p. 13, NCL/2.
82 J. Baxter to J.S. Middleton, 30 December 1943, LP/MAG/153.
83 Minutes, NCL, 26 October 1943, p. 13, NCL/2.
84 J.S. Middleton to W. Howard, 7 December 1944, LP/MAG/360.
85 A declaration which did not, apparently, impede the appointment of 40 (largely Tory) new Justices in Kent. See J.S. Middleton to H.W. Watling, 10 November 1944, LP/MAG/167.
86 J.S. Middleton to Leo Page, 4 December 1944, LP/MAG/436.
87 P.P. 1947/48, xii, 302.
88 See, e.g. Whitely (1942: 120); Sprott (1942); President of the Association of Welsh Law Societies (*The Times*, 15 January 1944); Lord Morris, 5 Pltry. Debs. (Lords), 163, 12 July 1949, 1177.
89 See Mannheim (1946: 197); Templewood, *Howard Journal*, 1946, p. 7.
90 P.P. 1947/48, xii, para. 302.
91 *The Times*, 20 October 1945, p. 2.
92 *The Times*, 23 October 1945, p. 5.
93 Commander Maitland, 5 Pltry. Debs., 416, 22 November 1945, 718.
94 5 Pltry. Debs., 424, 24 June 1946, 683.
95 See Page (1949: 69) who accuses it of 'shirking the issue'.
96 P.P. 1947/48, xii, pp. 18–21.
97 Ibid., pp. 9–10. See also Taylor (1981: 65).

98 A statutory retirement age of 75, payment of travelling expenses, the creation of Magistrates' Court Committees and the abolition of separate Commissions in the smaller non-county boroughs.
99 See 5 Pltry. Debs., 470, 22 November 1949, 885.
100 5 Pltry. Debs., 470, 7 December 1949, 1957.
101 5 Pltry. Debs. (Lords), 159, 18 November 1948, 421–2.
102 See *Howard Journal*, **1**, October 1921, p. 60 and Jones (1966: 118).
103 *The Magistrate*, **XXVI**, 1970, pp. 2 and 170. Evidence of the Howard League to the 1949 Royal Commission, P.P. 1947/48, Minutes, pp. 127ff.
104 *The Magistrate*, **1**, 1921, p. 1.
105 *Howard Journal*, **1**, October 1921, p. 60.
106 Quoted in *The Magistrate*, **XXVI**, September 1970, p. 1.
107 Article 11(a) of the 1921 Constitution.
108 Sir William Addison, *The Magistrate*, **XXXVI**, 1980, p. 169.
109 See *Howard Journal*, 1946, p. 72; *Justice of the Peace*, **cix**, 1 December 1945, p. 569.
110 *Justice of the Peace*, **cxii**, November 1948, p. 707.
111 *The Times*, 23 October 1948, p. 2.
112 5 Pltry. Debs., 470, 28 November 1949, 806–10.
113 S.17 required the new Magistrates' Courts Committees to set up optional training schemes. Arrangements were completed by 1954, but in 1961 the Magistrates' Association renewed its demand for obligatory training. After 1966, therefore, all newly appointed justices were obliged to give an undertaking to complete a prescribed course within a year (from 1980 the obligation was widened to include obligatory refresher courses). By 1974, training arrangements, under the auspices of the Association, had expanded to the extent that a Home Office Standing Committee was appointed.
114 *The Magistrate*, **V**, November/December 1940, p. 333.
115 *Howard Journal*, **xxi**, 1981, p. 133.
116 *The Times*, 7 January 1966, p. 6.
117 *The Guardian*, 17 August 1966, p. 14.
118 *Justice of the Peace*, **129**, 6 March 1965, p. 158.
119 *The Magistrate*, **24**, December 1968, p. 178.
120 *Justice of the Peace*, **134**, 1 August 1970, p. 580.
121 *The Magistrate*, **26**, September 1970, pp. 129–30.
122 See Justices' Clerks' Society (1983: para. 40).
123 Lord Chancellor's Department, *Report of a Survey of the Ethnic Composition of the Magistracy* (1988).
124 *Report of the Working Group on Magistrates' Courts*, 1982, Annex S.
125 *The Justices' Clerk*, **116**, September 1981, p. 92.
126 Ibid., no. 71, September 1966, pp. 90–1.
127 Justices' Clerks' Society (1983: paras 4.5 and 4.6).
128 Ibid., para. 4.8. Also *Report of the Working Group on Magistrates' Courts*, 1982, Annex S.
129 *The Sunday Times*, 22 January 1982, p. 3.
130 *The Times*, 28 April 1988, p. 5.

References

Anderson, P. (1964). Origins of the present crisis. *New Left Review*, **23**, 26–53.
Baldwin, J. (1976). The social composition of the magistracy. *British Journal of Criminology*, **16**, 171–4.
Barrister (1938). *Justice in England*. London: Victor Gollancz.
Broadbent, T.A. (1977). *Planning and Profit in the Urban Economy*. London: Methuen.
Burney, E. (1979). *J.P., Magistrate, Court and Community*. London: Hutchinson.
Chorley, R.S.T. (1945). The unpaid magistrate and his future. *Modern Law Review*, **viii** (1–2), 1–18.
Christian, L. (1985). Restriction without conviction. The role of the courts in legitimising police control in Nottinghamshire. In *Policing the Miners Strike*, (B. Fine and R. Millar, eds). London: Lawrence and Wishart.
Cockburn, C. (1977). *The Local State*. London: Pluto.
Cotterrell, R. (1984). *The Sociology of Law: An Introduction*. London: Butterworths.
Dear, M.J. and Clarke, G.L. (1978). The state and geographical process: A critical review. *Environmental Planning A*, **10**, 173–83.
Dearlove, J.N. (1973). *The Politics of Policy in Local Government: The Making and Maintenance of Public Policy in the Royal Borough of Kensington and Chelsea*. Cambridge: Cambridge University Press.
Duncan, S. and Goodwin, M. (1988). *The Local State and Uneven Development: Behind the Local Government Crisis*. Cambridge: Polity Press.
Foucault, M. (1977). *Discipline and Punish*. Harmondsworth: Penguin.
Fry, M. (1944). *The Future Treatment of the Adult Offender*. London: Victor Gollancz.
Griffith, J.A. (1966). *Central Departments and Local Authorities*. London: Allen & Unwin.
Hall, S. (1980). Nicos Poulantzas: State, power, socialism. *New Left Review*, **119**, 60–9.
Harries Jenkins, G. (1977). *The Army in Victorian Society*. London: RKP.
Heuston, R.F.V. (1964). *Lives of the Lord Chancellors, 1885–1940*. Oxford: Oxford University Press.
Hogg, R. (1979). Imprisonment and society under early British capitalism. *Crime and Social Justice*, **12**, 4–17.
Hood, R. (1972). *Sentencing the Motoring Offender*. London: Heinemann.
Jessop, R. (1982). *The Capitalist State*. Oxford: Martin Robertson.
Jones, E.H. (1966). *Margery Fry. The Essential Amateur*. Oxford: Oxford University Press.
Justices' Clerks' Society (1983). *The Working of the Magistrates' Courts*. Bristol: JCS.
Keith-Lucas, B. (1977). *English Local Government in the Nineteenth and Twentieth Centuries*. London: Historical Association.
King, M. and May, C. (1985). *Black Magistrates*. London: Cobden Trust.
Lee, J.M. (1959). Parliament and the appointment of magistrates. *Parliamentary Affairs*, **xiii** (1), 85–94.
Lee, J.M. (1963). *Social Leaders and Public Persons*. Oxford: Clarendon.
Mandel, E. (1975). *Late Capitalism*. London: NLB.
Mannheim, H. (1946). *Criminal Justice and Social Reconstruction*. London: Kegan, Paul, Trench, Tubner.

McLennan, G. et al. (1984). *The Idea of the Modern State*. Milton Keynes: Open University Press.

Mullins, C. (1948a). *Fifteen Years Hard Labour*. London: Victor Gollancz.

Mullins, C. (1948b). Should criminal courts pass sentence? *Quarterly Review*. October, 485–94.

Mullins, C. (1949). Psychology in sentencing. *Journal of Science*, xcv, 263–74.

Mullins, C. (1950). New methods for sentencing the guilty. *Howard Journal*, viii (2), 118–20.

Mungroo, I.P. (1980). *Magistrates within the English Judicial System*. Private Publication.

Nairn, T. (1977). *The Break up of Britain*. London: NLB.

Napier, Sir W. (1957). *The Life and Opinions of General Sir Charles James Napier*. London: John Murray.

Osborne, B. (1960) *Justices of the Peace 1361–1848: A History of the Justices of the Peace for the Counties of England*. Dorset: Sedgehill Press.

Page, L. (1949). Justices of the Peace: Some reflections on the Royal Commission's Report. *Quarterly Review*, January, 66–77.

Pearson, R. (1980). Popular justice and the lay magistracy: The two faces of lay participation. In *Essays in Law and Society* (Z. Bankowski and G. Mungham, eds). London: RKP.

Percy-Smith, J. and Hillyard, P. (1985). Miners in the arms of the law: A statistical analysis. *Journal of Law and Society*, 12, 345–54.

Petras, J. and Gundle, S. (1982). A critique of structuralist state theorising. *Contemporary Crises*, 6, 161–82.

Poggi, G. (1978). *The Development of the Modern State*. London: Hutchinson.

Poulantzas, N. (1969). The Problem of the Capitalist State. *New Left Review*, 58, 67–78.

Poulantzas, N. (1973). *Political Power and Social Classes*. London: NLB.

Poulantzas, N. (1974). *Classes in Contemporary Capitalism*. London: Verso.

Poulantzas, N. (1978). *State, Power, Socialism*. London: Verso.

Pritt, D.N. (1971). *The Apparatus of the Law*. London: Lawrence and Wishart.

Quinault, R. (1974). The Warwickshire County Magistracy and public order 1830–1870. In *Popular Protest and Public Order* (J. Stevenson et al., eds). London: Allen & Unwin.

Saunders, P. (1979). *Urban Politics: A Sociological Interpretation*. London: Hutchinson.

Saunders, P. (1986). Reflections on the dual politics thesis: The argument, its origins and its critics. In *Urban Political Theory and the Management of the Fiscal Crisis* (M. Goldsmith, ed.). London: Gower.

Solicitor (1932). *English Justice*. London: George Routledge and Sons.

Skyrme, Sir T. (1979). *The Changing Face of the Magistracy*. London: Macmillan.

Sprott, W.H.J.S. (1942). A plea for trained magistrates in the juvenile courts. *Howard Journal*, vi (2), 98.

Steedman, C. (1984). *Policing the Victorian Community: The Formation of the English Provincial Police Forces 1856–80*. London: RKP.

Sugarman, D. (1983). Law, economy and the state in England 1750–1914: Some major issues. In *Legality, Ideology and the State* (D. Sugarman, ed.). London: Academic Press.
Taylor, I. (1981). *Law and Order: Arguments for Socialism*. London: Macmillan.
Tracey, H. (1925). *The Book of the Labour Party*. London: Caxton.
Vogler, R.K. (1982). Magistrates and civil disorder. *LAG Bulletin*, 12–15.
Vogler, R.K. (1984). *The Development of Summary Jurisdiction in England and Wales in relation to Civil Disorder*. Ph.D. Thesis. Cambridge University: Institute of Criminology.
Vogler, R.K. (1986). Anti-nuclear defences: Aspects of legality and the Peace Movement in England. In *Nuclear Weapons, the Peace Movement and the Law* (J. Dewar *et al.*, eds). London: Macmillan.
Webb, S. and Webb, B. (1920). *A Constitution for the Socialist Commonwealth of Great Britain*. London: Longmans, Green and Co.
Webb, S. and Webb, B. (1963). *English Local Government*. London: Frank Cass.
Whitely, C. (1942). *Brief Life*. London: Macmillan.
Zangerl, C.H.E. (1971). The social composition of the magistracy, 1831–1887. *Journal of British Studies*, 113–25.

5 The censure of 'communism' and the political trial in South Africa

Cathi Albertyn and Dennis Davis

The trial of political offenders in South Africa has become a regular feature of the political process, although the form thereof has undergone modification at various times (Suttner, 1984: 63). A major change in the character of political trials over the past few years has been the increase in the number of treason trials. Only one treason charge was brought between 1945 and 1979, that of 156 leaders of the Congress Alliance in 1956. The pattern has subsequently changed, with 22 such trials between 1979 and 1984, mostly involving members of the banned African National Congress (Institute of Race Relations, 1983: 806).

The announcement in February 1985 that treason charges were to be brought against 16 leaders of the United Democratic Front (the extra-parliamentary political front that has grown, since its inception in 1983, into a mass national movement), once more highlighted the political trial as a means of crushing popular opposition to the State.

In this essay, we attempt to develop a theoretical understanding of the character and role of political trials within the South African social formation. We illustrate our argument by way of the two major treason trials of 1956 and 1985. While they are not necessarily typical of the range of political trials in South Africa (e.g. public violence cases were far more common in 1985), we would argue that the 1956 and 1985 trials of opposition leadership condense many of the political and ideological issues of their respective periods, thereby providing an insight into the relations between the trials and political struggle at a particular historical conjuncture.

A theoretical framework

In *Political Justice* (1961), the most systematic analysis of political trials to date, Kirchheimer attributes a political role to law by addressing the central question of the role of the courts in the fight for political domination. The thrust of his argument is that the courts play an important political role in the ideological fight for domination over the minds of the citizenry. The trials of political opponents

> . . . serve to authenticate and thus to limit political action . . . [and] . . . have become a new dimension through which many types of political regimes, as well as their foes, can affirm their policies and integrate the population into their political goals. (Kirchheimer, 1961: 17)

The courtroom is not the exclusive arena in the fight for political domination. Kirchheimer explicitly links the courts with other agencies and methods of political control, such as military action, informal violence, bribery and media propaganda. However, the trial is seen to play a specific role in the authentication of political repression, operating as a political weapon in the struggle for 'spontaneous consent' to the political programmes of the state by the selection of suitable targets for public degradation and criminalization. Hence:

> . . . court action is called upon to exert influence on the distribution of political power. The objectives may be to upset – fray, undermine or destroy – existing power positions, or to strengthen efforts directed at their preservation. (Kirchheimer, 1961: 4)

Kirchheimer appears to suggest that as 'a staging-area for clashes between conflicting political aims', the courtroom constitutes a potential site of political and ideological struggle. Political trials, he argues:

> . . . operate in the same zone of seemingly endless thrusts and counter-thrusts through which power positions are strengthened and the incumbent regime's authority is impressed upon friend and waverer; but often at the same time, new images and myths are pressed forward by the foes of the regime who try to erode and expose established authority. (Kirchheimer, 1961: 49)

Even this brief summary of Kirchheimer's analysis illustrates its value, particularly in the emphasis placed upon the political nature of law, the ideological significance of the political trial and the struggles combined within it, and the location of the political trial within a range of political controls. Notwithstanding this, the work does suffer from two major weaknesses:

1 Perhaps the most crucial problem with *Political Justice* is that it does not

provide a clear definition of political crime. It is the actions and ideas of the defendants, and their organizations, that provide the content of a political trial. Without examining the form and content of political crime within the context of political struggle and power relations in a given social formation, it is not possible to develop an understanding of a political trial. Kirchheimer, however, proceeds to analyse the political trial without addressing this important prior question, namely what can be defined as the political crime, which *then* becomes the subject of the political trial.

Consequently, there is considerable confusion in distinguishing a political from an ordinary criminal trial. He argues that a political trial is distinguished by:

> ... the direct involvement in the struggle for political power, rather than the long-range political effect of socio-economic power-contests or the derivative effect of the confirmation or destruction of personal power positions. (Kirchheimer, 1961: 4)

Despite this statement, there is no attempt to define and explain the concept of 'political power' as opposed to 'socio-economic' power. Kirchheimer fails to provide a clear category of political trials, and a theoretical context within which to locate them. This reflects a general tendency in his work to view such important concepts as 'political power' and 'political crime' as uncontroversial and uncontested categories.

2 Although Kirchheimer identifies the political trial as linked to a range of political controls, he does not describe or explain the nature and operation of these connections. There is no theory of 'the political' in which the political trial may be seen to operate in a complex relationship of mutual reinforcement, support and legitimation with other controls, agencies and institutions. The nature of the strategies employed by the state to reproduce the cohesion of the social formation, and the impact of political struggle thereon, are ignored by Kirchheimer. Hence, one is never certain of why the political trial becomes an important means of authenicating and limiting political action. It is surely not sufficient to state that:

> ... whatever the dominant legal system, both governments and private groups have tried to enlist the support of the courts for upholding or shifting the balance of political power. (Kirchheimer, 1961: 47)

Given these omissions, *Political Justice* tends to lapse into considerable moments of instrumentalism. The use of the political trial, and the entire criminal justice system, is largely seen as a choice open to the state as it deems fit.

Where he does concern himself with prevailing institutional structures, he analyses the differences of the political trial in totalitarian and in constitutional regimes. Referring to 'Stalinist' political trials, he argues that within a totalitarian regime, the political trial has only its outward form, at best, in common with 'genuine judicial proceedings'. The mechanical and ideological manipulations of the trial by the ruling party leadership completely eliminate the elements of chance, conflict and confrontation in the courtroom, as defendant, prosecution and judge co-operate in the presentation of a 'prefabricated and alternative reality'. This is an extreme example of the image-creating effect of the trial which serves the purpose of manipulating and rallying public opinion. It is the element of uncertainty and risk that separates the constitutional trial from the administrative action of totalitarian regimes. In the former, the political trial is more of a contest and less of a unilateral reaffirmation of unassailable power positions.

Even within this characterization, the instrumentalism of Kirchheimer's analysis is well illustrated in his description of the form of the political trial. He suggests that:

> The instigators of a political trial will face many uncertainties if they want to use the legal form for purposes beyond harassment or elimination of a political foe, and if they want to advance into the territory of image-creating or destroying. . . . The narrower the scope of the theme selected for proof, the greater the likelihood that the operation will succeed, but the less chance that the result will do more than serve momentary political purposes. . . . The morality play, after serving the political needs of the day, will survive mainly as a testimony to its initiators' own frame of mind, which may well prove more distorted than that of the victim (Kirchheimer, 1961: 118)

The form of legal procedure followed in the trial, and the legal definition employed, are explained by Kirchheimer exclusively in terms of choices open to the state. He sees law and its forms as being shaped by the decisions of the state. Because this theoretical area of *Political Justice* is underdeveloped, little indication is given of other constraints which might shape or influence the form of the trial.

This weakness is particularly surprising when we examine Kirchheimer's reference to South Africa, where he alludes to the importance of political struggle in shaping the nature of legal control, but does not extend such insights to the theoretical basis of the work. In explaining the form of political control which operated in South Africa during the 1950s, Kirchheimer described the period as a 'war of position':

> The leaders of the majority clung to legality in their actions because they counted on a mass reservoir of potential adherents whom they

hoped to turn into reliable and disciplined followers; they wanted to do this by education and by drawing them into the ever-widening campaigns of disobedience directed against selected features of the minority regime. . . . Conversely, in tolerating and using the cloak of legality, the leaders of the ruling minority trusted in the durability of prevailing social arrangements; they counted on being able to continue covering with legal forms the proper social and administrative weapon for obstructing the majority's ascent to power. (Kirchheimer, 1961: 124)

However, the use of legal forms of control was not likely to reduce the basic tensions between the state and the black majority:

Weakening the minority's position without being willing to accept compromise would call the tune; the ruling group would feel impelled to scrap legal repression and introduce stronger, more pervasive, and less law-beholden controls; the courts, perhaps even then speaking for elements not fully in sympathy with the minority's present political leadership, would either be packed or sidetracked and stripped of the residual power which permits them to act as stabilizers. (Kirchheimer, 1961: 124–5)

In these passages, Kirchheimer locates the forms of state control in terms of the nature of political struggle. For this reason, writing in 1961, he is able to predict (accurately) that as the mass organizations familiarize themselves with increasing techniques of resistance, and cautious leadership was challenged by the emergence of more radical groups, repression would tend to move beyond the existing legal framework.

In summary, Kirchheimer's analysis is based on undeveloped concepts of law and the state. He fails to question or define the relationship between law, the state and the institutions of the state. Despite the richness of his data, Kirchheimer's work suffers from the use of ill-defined theoretical concepts in general, and the lack of a theoretical framework within which the political can be analysed accurately so as to develop a clearer understanding of (1) what constitutes a political crime, (2) when and why a political trial occurs, and (3) the nature of the political struggle forming the context of the subsequent trial.

Beyond Kirchheimer

The problems of providing an accurate theorization and analysis of the political is not limited to Kirchheimer's work, but has constituted a major problem for Marxist scholarship in general. Laclau and Mouffe (1981: 17) have suggested that there are two broad strands within Marxist thought:

. . . texts which present class-struggle, in its concrete historical specificity, as the motor of history and as an essentially active and creative element, whilst other texts present it as the passive manifestation of an underlying structural process – the development of the productive forces and the contradictions inherent in them.

The former perspective has tended to assert the primacy of the political, whereas the latter perceives political struggle not as being constitutive of the social order, but merely part of the superstructure of an inexorable economic process.

Laclau and Mouffe argue that the latter perspective has held ascendancy for too long, and that there exists a pressing need to break away from the economism of such a view, and to assert the primacy of the political within the economy itself. This would allow scope for a developed analysis of the political in which:

> ... the economy like all other spheres of society, is the terrain of a political struggle and ... its laws of motion are not governed by a simple logic, but by the hegemonic articulation existing in a given society. (Laclau and Mouffe, 1981: 22)

In order to develop a theory of the political, Nicos Poulantzas' (1978) *State, Power, Socialism* provides a rich and complex starting-point.[1]

Poulantzas (1978: 17) rejected the notion of an economic base as a hermetically sealed entity capable of self-reproduction, functioning in terms of its own internal laws. He suggests that the political field of the state (as well as the sphere of ideology) has always been present in the constitution and reproduction of the relations of production in different forms. He argued that there is an inextricable link between the economic and the political in which the relations of production (which have primacy over productive forces in that the latter are always organized under given relations of production) play a determining role in fixing the boundaries of the economic *and* the political within a social formation. This approach allows Poulantzas to move away from 'traditional economism' where the base/superstructure metaphor becomes the central means of explaining the social formation.

Having explained the primacy of the relations of production, Poulantzas argues that political and ideological relations are present within the relations of production, indeed in their very constitution and reproduction. Relations of production find expression in class powers which are shaped by political and ideological relations. These relations do not constitute a passive reflection of already existing relations of production, but are themselves present in the actual constitution of the relations of production. This analysis becomes particularly important in considering the nature of social classes. For Poulantzas, the determination of classes depends on the relations of production, which relate directly to the social division of labour and which include political and ideological relations. Hence, economic criteria are not sufficient to determine and locate social classes.

Consequently, even at the level of relations of production, class positions find expression in class powers:

> ... as the relations of production and the social division of labour do not constitute an economic structure outside (before) social classes, *so they do not belong to a field external to power and class struggle*. ... There are no social classes prior to their opposition in struggle. (Poulantzas, 1978: 27)

Thus, class struggle is analysed in terms of the capacity of one or several classes to realize their specific interests, a capacity which is in opposition to the capacity of other classes to do likewise. For this reason, power is strictly relational, located in a 'network of relations between exploiters and exploited' (Poulantzas, 1978: 35).

Although power finds its roots in the relations of production, it can exist only in so far as it is materialized in certain apparatuses. These are not only apparatuses of the state, although power is pre-eminently concentrated and materialized by the state. The nature of the state reflects the relationship of forces among social classes (Poulantzas, 1978: 128–9); it is neither subject nor instrument, but 'the specific material condensation of a relationship of force among classes and class fractions'. For this reason, state policy must be seen as a result of the class contradictions inscribed in the very structure of the state. The state is itself divided, and contradictions are present in its material framework. Poulantzas concludes that not only inter-fractional divisions but also popular struggles are:

> ... inscribed in the institutional materiality of the state, even though they are not concluded in it; it is a materiality that carries the traces of these muted and multiform struggles. (Poulantzas, 1978: 144)

Even where the specific framework of the state might involve the exclusion of the popular masses from a directly physical presence in certain of its apparatuses, such as the judiciary and bureaucracy, popular struggles will always have an effect within such apparatuses (Poulantzas, 1978: 141).

Poulantzas' work provides the basis of a theory of the political and an understanding of struggle and its effects upon the state. Power relations and struggle become the forms of analysis as the state is viewed as a material condensation of the relationship of forces between the dominant and dominated classes. In this context, the state is a site of struggle, with power struggles traversing the state and the dominated classes existing within the state in the form of centres of opposition to the power of the dominant classes. An analysis of the political must grasp the manner in which the prevailing political struggles are inscribed in the institutional structure of the state, while exploring the differential forms and precise historical transformation of the state (Poulantzas, 1978: 152).

However, while Poulantzas emphasizes the role of political and ideological relations in class formation (and the role of struggle in general), he does not develop the argument that classes are more than economic categories. This renders his work vulnerable to criticisms of class-reductionism, for example:

1 There is no detailed enquiry into the role of struggle in class formation and reproduction; classes are seen as determined by a totality of objective conditions – political, economic, ideological. In the analysis, classes are seen as existing prior to struggle, not as an effect of struggles among class-forces. Although he argues that classes can only exist in relation to each other (i.e. in opposition and struggle), this is only at the level of the relations of production and thus at the level of capital, as opposed to labour, whereby classes are inevitably conceptualized as unitary and homogeneous and the relations between them as an undifferentiated relation of exploitation.
2 The presence of political and ideological relations in class constitution and reproduction presupposes classes in a state of flux, as continually constituted and reconstituted. As Burowoy (1958: 260) writes:

> The patterns we discover in history are not immutable, nor are they tendential toward some ultimate 'true' pattern; they are continually reconstructed as part of the historical process.

However, this view of class formation as a continuous process is only implicit in Poulantzas' work. Furthermore, class organization and reorganization must be viewed as the effect of a totality of struggles – including popular struggles, struggles around race and gender. Poulantzas does not sufficiently theorize the nature and role of struggles which affect the class struggle, but which focus on issues other than class.

In order to develop our analysis, it is necessary to meet such criticisms. Wolpe (1985) argues that the relations of production provide a necessary but not a sufficient basis for the analysis of classes and class struggles. At the level of the relations of production, classes can only be conceptualized as unitary and homogeneous entities and the relations between them as an undifferentiated relation of exploitation. However, classes must be seen as the effect of the totality of struggles. Thus they are:

> ... fragmented and fractured by politics, culture, ideology and, indeed, the concrete organisation of production and distribution itself. A class is constituted not as a unified social force, but as a

patchwork of segments which are differentiated and divided on a variety of bases and by a variety of processes. (Wolpe, 1985: 23)

By using these developed notions of classes and the role of struggle, it is possible to analyse the significance of racial domination, and issues of 'national' liberation and popular struggle, without undermining that of the fundamental class divisions within a capitalist social formation. This conceptualization of class can be linked to Poulantzas' analysis of struggle and the state to provide a basis for analysis of political trials in South Africa.

Political struggle, political trials and hegemony

On the argument above, there is a need to show how political struggle affects the nature of a political trial. To do this, we analyse the political trial by employing a concept of hegemony. In the context of political trials, we understand hegemony as a complex, contradictory and dynamic process which is itself a site of struggle.

Raymond Williams (1980) is correct to define hegemony as a set of meanings and values which, as they are experienced as practices, appear as reciprocally confirming. However, 'except in the operation of a moment of abstract analysis', hegemony cannot be considered to be a static system, but must be regarded as a dynamic process of incorporation in the constitution of an effective and dominant culture. Within this process of incorporation, a selective tradition

> . . . is always passed off as the tradition, the significant past. But always the selectivity is the point; the way in which from a whole possible area of past and present, certain meanings and practices are chosen for emphasis, certain other meanings and practices are neglected and excluded. . . . [This process] is continually alive and adjusting. . . . Thus we have to recognise the alternative meanings and values, the alternative opinions and attitudes, even some alternative senses of the world, which can be accommodated and tolerated within a particular effective and dominant culture. (Williams, 1980: 39)

It is logical that the process of incorporation presupposes the process of exclusion, but it is necessary to include additional processes in order to understand the hegemonic struggle, viz. subversion, legitimation and redefinition (see Mathiesen, 1980: 224–6). Such a process is confronted continuously with the problem of new meanings and values, new practices and significances, and the extent to which it is possible to incorporate, exclude, redefine or subvert these things. As Laclau and Mouffe point out, and in accordance with our view of the diversity and changing nature of struggle, the process of hegemony does not necessarily presuppose a dichotomically divided political space, but a proliferation of political spaces with a complex and difficult articulation. There is no single site of hegemony; on the contrary, within a given social formation, there can be a variety of hegemonic nodal points.

Such a concept of hegemony accords with an analysis of power in which primacy is given to concrete political struggles. The process of incorporation and exclusion is consistent with the view that the nature of power struggles between different classes and class fractions (however fractured and fragmented at the concrete level) will shape the nature and extent of these processes, and hence the form and content of the central system of practices, meanings and values which can properly be called dominant and effective (Williams, 1980: 38).

Williams' concept of hegemony and Poulantzas' analysis of the state provide the tools to develop Kirchheimer's work in relation to the meaning of political crime, the role and meaning of political trials, and political control. It is to the concepts of political crime and political trials that we now turn.

Political crime

Contemporary sociology of deviance has contributed greatly to the debunking of the idea that the concept of crime is an uncontested one. As Hall and his colleagues made clear in *Policing the Crisis* (1978), crime is defined differently (in both official and lay ideologies) at different historical moments. This reflects both the changing attitudes among different sections of the population to crime, and real historical changes in the social organization of criminal activity. In addition, it shows the shifting application of the category itself, by the ruling classes, to different groups and activities in the course of, as well as for the purpose of preparing the ground for, the exercise of legal restraint and political control (Hall *et al.*, 1978: 189).

Given the difficulties of employing objective categories of crime and deviance, Sumner makes the useful suggestion that crime and deviance should be analysed as 'negative ideological categories with specific material application', termed censures (Sumner, 1983: 187; see also p. 26, this volume). Thus:

> . . . in societies which are substantially divided by class in terms of wealth and power, it is inevitable that the class which dominates the economy, owns the means of mass-communication and controls the reins of political power will find its censures pre-eminent in the legal and moral discourses of society. Hence enunciated in the mass media, practised in the courts and other political-policing institutions and materially rooted in the dominant social relations of the epoch,

such censures must soon take a more generalised character as other people internalise them. And if the subordinate classes do not learn, we can expect the dominant class agencies of control to destroy, colonise or police the institutions of lower class culture so that ideological resistance is weakened. (Sumner, 1983: 187)

Social censures are thus not simply labels without a point of reference or justifiability. They cannot be understood without reference to:

(a) the ideological discourse and social interests which support and constitute them;
(b) the phenomena they interpret and classify;
(c) the historical conjuncture within which they are applied. (Sumner, 1983: 196; see also pp. 28–9, this volume)

Sumner and Sandberg (this volume) contend that the censure is a composite category with definite and predictable political targets. It is not just an abstract principle applied equally to all. It is often targeted against what it downgrades as 'dissident minorities', i.e. those political movements that challenge dominant social relations of class, gender and race. Social censures, particularly those which are connected to hegemonic struggles, will thus condemn a wide range of dissent. They will appear as 'composite denunciations' unified by their class origins and hegemonic purpose in legitimating the state claim against alternative claimants to power. Furthermore, embedded within dominant ideologies, social censures can constitute an 'important feature of the process whereby a dominant class bloc reconstructs its hegemony within the nation-state' (see p. 187).

This use of the social censure is particularly pertinent within the context of political crime, as it emphasizes the contested nature of the classification of behaviour which the state portrays as founded upon universally accepted moral principles, while other concepts of behaviour are excluded, subverted and criminalized. It presupposes a number of political spaces and struggles around diverse issues. At a specific historical conjuncture, a particular censure will reflect these struggles, constituting an ideological form in which such conflicts are fought out.

By welding the theoretical developments of Poulantzas in relation to the state, and the concept of hegemony developed by Williams, together with Sumner's notion of censure, it is possible to connect the selectivity of the classification and contested nature of the social censure to the state's attempt to reconstruct its hegemony in the face of deep-rooted political struggle, to provide a comprehensive theoretical basis for understanding the notion of a political crime.

The political trial

If the criminal labelling of political activity is contested, the political trial should be viewed similarly as a site of struggle. The trial becomes a condensation of a point in political struggle in which opposing worldviews are brought sharply into focus both inside and outside the courtroom. If, as we have argued, the state is a material condensation of a relationship of struggle between different classes, and if the nature of social censures can be understood best in terms of the social relationships which generate opposing ideas and interests, the nature and proceedings of a political trial should be viewed in terms of a similar material condensation of struggle in which the fight concerns the nature of the censure of political programmes and political activity. A political trial is always retrospective in some sense, freezing and reflecting past political struggles, and seeking to interpret and reconstruct historical images.

Furthermore, these struggles are materialized in specific and limited forms, mediated and structured by institutional and organizational factors such as the ties between the judiciary and the executive, legal procedure and discourse, the relations between the defendants, the judge and their defence counsel.

The legal form of the trial

Reference has already been made to Kirchheimer's observations that the more apparently neutral the legal procedure adopted by the court, the greater is the chance that the ideological objectives of the state may be fulfilled, and that the accused may successfully urge their own interpretation on judge or jury (Kirchheimer, 1961: 118).

The nature of the legal form employed in a particular trial is thus important. On the basis of our analysis, there is a relationship between political struggle and legal form. In canvassing this issue, Balbus (1973: 100) suggests that 'the immediate pressure to end violence unavoidably dictates the serious abrogations of the principle of formal rationality, and here precisely lies the risk of delegitimation and maximisation of revolutionary potential'. The intensity of political struggles increases the pressure for using extra-legal forms of repression which in turn diminishes the ideological advantage of the political trial for the state.

Habermas provides the basis for a conclusion to the theoretical section of our paper when he writes that 'the technical legal form alone, pure legality, will not be able to guarantee recognition in the long run if the system of authority cannot be legitimized independently of the legal form exercising authority' (Habermas, 1976: 100). The political trial must be seen as part of the general struggle for the legitimization of a political system. This process cannot depend solely upon the perception that fair legal procedures have been adopted, but also on 'generally recognized norms' and interpretations which the censures of political criminalization mould and reinforce. It follows that the legitimating effects of the political trial can only be effective in relation to the degree to which there is consensus as to the norms which support and justify the entire system of authority. Should the censures not be internalized by sufficient members of the dominated classes, 'we can then expect the dominant class agencies of control to destroy . . . or police the institutions of working class culture' (Sumner, 1983: 187).

Implications for South Africa

Our analysis suggests that a political trial can be examined most accurately within the context of the dynamics of the social formation in general and the nature of the political struggle in particular. The rest of this essay employs the theoretical analysis to examine two of the major political trials which have been held in South Africa since 1945, the 1956 treason trial and the 1985 trial of 16 United Democratic Front leaders. Within this context, the criminal justice system can be seen as both a practical and ideological force to construct and restructure the state's hegemony.

South Africa post-1948

It has become accepted wisdom within South African sociology (Wolpe, 1984: 232) that the post-war South African social formation should be periodized into three periods:

1 *1948–60*: A period in which the possibilities for mass mobilization and political action existed, and during which a series of major campaigns and forms of mass protest against state policy were organized.
2 *1961–73*: The terrain of extra-parliamentary, mass-political struggle was abolished, such that the opposition movements were driven into the 'narrow confines of sporadic acts of violence' (Wolpe, 1984: 238).
3 The period from 1973 to the present in which, as a result of a series of large-scale African strikes, the extra-parliamentary political sphere was reconstituted despite the strong tendency towards militarization of an increasingly powerful executive of the state.

This provides a broad context for the comparison of the 1956 and 1985 treason trials.

The 1956 treason trial

The 1950s had witnessed a growing intensity in political opposition to the segregated South African social formation, particularly in the light of attempts by the Nationalist Government to develop and impose its policy of apartheid.[2]

While the organized campaigns of the 1950s were predicated upon non-violence, boycott and non-collaboration, the political struggle increasingly took on a mass character, unlike the formal style of negotiations between the ANC and the government which characterized the 1940s. The campaign of the 1950s focused upon the call for the abolition of a law, or series of laws, by way of passive resistance, boycotts, stay-at-home strikes and non-collaboration, and attempted to politicize the masses and broaden the base of political struggle.[3] The goal of these campaigns was to alter the racial character of the constitution. As Chief Albert Luthuli, President of the ANC said, the purpose of the Defiance Campaign was:

> To arouse sympathy and support amongst whites, and for them to press the government to open equal opportunities to all according to their abilities . . . [we] believe that the spirit of Christian goodness will ultimately come to our rulers. (Luthuli Papers, 1952)

In this statement, Luthuli captured the spirit of many of the ANC political campaigns of the 1950s. As he said on a later occasion, 'we hoped to bring pressure on the majority of the electorate so that they would come to see the justice of our claims' (*Cape Argus*, 29 March 1960).

The belief in campaigning to persuade whites peacefully of the truth of the ANC cause lasted into the early 1960s. A year after the Sharpeville unrest, in April 1961, Nelson Mandela launched a campaign against the Referendum on whether South Africa should become a Republic. He wrote to Sir De Villiers Graaff, the leader of the white opposition to elicit support for a national convention claiming, *inter alia*, that 'a call for a national convention from you could well be the turning point in our country's history' (Karis and Carter, 1977: 635).

During this period, white South Africa was divided on the question of the shape of capitalism. The incorporationist ideology, with its strains of liberalism, and probably best represented by the Fagan Commission of 1948, was still rooted in the consciousness of sections of white South Africa. None the less, by the late 1950s, white parliamentary politics was beginning to operate in a more closely defined framework of consensus. Not only the National Party was concerned to defend white rule. In a revealing speech to Parliament in 1957, Harry Oppenheimer, a leading 'liberal' member of the United Party, said:

> Investors overseas are not lunatics. They know very well that if

discrimination of all sorts were stopped in South Africa, if the running of this country were handed over to races and groups who obviously are not capable of carrying it out, that would be a disastrous thing for South Africa. (House of Assembly Debates, 1957, col. 8817)

As the government began to impose 'apartheid' upon the social formation, it met with increasing resistance from small sections of the white community who aligned themselves with black demands. This is best evidenced by the emergence, in 1953, of the South African Congress of Democrats, to support the black struggle in the extra-parliamentary sphere, and the South African Liberal Party, to pursue change by parliamentary means. In the same year, the South African Communist Party was reconstituted as an 'underground' organization.

The state responded to the struggles and resistance of the late 1940s and early 1950s in an increasingly repressive manner. The Suppression of Communism Act of 1950 was followed in the early 1950s by increased repression and reactionary laws. The 1954 Annual Report of the ANC National Executive commented on the banning of almost all the active workers of the Congress of the People from political activity, the banning of meetings, persons being exiled and deported without trial, the banning of newspapers, intimidation of blacks by armed police, raids and searches of homes and offices. As the struggle intensified, there was talk of banning the ANC. At the Annual Conference of the ANC in 1955, Luthuli warned of the possibility of the ANC being banned as an organization, a view which was shared by a number of delegates at the conference. In the wake of all this, the struggle moved to the courtroom when 156 leaders were charged with treason.

The 1956 trial focused heavily upon the Freedom Charter, the major policy statement of the Congress Alliance. Conceived of initially by Z.K. Matthews in 1953, the Freedom Charter was accepted by the Congress of the People in 1955 as constituting the demands and vision for a future South Africa. It became the ideological banner of the Congress Alliance movement, or, as Matthews wrote, it 'instilled political consciousness into the people and encouraged political activity' (Karis and Carter, 1977: 57). The prosecution attempted to show that the Charter's aims – the abolition of all racial discrimination and the granting of equal rights to all – were unrealizable in South Africa without violence. As State Counsel, Oswald Pirow, told the court:

> They [the ANC] knew that to achieve the demands of the Freedom Charter in their lifetime would necessarily involve the overthrow of the State by violence. . . . The evidence of the Crown's expected witnesses will be that the demands contained in the Charter fit perfectly in the intermediate programme of the Communist Party in a country

described by them as 'colonial' or 'semi-colonial country'. (Treason Trial Record, 1958)

Defence Counsel argued that the Freedom Charter was no more than a blueprint for a bourgeois democracy, a view confirmed earlier by Nelson Mandela writing in 1956:

> Whilst the Charter proclaims democratic changes of a far-reaching nature it is by no means a blueprint for a socialist state – but a programme for the unification of various classes and groupings amongst the people on a democratic basis . . . Its declaration 'The People Shall Govern' visualizes the transfer of power . . . to all the people of this country be they workers, peasants, professional men or petty bourgeoisie. (Karis and Carter, 1977: 247)

In short, the 1956 treason trial was a condensation and reflection of the struggles of the 1950s, and constituted, in material form, one of the state's responses to the demands of the Congress Alliance for changing South African society. During a period of extra-parliamentary struggle protected by law, and within a white community which retained a strong belief in the rule of law, the court was an effective mechanism in which to present the alternative as a simple stark choice for South Africa, namely the policies of the state predicated upon racial discrimination versus the violence which was portrayed as the inevitable consequence of a campaign for the abolition of such discrimination. Treason became a contested censure, targeted against a wide spectrum of political opposition whereby the state sought to portray the adoption of extra-parliamentary means of political opposition as violent and treasonous. By contrast, the defence asserted 'the right of people to express themselves openly in criticism of the government . . .'.

From the commencement of the preparatory examination the political nature of the trial was made clear. Defence Counsel, Vernon Berrange, told the court in his opening statement:

> That this was not an ordinary trial can be gathered from the fact that the accused are in themselves no ordinary persons . . . they constitute a cross-section of the members of our population . . . all of them have one thing in common . . . and that is the belief in the brotherhood of man and a desire to work for his betterment and towards his ultimate freedom. A battle for ideas has indeed been started in our country – a battle in which on one side – the accused will allege – are poised those ideas which seek equal opportunities for, and freedom of thought and expression by, all persons of all races and creeds; and on the other side those who deny to all but a few the riches of life, both material and spiritual, which the accused aver should be common to all. (Sampson, 1958: 19)

By contrast, Oswald Pirow, the leader of the prosecution, described the case as one:

> ... in which the evidence quoted is sufficient to disclose the existence of a dangerous Communist conspiracy aimed at the overthrow of the State and its re-placement by a Communist People's Republic. (*Cape Argus*, 30 January 1958)

Similar sentiments were expressed by Nationalist cabinet ministers. Within two weeks of the arrests of 156 Congress Alliance leaders, Dr Donges, the Minister of the Interior, spoke of a certain association, including the African National Congress, forming a spearhead of the Communist attack of South Africa (*Cape Times*, 19 December 1956). In justifying government policy, the Minister of Native Affairs referred to the treason trial in early 1958 when he told Parliament:

> As far as the Union is concerned, insofar as there are liberalists and Communistic Whites and Indians and Coloured and Natives who co-operate, their efforts are directed just as much against White leadership with discrimination as against Apartheid. Those classes of people – agitators, leftists and people who have been uprooted – who form themselves into a group, view the United Party with as much hostility as they view Apartheid. (House of Assembly Debates, 1958, col. 159)

In an interview in 1959, Oswald Pirow, the chief prosecutor, claimed that the trial was largely responsible for a rapid decline in 'agitation' in December 1956 and a generally quiet period during 1957 and 1958. The trial also bought the government 'valuable time', during which the police could become more efficient in dealing with 'small numbers of agitators' who played upon an 'hysterical native population'. The government now had time to go ahead with plans for separate development that appealed to the natives, '90 per cent of whom were good' (Karis and Carter, 1977: 275).

In the context of the state's attempt to construct a new hegemonic process, that is to select, emphasize and incorporate a new configuration of meanings and values around the concepts of apartheid and racial discrimination, the trial form provided the occasion for attempting to legitimate and authenticate state policy. In this way, the trial constituted a site of struggle over the legitimacy and plausibility of a political censure, the effects of which were important in weakening the particular form of the white incorporationist ideology; delegitimating black aspirations; legitimating more severe state action (past and future); and attempting to undermine the Freedom Charter in the eyes of black liberals and conservatives, who were to form the focal point of the state's policy of class-stratification, developed from the late 1950s in the form of the Bantustan policy.

In reviewing the trial shortly after the accused had been acquitted in 1961, Thomas Karis wrote that:

> Three differing conclusions may be drawn about the trial's political importance, each of which has some validity. The Afrikaner Nationalist sees the trial as necessary. It stigmatizes subversive forces that are undermining racially separate development, the only policy that can prevent the submergence of Whites by Blacks. The liberal or multi-racialist sees the trial as tragic. It excommunicates moderate forces with whom Whites must consult if they are to bring about the conciliation and eventually win the consent that is the only hope for multi-racial peace. The realist or defeatist sees the trial as symptomatic. It epitomizes the conflict of Afrikaner nationalism and African nationalism – or more ominous, White racialism and Black racialism – forces that cannot be separated or reconciled. (Karis, 1960: 227)

On the surface, the trial proved a failure for the state. The inability to frame charges, the ability of the defence team to exploit the legal procedure for the benefit of its clients, the fact that the case continued for almost 5 years, and the eventual acquittal meant that the trial was considered a failure even by the Afrikaans language press. Its failure to legitimate state action either in the eyes of the black or the associated white opposition reflected upon the nature of the social formation and the position of political struggle as outlined above. However, Karis is correct to have viewed the trial as 'excommunicating moderate forces with whom Whites must consult'. The state's presentation of the ANC and its Freedom Charter programme as 'Marxist and revolutionary', reinforced an existing discourse which made difficult any potential cooperation between the white opposition United Party and the Congress Alliance. Indeed, the Nationalists used ANC attempts at cooperation to undermine the United Party's support base; for example, the Prime Minister, Dr Verwoerd, told a National Party election meeting in March 1958:

> . . . a political party could be judged by its friends . . . there was a reason why organisations like the African National Congress . . . and other similar organisations were siding with the United Party. They knew that a United Party government would be weak and that they would be able to apply their stranglehold on the country much easier. (*Cape Times*, 17 March 1958)

Shortly thereafter, Anthony Delius wrote a leader article on this campaign by the National Party entitled 'ANC threat seized by the Nationalists for election purposes' (*Cape Times*, 1 April 1958). Opposition newspapers responded by attempting to distance the ANC from white opposition. The *Cape Times* replied to the Nationalist attack on 23 March 1958 in an editorial:

... the stated aims of the African National Congress to obtain full rights of citizenship and franchise for all is revolutionary whether the National Party or the United Party with its present programme, be in power.

The censures employed during the trial had been directed against specific targets, namely the Congress Alliance and its supporters. The verdict of the treason trial court might have been disappointing for the state, but in bolstering its hegemony over white South Africans it proved successful, in the manner described above.

The 1985 trial

The 1985 treason trial took place within the context of the reconstituted terrain of extra-parliamentary struggle. This terrain was significantly different to that of the 1950s, particularly in the context of widespread worker militancy and trade union activity, and escalating forms of protest and resistance, which increasingly have pervaded all sectors of black South African society. Although a comprehensive examination of these developments, of necessity, falls outside the scope of this essay, it is important to allude to the major changes that have taken place within the South African social formation. Despite the increased militarization of the state during the post-Sharpeville period, the effects of the changing nature of the relations of production and the intensity of the class struggle have created a more deeply fragmented state than at any time since the early 1960s.

The period of the post-Sharpeville boom saw the consolidation of monopoly capitalist relations of production, particularly in manufacturing, the output of which constituted 22 per cent of the GDP by 1977 (Davies *et al.*, 1984: 54). The result of economic growth in the 1960s was a concentration of industry and population in and around the major metropolitan areas. The development of the metropolitan centre and more extensive regional sub-economies, during the 1970s, eroded the premise of the division between white and Bantustan South African upon which the Apartheid policy had been predicated. Within these changing conditions, South Africa experienced worker militancy during the 1970s for the first time since Sharpeville. These developments, combined with the demand for an urbanized workforce more suitable to the needs of the increasingly mechanized manufacturing economy, have resulted in monopoly capitalist forces advocating a strategy of restructuring some of the institutions of Apartheid constructed in the 1960s. This has come to be known as 'Reform' within the South African political discourse.

The pressure for this restructuring has been exerted by both English and Afrikaans capital, Afrikaans capital having loosened its ties with its traditional allies within the Afrikaaner nationalist movement. Concerted pressure by capitalist forces, and the growing intensity of the class struggle, has brought the relaxation of labour controls and the more flexible use of labour, to permit its more productive utilization in capital-intensive forms of production, as well as the abolition of more overt forms of discriminatory control.

The government's major responses included the implementation of labour 'reforms' as recommended by the Wiehahn Commission, the thrust of which was to de-racialize the legislative framework for collective bargaining. Another important element of the reform process concerned the reorganization of local government in the black townships. The 1982 Black Local Authorities Act extended the powers and duties of the Community Councils in an attempt 'to co-opt a wide segment of the African dominated classes' (Hughes and Guest, 1983: 131).

In 1983, a new Constitution Act was passed creating an elaborate tricameral Parliament for Whites, Coloureds and Asians, in which the two latter groups were given a minority share in the running of the legislature and executive. In short, the state strategy of the late 1970s and 1980s has been to seek a way in which the basis for a stable capitalist rule could be reconstructed in such a way as to defuse mass struggles, and incorporate specific strata of the African masses into a new 'historical bloc', albeit within clearly defined limits (Davies *et al.*, 1984: 38).

By early 1985, the hegemony of the Nationalist Government over white South Africa was more secure than it had been in 1956.[4] This unity was exemplified by the speech of Mr Harry Oppenheimer, retired chairman of Anglo-American Ltd, to a London audience of businessmen in which he said:

> Now at long last, President PW Botha is, I believe, making a genuine though slow and cautious effort to reform. For a man of his background this has needed the greatest courage. . . . Now such changes while no doubt inadequate cannot reasonably be dismissed as cosmetic. What is more they will make further changes inevitable. (*The Citizen*, 7 March 1985)

The Association of Chambers of Commerce issued a statement in 1985 in which they claimed that:

> . . . no real progress in stabilising and normalising relations between people within South Africa or between South Africa and other countries can be made unless legal racial discrimination is removed in the political institutions of this country. The future legitimacy of the Republic of South Africa both internally and externally depends on this issue. (Quoted in Cobbett *et al.*, 1985: 13)

Unlike the situation in the 1950s, an incorporationist ideology was not only articulated by a liberal opposition. The ruling class in general perceived that it was essential to find a wider base of support for capitalism among blacks as well as whites. As Legassick (1985: 597) wrote recently, black support for state policy is 'not just a desirable luxury but a vital necessity'.

The state's attempt to incorporate a black bourgeoisie into a 'historical bloc' placed it in direct opposition to the mass movements, such as the ANC and the UDF, which are supported by major sections of black South Africa. In 1984–5, a policy of repression similar to that adopted during the 1950s and 1960s would not succeed in drawing significant black support for the new 'reform' policies. A strategy of delegitimation of mass movements became an important component of the reform programme. This delegitimation was equally important in respect of white South Africa, as the state attempted to consolidate support for its policy of co-option of a black bourgeoisie within strictly defined limits.

During 1984 and 1985, government ministers and state-controlled media had developed the thesis that the ANC and, what the state claims to be its front organization, the UDF are trying 'to render South Africa ungovernable'. As President Botha stated in April 1985, 'the aim of the UDF was not peaceful change but the destruction of our system of government and civilised values' (*Cape Times*, 20 April 1985). In similar fashion, the Minister of Law and Order, Louis le Grange, said during the same Parliamentary session, 'experienced and seasoned advisors were behind the disturbing internal security onslaught which was aimed at creating a revolutionary climate'. He appealed to black people to fight the UDF and other organizations which tried to make the country ungovernable through violent or illegal methods (*Cape Times*, 30 April 1985).

Such statements have not only been issued by government ministers. The leader of the Inkatha movement, Chief Buthelezi, has accused the ANC and the UDF of becoming 'even more suicidal by urging Black Africans to expand their orgy of killing into white suburbs. But Black South Africans do not want to conduct their struggle in this way' (*South African Digest*, 4 October 1985).

The 1985 treason trial became an important reflection of a political and ideological struggle that had grown in intensity since 1973, when worker militancy began to have a profound effect upon the re-establishment of the extra-parliamentary opposition. The state used the occasion to reiterate its language of reform, while trying to discredit and subvert the values and aspirations of the opposition. An attempt was thus made to reinforce the emerging incorporationist strategy, and the ideology of reform, progress, and reasonable, peaceful development, within the context of the new constitutional proposals and increasing political opposition.

The 1985 trial put on trial the values which the ANC has espoused over the past 30 years, particularly as contained in the Freedom Charter. Once more, the courtroom became a site of struggle in which the state sought to portray the UDF demands as irreconcilable with non-violence. The charges brought against the 16 UDF leaders reflected accurately the nature of the discourse referred to above. According to the charge sheet, the state alleged that the 16 individuals had conspired together to assist in the formation of

> ... a revolutionary alliance which aims at overthrowing the government by violence, means which envisage violence, and other unlawful means. It is alleged that the Revolutionary Alliance considers the Freedom Charter as its political programme and policy, and believes that it can only be implemented through a violent revolution. The Alliance also aims at encouraging non-violent forms of political struggle to create a climate favourable to its aims. These non-violent forms of political struggle include
>
> - the popularisation of the Freedom Charter;
> - mass mobilisation and politicisation;
> - calls for the release of political prisoners;
> - calls for the return of exiled leaders;
> - the popularisation of leaders of the Revolutionary Alliance;
> - the popularisation of the Freedom Charter.

The state alleged further that the Revolutionary Alliance used the National Executive Committee of the UDF, and other UDF affiliates, such as the Natal Indian Congress, the Transvaal Indian Congress and the South African Allied Workers Union, to fulfil these aims.

As the charges made clear, the trial purported to portray the oppositional movements as violent and subversive. Given the greater political sophistication of the masses, and the organized and widespread nature of the mass movements in South Africa in the 1980s, the trial was unlikely to succeed in delegitimating the UDF or diminishing black support for the Freedom Charter. The contested nature of the legal categories employed in the charge sheets at the trial was exemplified by a statement issued by the South African Catholic Bishops' Conference shortly after the announcement of the trial:

> Their trial ... is likely to be a protracted one, which means that whether innocent or guilty they are effectively removed from active life and involvement for a lengthy period. Is this a repetition of the tactics of 1956 and 1961 when 156 persons were arraigned for treason and none found guilty? If this turns out to be the case, and there is the strongest expectation that it will, the South African government will have proved itself guilty of using the process of 'justice' to perpetuate injustice. Talk of reform has little meaning when brave men and women are prevented in this way from striving for freedom. The

crime attributed to them become the crime of all who share their hopes and endeavours. (Catholic Institute for International Relations, 1985: 1)

Conclusion

In reviewing two of the major trials of Apartheid's political opponents, it becomes clear that the South African state aimed 'not only at eliminating political adversaries from the political arena . . . but at the creation of a picture of political reality in which the defendant incarnates socially undesirable tendencies' (Kirchheimer, 1969: 410). In both trials, the contested censure reflected the struggle over political ideals and programmes. But the failure of the state to pull the ideological rug from under the extraparliamentary opposition's feet reflected the balance of power; it was unable to re-create reality. In both trials, the censure was overtaken by political events, and remained a mere commentary on an earlier phase of struggle. In 1960, the state of emergency ushered in a phase of greater repression and armed struggle, and the 1985 trial has been superseded by what can be identified as a fourth phase of political struggle – the control of extra-parliamentary organizations by greater repression (successive states of emergency) and by the use of extra-parliamentary forces (vigilantes, Joint Management Committees).

The examination of both the 1956 and 1985 trials reveals that the state's choice of the courtroom reflected both the prevailing relations of production and the political struggles taking place during the periods in question. Within this framework the differences between the two trials can be analysed. In particular, the theory of the political censure developed earlier can assist in explaining the differences in the purpose and effect of the censures employed in the two trials under review.

In 1956, the state was confronted by (1) an extra-parliamentary opposition, which, under the banner of the Freedom Charter, was beginning to campaign with greater ideological coherence for a future South Africa, and (2) a white population which was divided over the set of policies to adopt in order to reproduce white rule. The censure employed in the 1956 trial was thus targeted against a relatively small extra-parliamentary opposition. The trial, and the censures employed therein, attempted to delegitimate all black demands for a share of political power in a unitary state, while simultaneously legitimating the state strategy of consolidating white support for total white control by foreclosing the possibility of multi-racial cooperation between white political parties and the Congress Alliance. That the trial helped consolidate Nationalist hegemony over white South Africans is one matter; that it failed to diffuse black demands was another. But, with the shifts in political forces in 1961 and the subsequent use of direct repression to smash the Congress Alliance and the

Pan-African Congress, the censures of the 1956 trial, located within the struggles of the 1950s, had become historically irrelevant.

The 1985 trial took place in the context of very different relations of production. Unlike the 1950s, a settled and increasingly skilled, urban, black, labour force had become essential to the growth of the South African economy. Upon this new terrain, worker and popular militancy, particularly in the urban areas, had broadened and deepened far beyond the narrow-based Congress Alliance of the 1950s. Within this context, state strategy has been directed at deflecting and diffusing this opposition. For example, Nationalist economic expert, Jan Lombard, recognized explicitly that state attempts to renew and diversify control over the black population would require a new form of state discourse:

> South Africa must 'normalise' the character of its socio-economic regime. . . . If the maintenance of order requires discriminatory provisions in our legal system, these provisions must be defined in terms of other characteristics correlated to the maintenance of order. To declare or imply that racial differences as such are, in themselves, a threat to political order or socio-economic stability is simply no longer accepted. (Lombard, 1978: 19)

In 1985, Nationalist hegemony over white South Africa was more secure, but the growth of extra-parliamentary opposition has severely threatened the state's co-optive strategy, which itself had developed as a response to increasing black political organization during the early 1970s. The battle for legitimacy extended beyond the borders of South Africa. In defending its links with its major trading partners, the South African state has been engaged in a major ideological battle with the ANC which it has tried to present as an anti-democratic, violent, Marxist organization controlled by the South African Communist Party, which, it alleges, 'takes orders' directly from Moscow. By bringing 16 leaders of the UDF to trial, the state claimed that the conduct and programmes of its opponents would be tested in an open and impartial court of law.

The 1985 censure was therefore targeted against opposition forces which were presented not as anti-white, but as anti-democratic and anti-reformist. The 1985 trial took place within a discourse which attempted to divide the black population by rendering legitimate certain demands for political participation, reinterpreting them to fit within the framework of reform, and simultaneously criminalizing all demands which cannot be so interpreted.

Both trials illustrate how the *choice of state strategy* was dependent on the nature of the political struggle; whether in a period when the state was too weak to clash head on with black oppositional forces, or whether in a period when the nature of the social formation necessitated a state policy in which long-term repression, such as that between 1960 and 1973, will not obtain the widespread support of capital operating in different relations of production.

As mentioned above, the state strategy of the 1980s has taken as its starting point the inevitable political incorporation of black South Africans into a single nation-state, with real power remaining in the hands of the existing ruling classes. The fate of the 'reform process' is extremely uncertain at the time of writing. Whether or not this process reshapes the political terrain will depend on struggles within the governing political party, as well as struggles between reformists and their opponents on the right and in the popular movements, all of which will be taking place within increasingly monopolistic relations of production (Cobbett *et al.*, 1985: 21).

The social censure of 'undemocratic, violent, Marxist organizations' should be seen as part of the attempt to establish the centrality of the 'reform' process. The censure also justifies a more repressive and pro-active criminal justice system in the eyes of whites, and possibly certain sections of black South Africa. Our argument is that, notwithstanding massive state repression of the most brutal kind, any attempt to restructure the political terrain takes place within the context of a political struggle in which the state is trying to restructure its hegemony. In the context of the state repression since 1985, this conclusion might appear to be misplaced. However, it is our contention that increased repression alone is unlikely to resolve the crisis, even in the short term.

A comparison between the two states of emergency illustrates this conclusion. After the Sharpeville state of emergency was lifted, the state had already smashed the Congress Alliance. In 1986, the emergency was lifted without any indication of a tangible weakening of popular organizations. Unless the state is to render South Africa into a complete wasteland, repression alone will not solve the present crisis, given the widespread level of political organization in South Africa at present. It is within this context that the political trial of 1985 should be viewed.

However, to be successful, the censure employed at the trial needs to be socialized, and this can only happen when its generalized and authoritative dissemination is unopposed by the ideologies and political organizations of the subordinate classes. In South Africa, this did not occur in 1956, neither has it happened during the 1980s, notwithstanding the most concentrated attempt to co-opt a black bourgeoisie in South African history. In the final analysis, the study of both trials, and the censures employed by the state within them, provides an understanding of the nature of the political struggle during the two periods, the form of strategy adopted by the state in differing political and economic conditions, and the nature of the political struggle waged in the 1950s and 1980s. If as

Cobbett *et al.* (1985: 18) conclude, the state's new initiative is to help the reimposition of law and order, secure a degree of popular quiescence, and regain control of the pace and direction of political developments, the use of the social censure and hence the political trial will remain important elements of state strategy in contemporary South Africa.

Postscript

Charges against 12 of the 16 accused were withdrawn in December 1985, after the state failed to prove the basis of its case, and the four trade unionists were acquitted in mid-1986.

Acknowledgements

Thanks to Stan Cohen, Bob Fine, Harold Wolpe, Raymond Suttner and, in particular, Colin Sumner for valuable comments on earlier drafts. Cathi Albertyn would like to acknowledge the financial support of the Institute for Research Development at the Human Sciences Research Council, in South Africa. Opinions and conclusions expressed in this essay, however, are those of the authors, and are not to be attributed to the IRD or the HSRC.

Notes

1 Poulantzas' work has been criticized severely (see, e.g. Giddens, 1981). Giddens criticizes Poulantzas' concept of the state and suggests that the state is directly:

> enmeshed in the contradictions of capitalism. By undervaluing the power of the working class, functionalist Marxists curiously may lead to overestimate the 'relative autonomy' of the state. . . . The important point is that the state, if it participates in the contradictions of capitalism, is not merely a defender of the status quo. The state can in some part be seen as an emancipating force; neither a class-neutral agency of social reform . . . nor a functional vehicle of the 'needs' of the capitalist mode of production (Giddens, 1981: 219–20).

Ironically, Giddens's prescription for analysing the state is very close to Poulantzas' project (1978), which reveals the extent to which Poulantzas' important work has been ignored by even distinguished commentators.

2 The 1950s saw the enactment of the Group Areas Act (1950) and the subsequent 'removals' under the Act; the Population Registration Act (1950); the Reservation of Separate Amenities Act (1951); various labour acts, including the Black Urban Areas Amendment Act and Black (Abolition of passes and co-ordination of documents) Act in 1952; the Industrial Conciliation Act of 1956; and the Bantu Education Act of 1953.

3 The major campaigns of the 1950s included the Defiance Campaign (1952–3); the Congress of the People and the drawing up of the Freedom Charter (1955); the Women's anti-Pass Campaign (1956); and sporadic anti-pass campaigns,

stay-at-homes and days of protest. Community resistance to removals (Sophiatown) increased as the 1950s progressed. Protests against Bantu education elicited mass support, and several intensive community campaigns were waged against transport costs (Evaton and Alexandra, 1955–7).

4 For example, in the 1983 Referendum, 65.95 per cent of all those who voted, supported the new constitution. In the referendum, 76 per cent of the total white electorate voted (Institute of Race Relations, 1983: 88).

References

Albert Luthuli Papers, University of Cape Town Manuscripts Collection.
Treason Trial Records, Unsorted Files, University of Witwatersrand Manuscripts Collection.

Balbus, I. (1973). *The Dialectics of Legal Repression*. New York: Russell Sage Foundation.
Burowoy, M. (1985). *The Politics of Production*. London: Verso.
Catholic Institute for International Relations (1985). *Treason Against Apartheid*. London: CIIR.
Cobbett, W., Glaser, D., Hindson, D. and Swilling, M. (1985). South Africa's regional political economy: A critical analysis of reform strategy in the 1980s. Unpublished seminar paper. Johannesburg: University of Witwatersrand.
Davies, R.H., O'Meara, D. and Dlamini, S. (1984). *The Struggle for South Africa*. London: Zed.
Giddens, A. (1981). *A Contemporary Critique of Historical Materialism*. London: Macmillan.
Habermas, J. (1976). *Legitimation Crisis*. London: Heinemann.
Hall, S., Critcher, C., Jefferson, T., Clarke, J. and Roberts, B. (1978). *Policing the Crisis*. London: Macmillan.
Hughes, H. and Guest, J. (1983). The local state. *South African Review*, **10**.
Institute of Race Relations (1983). *Survey of Race Relations in South Africa*. Johannesburg: IRR.
Karis, T. (1960). The South African treason trial. *Political Science Quarterly*, **76**, 217–39.
Karis, T. and Carter, G. (1977). *From Protest to Challenge*. California: Hoover Institution Press.
Kirchheimer, O. (1961). *Political Justice*. Princeton, N.J.: Princeton University Press.
Kirchheimer, O. (1969). Politics and justice. In *Politics and Social Change* (F.S. Burin and K.L. Schell, eds). New York: Columbia University Press.
Laclau, E. and Mouffe, C. (1981). Socialist strategy. *Marxism Today*, **25**, 17–23.
Laclau, E. and Mouffe, C. (1985). *Hegemony and Socialist Strategy*. London: Verso.
Legassick, M. (1985). South Africa in crisis: What route to democracy? *African Affairs*, **83**, 87–603.
Lombard, J. (1978). The economic aspects of security. In *National Security: A Modern Approach* (M.H. Louw, ed.). Pretoria: Institute of Strategic Studies.
Mathiesen, T. (1980) *Law, Society and Political Action*. London: Academic Press.
Poulantzas, N. (1978). *State, Power, Socialism*. London: Verso.

Sampson, A. (1958). *The Treason Cage*. London: Heinemann.
Sumner, C. (1983). Rethinking deviance: Towards a sociology of censures. In *Research in Law, Deviance and Social Control*, Vol. 5 (S. Spitzer, ed.). Greenwich, Conn.: JAI.
Suttner, R. (1984). Political trials and the legal process. *South African Review*, **11**, 63–75.
Williams, R. (1980). *Problems in Materialism and Culture*. London: Verso.
Wolpe, H. (1984). Strategic issues in the struggle for national liberation in South Africa. *Review*, **8**, 232–46.
Wolpe, H. (1985). Class concepts, class struggle and racism. Unpublished paper.

Media, censure
and politics

6 Dramatic power: television, images of crime and law enforcement

Richard Sparks

Crime drama and soap opera are the dominant generic categories of fictional television series in the UK and USA and, consequently, through the mechanism of syndication, in much of the rest of the world as well. In this essay, I suggest some ways in which this fact may bear upon certain key themes in criminological theory: the ideological constitution of criminal justice; the political correlates of the fear of crime; and the continuing vitality of the will to punish.

It is, of course, quite unnecessary and inappropriate to argue that the crime drama is uniquely responsible for these dynamics. Indeed, I want to argue that one problem of much existing research in this area is that, in overstating its case about the calculable 'effects' of television, it has obscured and neglected more fruitful lines of enquiry. Instead, I want to suggest, albeit in only programmatic form,[1] that the crime drama has achieved its prevalence and popularity by offering a set of stories which address certain social anxieties in its audience. The narrative is able to render the messy and troubling complexities of law enforcement pleasurable by assigning them to the ancient simplicities of crime and punishment. The story offers punishment as a kind of consolation in the face of a world which, it also asserts, is violent, dangerous and difficult to comprehend. In a sense, therefore, even the 'happy ending' of these moral tales is pessimistic and conservative: it results from the saving act of an heroic individual in the face of intractable wickedness. Within this logic, civilization cannot develop, it can only ever be provisionally rescued until next week at the same time.

The politically interesting question is whether we, as audience, must share these presumptions in order to participate in the story. To what extent does their orderly and predictable repetition limit our horizons, preparing us for punishment and discouraging us from innovation?

Clearly, the very prevalence of the crime drama has strongly influenced the ways in which television has been thought of and studied, both within the academy and elsewhere.[2] The effects tradition of research, which has sought to describe and quantify the consequences of exposure to television on subsequent conduct and on specific items of belief or attitude, in a sense responds very directly to this ubiquity. Its arguments and concerns have tended to revolve around the question of quantities – in terms of excessive numbers of violent incidents viewed (Belson, 1978; Eysenck and Nias, 1978), or of the deleterious consequences, for civility, articulacy and other aspects of personal conduct, of excessive hours spent in front of the television screen (Winn, 1977; Sohn, 1976).

In another sense, however, this very prevalence, and its sequels in terms of received opinions and customary reactions, can be the source of a blindness, of an 'invisibility' (Bigsby, 1976) of popular culture, which is, paradoxically, the very criterion of the extent of its insinuation into our everyday lives. We inhabit what Gerbner (1970) calls the 'mass-produced symbolic environment'. The apparatuses of mass communication punctuate (or at least form the background to) the daily rhythms of the lives of many millions of people both in public spaces and in the most intimate domestic settings. Their products are no longer discrete 'bits' of information which enter our lives only periodically, like horsemen returning with news of some ancient battle, or beacons on hilltops; rather, they focus and organize routine uses of time and money (Kellner, 1981) and alter patterns of interaction within the home (Csikszentmihalyi and Kubey, 1981).[3]

Television sharply attenuates the inherited distinction between public and private spheres of life. Television sets are for the most part, in the UK and USA at least, privately owned or rented and watched either alone, in the family home or among friends and peers. And yet this most private activity simultaneously constitutes the viewer as a member of a public (in some versions as a part of the 'mass') in that he or she is one among an indefinitely large number of subjects, indiscriminately addressed from a single source. Is it then the case that the perspectives on the world which the institutions of mass communication advance, whether authoritatively factual in the form of reportage or trivially fictional in the form of popular narratives of family conflict or of heroism, permeate our lives so regularly and so intimately that the institutional and ideological particularities of their sites of production are lost or forgotten? If so, how does this bear upon our experience of watching television and, in turn, on other aspects of our ways of being in the world?

In the case of television crime fiction, to pose the question of 'forgetting' in this way is to suggest that the narratives to which we are exposed contain propositions about the nature of society and about human conduct which operate 'behind our backs' without reaching the level of articulate opinion.

Much has been written on the homogenizing or 'mainstreaming' influences of the mass media (Gerbner *et al.*, 1980, 1984) and on alleged tendencies to obliterate minority opinion and to inhibit critical reflection on public concerns (Marcuse, 1964). Naturally, attempts to demonstrate that this is so, and materially important, in the public sphere are fiercely contested (Altheide, 1984; Anderson and Sharrock, 1979). The critical theory of television fiction, however, does not begin and end with those things which the indices typically deployed by social psychologists can quantify and enumerate. Rather, it is bound to broach the questions of form and meaning, and of why certain generic categories of programming, specifically crime drama, achieve the dominance which they enjoy.

As Raymond Williams (1974b: 35) has observed, 'Questions about forms in communications are also questions about institutions and the organization of social relationships.' For broadcasting institutions, programmes produced and marketed within accessible rubrics reliably provide large audiences and make for orderly administration. What tends to follow is a considerable degree of regularity in the 'flow' of television (Williams, 1974a); at the levels both of a certain consistency of contents and forms within 'kinds' of programming and of what sets of programmes are substitutable for one another at a given time of day. Broadcasting is carried on by companies which 'as open systems, must adapt to their environment or die' (Garnham, 1973: 10). The 'external environments' in which they exist are the world of explicit political discourse and legislative prescription of the state and the public sphere on the one hand, and the audience on the other. Their relation to the latter has, Garnham goes on to argue, been less publicly directed, leaving freedom to the institution to adapt according to its own requirements. The outcome of this has been an increasingly rigid structure of programming.

The same 'typification' of a public idiom which Hall and his colleagues (1978: 61) identify in newspaper coverage of law and order questions obtains in television fiction with similar insistence. If as Conrad (1982: 9) comments, television 'mimes our passage through the day', it does so by addressing its audience as members of a public and, thereby, as beings in community both with the television message and one another. This is what Hirsch (1976) has called a 'network effect' (cf. Williams', 1974a, notion of 'majority television'). The provision of a 'centrally produced, standardised and homogeneous common culture' is not a simple outcome of the medium's technological capacities. It is contingent upon its present organizational form. It is in the nature of the 'network effect' to 'present to diverse groups a set of common symbols, vocabularies and shared experiences' (Hirsch, 1976: 291).

Clearly, these perspectives on the economic and organizational imperatives of television production are of interest primarily for what they suggest about the position of the medium in domestic life and for the constraints which they impose on television content. It is the television text which represents the point of contact between the 'life-world' of the viewer and the 'surrounding environments' of the economic and political spheres (Giddens, 1987: ch. 8).

If, as Counihan (1975: 31) suggests, the analysis of television content seems 'at best, a rather dubious enterprise', by reason of its association with obsolete models of effect and viewing, work which has ignored or denied the necessity of the interpretation of content can only be yet more suspect.[4] Counihan shows that recent research, which has tended to argue against content studies, always implicitly falls back on some notion of content. In Counihan's view, approaches which stress either audience behaviour or production processes without some accountable attention to the meanings of the text 'elide' the necessity of thinking through the complexities of the relations between texts, institutions and audiences. The dangers of attempting to reduce any one of the moments in the processes of mass communication to the categories of the others are clear. On the one hand, one falls into 'an inept and reductive sociologism'; on the other, lies a 'closed formalism . . . equally one-sided' (1975: 35). He concludes that:

> A theory of content as discourses and texts is a partial but necessary precondition for an analysis of how dominant political and aesthetic ideologies are at work within the texts, dictating their silences as well as their statements. (Counihan, 1975: 36)

This, however, does not justify treating the television idiom in terms of an objectivist theory of codes, which are in turn enactments of some unitary or systemic 'dominant ideology' (cf. Corner, 1980: 75). Rather, we are concerned with the rhetorical means whereby the text works towards the assent of its audience, preferring certain responses over others, whether or not such cooperation is forthcoming (Eco, 1979).

Hence, rather than invoking a static notion of hegemony as what Gitlin (1979: 252) calls the 'magical explanation of last resort', we should consider some more modest, but more concrete, processes and reactions which the existing structures of television prescribe for us. Our interest is in what Gitlin (1979: 253) calls 'the hold and the limits of cultural products' and the senses in which people 'permit their life-worlds to be demarcated by them'.

We do not inhabit a culture which simply has television grafted on to it; rather it prescribes a set of central cultural practices, which variously foster, corroborate, coexist with and displace other practices. It does so, moreover, in its own (which increasingly become our own) accustomed and expedient ways. Lévi-Strauss, in *The Raw and the Cooked* (1970), makes the point, further elaborated upon by Kress (1976: 104), that while in the arena of myth each individual realization of the abstract form of the myth differs with the innovative act of telling, the very obviousness of the self-presentation of popular culture (especially the visual media) is disabling, cutting us off from this creativity, locating us as consumers rather than as participants. We are confronted by objects which are extremely familiar to us and in some ways gratifying to us, but in whose creation we have played no part (cf. Debord, 1983). We have already argued that relatively rigid structures of programming tend to become established. Such structures tend to impose characteristic patterns on fictions in terms of length, content and expectation. We can interrogate these texts and their patterns. I want to ask whether, in the case of crime drama, the simplification of the dramatic world projected in television fiction may be consequential for the simplification and dramatization of other political discourses on crime and law enforcement; in proposing an imagery of social order, of the sources of social threat and of appropriate response. To do this we must at some point deal with the texts themselves. This involves an act of interpretation, of criticism in a strict sense, not merely of 'decoding'.

Stephen Knight (1980: 4) argues that crime fiction ritually provides consolation to an anxious audience, implicitly demonstrating that their anxieties are resolvable within the terms of the 'ideology of the culture group dominant in the society'. The form of the fiction is of direct concern here: 'Plot itself is a way of ordering events; its outcome distributes triumph and defeat, praise and blame, to the characters in a way that accords with the audience's belief in dominant cultural values' (ibid.). Therefore, Knight concludes, it is possible to discuss 'how our anxieties are realised, but how ultimate realities are obscured by our crime fiction' (1980: 6).

The modern police story, Knight contends, using the example of the novels of Ed McBain, is about security and the community. At its centre is the image of the city as a special site of danger. The city is like a huge organism, none of whose members can see or comprehend it as a whole. The appropriate response to misfortune and victimization is a resigned pity rather than a cause-finding critique. In a world in which the individual is the inert plaything of a variety of hostile forces, murder results from rifts in private relationships. It is contained within the sphere of personal conduct, which is not seen as socially constituted. The expression of anxiety through the emblematic objects of a kind of fictionalized urban geography constitutes, in Knight's view, a 'disavowal of knowledge of human causes' (1980: 179). This fragmentation can only be ideologically rescued by 'magically' replacing the hero at the hub of the fictional world.

The distribution of triumph and defeat to which Knight refers is organized, as a consequence of the institutional structures and characteristic manner of address of the medium, within far more rigid narrative strategies in television fiction than in the crime novel, although many of its fundamental concerns are similar.

Crime drama on British television in 1983

What follows here is my interpretation of a number of crime drama programmes, all of which were broadcast on British television during one calendar month (September 1983). I assume that television drama employs (and anticipates that its audience takes part in) certain conventions and presuppositions. This means that the variety of stories, characters and moralities in television crime drama tend to make use of a rather limited number of underlying axioms or propositions. My aim will be to show how far the conventions and regularities of narrative structure and role relationship circumscribe the ways in which the conduct of policemen, detectives and criminals can be made to make sense.

My criteria for inclusion in the sample were simply that the programmes should be broadcast as part of a series, that they should take the activities of criminals and law enforcers as a predominant focus, and that they should take place in contemporary urban European or American settings. This therefore ruled out a number of adventure stories on broadly related themes but which were marginal in terms of their historical and geographical references.

It should be borne in mind that this is 'prime-time' television: it takes place in the early evening, which is the period when viewing is heaviest. The argument advanced by Murdock and Golding (1977) which links the social relations of television to programming priorities thus applies here with some force. There is a particular pressure (especially on the commercial stations given their dependence on advertising revenue) to produce reliably popular programmes at this time of day. Significantly, then, crime drama programmes are concentrated on the two 'majority' channels (i.e. BBC 1 and ITV) in the early evening. BBC 2 showed no such programmes during the study period and Channel 4 broadcast only *Out*, easily the most 'serious' of the programmes I watched. Later evenings, when audiences decline, contain a substantially larger number of repeats of programmes of proven popularity (like *Minder* and *Hawaii Five-O*). This represents a comparatively cheap way of slowing the drift of the audience off to bed.

If these are some of the commercial imperatives which give rise to the relatively predictable nature of television crime fiction, it remains to explore the implications of this for the genre by means of a set of readings of the programmes in question.

I argue that it is fruitful to examine television crime fictions in terms of certain organizing dimensions, in particular narrative structure and role relationships, in so far as these create the framework in which the actions and characteristics of criminals and law enforcers are established. This does not amount to claiming that all crime drama programmes are in some sense the same, although it does tend to direct attention towards similarities and patterns rather than differences. The argument then is that for the purposes of analysis, the range and diversity of a sample of such programmes may be simplified by looking at them in terms of certain partial but important organizing concepts.

Narrative structure

A one-hour crime drama programme typically consists of about 40 distinct scenes taking in a number of different characters and locations. Scenes decrease in length as the story progresses. For example, in *The Streets of San Francisco* and *Hawaii Five-O*, early scenes may be up to 3 or 4 minutes long and are often made up predominantly of dialogue. This serves to introduce the characters (in particular, where they are familiar, the opportunity is presented for them to reiterate their distinguishing features and relationships, often in a bantering way), and to set the scene for the subsequent movement of the plot (by giving information or speculating on possible criminal motivations). Scenes then decrease in length as the story progresses towards climax (to as little as 15–20 seconds). The moments leading up to the resolution of the plot, which is normally the capture, shooting or self-destruction of the criminal, are often characterized by ever more rapid cross-cutting, demanding more and more rapt attention from the viewer in order to follow the story. Music, running and shooting conventionally express an approaching moment of crisis; they act as indices of excitement.

Interestingly, actual contact or physical violence between antagonists tends to be suggested rather than demonstrated. Thus the policeman/ private eye often does not appear in the same shot as the criminal until the very moment of resolution. The chase or conflict is implied by rapid cross-cutting between distinct sequences of men running, cars skidding, etc. Gerbner is thus correct, I would suggest, to point out the relatively impersonal nature of violence within the conventions of the 'cop show' form. He is, however, mistaken in suggesting that the principal consequence of this is that the difference between the police/good guys and the criminals is thus reducible to one of efficiency, with success as equivalent to vindication. The relationship between success and moral worth, which I would identify, is rather more complex than this. The efficient use of violence is indeed a corollary of moral justification, but in a reciprocal sense: the efficient (necessary, provoked, judicious, altruistic) use of force is both constitutive of and consequent upon moral justification, so that the two stand for each other. In this sense, Williams (1974a) seems to me to be acute in arguing that crime drama programmes neither approve nor condemn violence as such (they are up to a point 'neutral' about it), but that only 'socially ratified violence' is presented as being justified and that this ratification is in part provided by the internal conventions of the narratives themselves as well as the ways they systematically deploy assumptions and references about the outside world.

The schematic nature of the narrative structure is thus unavoidably important. The story must fit into a particular slot in the evening's schedules, which is determined by considerations external to the programme itself. In the case of American productions, as well as those produced by British commercial television, this means in the first place that the story must be divisible according to the requirements of commercial breaks. This rigid programming structure constrains the narrative within a predictable set of movements or phases. In particular, the requirement is imposed that each episode (with the partial exception of some British series of a more ambitious dramatic intention like *Out* and *Killer*) form a unitary whole. Often the only characters to recur from week to week are the hero and a limited group of supporting players, colleagues, friends and family. This is especially the case where the eponymous hero is the sole focus of the series (viz. *Shannon* or *Bergerac*). The criminal's incursion into the hero's world is relatively peripheral. Thus in the case of *Shannon*, each episode is prefaced by what Fiske and Hartley (1978) call the 'ritual condensation' of a montage sequence. We see Shannon playing basketball, Shannon running, Shannon making an arrest, Shannon with his young son, Shannon shopping. Shannon is thus the only developed character. He is also represented as belonging to a certain social milieu and having definite affiliations and responsibilities. The consequences of this are noteworthy.

First, actions have no awkward consequences. Once captured or killed the criminal may not be referred to again, except for the purpose of tying up loose ends. There is rarely any suggestion of a grieving widow, mortgage payments, funeral expenses, etc.

Secondly, events are thus also radically decontextualized with regard to causes and motives. It is sufficient that the motive be plausible or explanatory for the purposes of the plot, which means that such accounts move within a narrowly specified conventional range. The principal qualification to this is where the other recurrent thread of the series (apart from the hero) is a particular urban environment: the streets of San Francisco, the melting pot of Hawaii, or the menace of Shannon's Chicago. This is reminiscent of a crude ecological sociology, with its vision of the polyglot city as a jungle peopled by exotic but threatening creatures.

The explanation of criminal action in television crime drama is thus no explanation at all but rather a plot function. Within this framework, the criminal seems generally to be represented as one of three things:

1. He may be wicked and clever, i.e. a professional crook motivated by greed and lacking principles or finer feelings (cf. *CHIPS*, *Out*, *Remington Steele*).
2. He may be compulsive, which may also be a form of wickedness and generally refers to sexual deviations. Of the programmes I studied, three concerned sexual psychopaths (*Shannon*, *Hawaii Five-O*, *Killer*), one an inadequate paedophile (*Juliet Bravo*) and one a wife driven to extremity by an unfaithful husband (*Streets of San Francisco*). A further mystery (a *Bergerac* episode) was caused by the unexplained death of an elderly homosexual who, as it turns out, died of a heart attack brought on by over-indulgence.
3. He may be mistaken, misguided or deluded. In this category, I include one ethically compromised policeman (*Out*) and one example of political insurgency (*Simon and Simon*). This is especially interesting since it concerns a survivalist-cum-mercenary band, i.e. a group which in other fictional contexts could be heroic. This, however, only applies on foreign territory (cf. *The Wild Geese*).

For all their range in terms of lightness or heaviness, fantasy or veracity, crime drama programmes seem to me to exhibit certain characteristic features at the level of narrative structure. An image of relative normality, of routine (often established within the policeman's office or home) or familiarity, is presented. This is then disturbed by the commission of a crime. The crime is thus not exactly arbitrary (as the hero of *Hawaii Five-O*, Steve McGarrett comments, 'even a psycho needs a motive'), but is generally a violent, unexpected and frequently rather random intrusion, which upsets the implied equilibrium. The crime thus poses a problem and the hero's task is its solution. This applies even where the hero is himself to some degree outside the law (e.g. *Out*), or socially marginal (e.g. *Minder*), in so far as his function for the plot resembles that of the policeman. The hero, then, is fundamentally a problem-solver, an agent of retribution or instrument of vengeance, who serves to bring about a return to the former state of things.

The resolution of the plot generally occurs with between 5 and 7 minutes of programme time left to run. We then meet the heroes again in more relaxed mood, e.g. bantering with friends or colleagues (c.f. *CHIPS*, *Minder*, *Shannon*). Normality thus frames the criminal event on either side. The criminal himself is generally absent by the time we arrive at the coda, put out of sight and mind – either by death or the machinery of justice. The story is thus predominantly about the hero, as problem-solver, as himself a repository of significances and in his relation to his supporting cast of allies who are often endearingly eccentric and generally ethnically diverse. For instance, in *CHIPS* the movement of the story is interspersed with a light-hearted sub-plot about the search for a skunk which has crept into the police garage. Meanwhile, both *Remington Steele* and *Minder* depend heavily on a comic dimension to the relationship between two central characters for their appeal and for a recurrent thread from week to week.

We have moved some distance, then, from an analysis which sees violence as the predominant or unique focus of investigation. It seems to me particularly apposite to view crime drama as representing, in Ricoeur's terms, the projection of a world, a world with its own variants on what is taken to be a societal moral order and one whose essential features remain unchanged from week to week, riding out the vicissitudes of the violent episodes which monotonously punctuate its comparative calm.

Role relationships

The hero is generally represented as being in one of three kinds of position in relation to other characters, each of which offers the opportunity of showing different positively sanctioned qualities.

1 He may be one of a male pair (as in *CHIPS, Streets of San Francisco, Simon and Simon, Killer, Minder*). In this case, the stress tends to fall on the pair's mutual loyalty, on the unity of complementary opposites (even where there is personal antagonism), and provides the opportunity for comic banter and horseplay. What is at stake is the pair's joint affirmation of a shared value system; an affirmation which is strengthened rather than compromised by differences of age, temperament, class or ethnic, origin. Thus, in *Simon and Simon,* the big boyish brother and the smooth, 'intellectual' brother are inseparable – each having qualities which save the day in different situations and which make up for the other's lacunae. Likewise, in *The Streets of San Francisco*, the differences between the elder partner Mike (slightly dowdy and awkward, highly experienced and intuitive, a lover of baseball, a man of practical intelligence) and his younger colleague Steve (smart, sexy, college educated, a reader of book reviews who also runs quickly and shoots straight) is played out within the context of their mutual admiration and affection. Meanwhile, in *CHIPS*, the blue eyed w.a.s.p. and the Chicano are united in a non-antagonistic relationship of trust and cooperation by their involvement in the fight against crime, but also by the more important dimensions on which they resemble one another (their youth, their masculinity). As Fiske and Hartley (1978) suggest in relation to *Starsky and Hutch*, the implied mutuality of differences can be taken as implying an inclusiveness in the wider culture. Potential

sources of dissonance are introduced but overcome and, in so far as it utilizes disparate talents, the resulting whole is fairer and more efficient.

2 He may be a leader or superior officer. This is the case in *Hawaii Five-O* and *Juliet Bravo*, and in a sense in *Out*. Here the constellation of relationships set up by the drama centres around the leader's efficiency, decisiveness and competence, and the loyalty and willingness to serve in a shared enterprise of his subordinates. So, in *Hawaii Five-O*, McGarrett is surrounded by a team of detectives who rush hither and thither at his behest, rarely acting on their own initiative. They provide him with a mass of anecdotal and forensic evidence which can be marshalled to produce the solution to the mystery ultimately only by McGarrett's intuitions. When one of his subordinates suggests they may be dealing with a 'psycho', McGarrett nods grimly and replies 'I feel the rumblings'. He is of course correct, and the malefactor is duly intercepted as a result of Steve's rumblings and flashes of inspiration. Meanwhile, in *Juliet Bravo*, inspector Kate Longton, labouring under the disadvantage of being a woman, succeeds in gaining the loyalty and cooperation of a recalcitrant group of subordinate males by virtue of her shrewdness, integrity and dedication. In both these instances, episodes revolve around direct challenges to the leader's personal authority by criminals who see themselves as having a score to settle. Thus, the young sexual murderer of *Hawaii Five-O* is motivated by a desire to outwit the famous Steve McGarrett, while in *Juliet Bravo* Kate is faced with being taken hostage by a man whom she once arrested. In each case the resolution of the plot is effected by the restoration of the central character's authority after the death or apprehension of the adversary.

3 He may be a loner, somewhat at odds with authority and perhaps himself socially eccentric (as is the case in *Shannon* and *Bergerac*). What is most strongly at stake in these cases is the self-reliance, integrity and determination of the hero, as against the malevolence of his criminal counterpart, and the bureaucratic inefficiency of the parent organization. Superior officers tend to be obstructive and hidebound by rules, and the central figure may have to disobey orders, work out of hours and use unconventional means to make his arrest. The hero is clearly marked out as different from his colleagues. Thus Bergerac is a reformed alcoholic, while Shannon is a widower and single parent. Their relations with the public are individualized, even idiosyncratic, so that their crime-fighting activities carry a distinct personal and moral emphasis, rather than being a simple question of doing a job or fulfilling a professional obligation.

The criminal, on the other hand, figures predominantly in two ways. First, he is, as I have suggested, a plot-mover – he poses the problem but the story is the hero's story as problem-solver. Secondly, he represents a metaphorical parallel or antipode to the hero within a set of narrative and moral conventions and structures according to whose internal logics the criminal/villain represents disruption and the hero/detective the restoration of the moral universe.

One might therefore contend that, at a thematic level, the relationship of the hero to the villain, and their different positions within a given social milieu, express their respective relations to authority and order (and only secondarily or incidentally to the law). It is the exploration of this kind of issue which places the nexus of relationships proposed within television crime drama in an important position in mass entertainment. Relationships, which according to other criteria (some might say 'in reality') are importantly about status and authority as vested by membership of a special body with particular political and constitutional constraints and obligations, are, via the central focus on the hero, personalized and individualized to a point where the politics and morality of the enforcement of the law are conflated with the personal moral qualities of the hero. The hero ceases to be the agent of law enforcement, and becomes its personification.

Where the offence is the province of the policeman as leader of a body of men, it represents a challenge to the rightful exercise of authority, an authority which is then ratified and restored by the successful capture or killing of the malefactor. Where the policeman is presented as a rugged individualist, he tends to become one party to a personal vendetta, in which the affront given by the criminal becomes an increasingly personal one as he establishes contact with victims or is himself threatened or victimized. Thus, in the case of *Shannon*, the conflict between Jack Shannon and the villain, an ingenious sexual psychopath, centres around their treatment of the same woman, the actress Pam, whom Shannon protects and the other menaces. Shannon and Pam are attracted to one another but argue. He criticizes her for flirting, and maintains a certain aloof and reproving distance, until she succeeds in convincing him of her sincerity. The killer, on the other hand, poses as a policeman, is flattering to the point of sycophancy, asks Pam for dates, and all the time is just waiting for an opportunity to pounce. The constant contrast is between the incorruptibility of the one and the scheming wickedness of the other – the device is thus not unlike the good/bad twinning metaphor which occurs in fairy stories, in which the 'seeming fair' is counterposed to a genuine heroic goodness which is revealed only later. It is a simple and powerful moral motif, but one which, for present purposes, at the same time subordinates Shannon's role *qua* policeman to his symbolic status in the drama – his moral justification and his personal qualities are one and the same thing.

In summary, the organizing principles of narrative structure and role relationships are partial analytic constructs, but do reveal important features of the real processes of representation at work in television crime fiction. Such an initial task of interpretation is an essential prerequisite to the proper understanding of what the 'effects' of television might comprise. Television (crime) fiction deals with issues of crime and law enforcement in a way which is relatively internally consistent. We may not 'believe' in it, but few of us have much first-hand experience outside it; nor can we state with any great confidence that our expectations of 'real' crime are in no sense framed by our vicarious and fictitious experiences of it in the mass media.

Within the context of television crime fiction, policing appears to be justified in terms of linkages between its effectiveness and identification with the personal characteristics of the hero, rather than in terms of elaborated ideas of justice, due process or law. Indeed, law is secondary (if not irrelevant) when there is a presumption of absolute confidence in the probity and competence of the hero as rugged individualist. Good policing is creative, interventionist, individual and, if necessary, violent.

The imagery of social order

W.H. Auden (1948) saw the detective story as a substitute for religious patterns of certainty. The subsequent inflections which television has lent to the accustomed flow of transgression and retribution in crime fiction have served to bolster the certainty which they offer, both in terms of the categories of virtue and malignity which they ratify and underwrite and the regularity and frequency of their occurrence.

The objection that these fictions are trivial matters says effectively nothing except that, as a matter of habit and compliance, we commonly watch within the frames of reference laid down for us by broadcasting institutions. Indeed, this very triviality is central to our present concerns, in that it is the outcome of a particular mode of production and presentation. For, as Bourdieu (1980) comments, part of what constitutes forms of public representation as 'political' is exactly this 'denial of the social' in the sphere of entertainment, and which provides for the invisibility of what stands directly before us.

Bourdieu holds that the dominion of 'symbolic power' is most complete where it is least recognized, and therefore admits of fewest challenges; that is, when it takes place within the field of 'doxa' as opposed to orthodoxy or heterodoxy. Doxa comprises an 'underlying complicity' which forms the 'unthought element common to all individual thought' within a cultural field (Bourdieu, 1971: 183). This doxic level of practice is most characteristic of simple and traditional societies whose operative principles, Bourdieu argues, are the 'gentle exploitation' of custom, kinship and courtesy. In advanced societies, where competition and conflict manifestly exist, the doxic is brought into crisis by competing discourses, whether orthodox or heterodox, majority or minority.

Orthodoxies, of which I take television to be predominantly a vehicle, always aim, Bourdieu holds, at 'restoring the primal state of innocence of doxa' (1977: 169), thereby magically reversing the crisis of the differentiation of society. Within this context, the industrial production of conventional narratives operates in confirmation of existing frames of reference, serving to delimit the universe of discourse, creating and maintaining shared sensibilities (cf. Chaney, 1977: 447). The aim of popular television fiction is effortless comprehensibility, transparency. Eco (1972) is thus correct to argue that, while understandings may not match between producers and audiences, the sender of mass communications must take for granted a range of assumptions and expectations in its audience which, in turn, may serve in some degree to promote exactly that commonality which it assumes. The obviousness – the redundancy – which the television message achieves must be construed as an ideological, and not just a technical matter.

The plurality which is intrinsic to communicative action is, therefore, reduced to a minimum in television fiction – excised in pursuit of an ideal of transparency. It is therefore inescapable, *pace* both the technicist theory of discourses and the pedestrian, actuarial procedures of content analysis, that we should broach the question of quality and of the relative merits of different kinds of portrayal.

In the case of television crime fiction, what is at stake is that its simplification of the dramatic world of crime and law enforcement is the operation by which dominant perspectives are relayed and reaffirmed; together with the extent of the mutual corroboration between these fictions, other media projections of crime, the city, heroism and villainy and existing political stances on crime and policing. We are concerned with mapping the contours of the cultural field in which fictional representations of crime and law enforcement currently exist, and the ways in which the force of their rhetorics is enacted on a ground which has *already* been prepared to receive them.

It seems to me then that there are three good reasons why students of criminal justice in its relation to politics should take an interest in television crime fiction:

1 Television crime fiction represents a massive potential source of falsehood about crime and law enforcement. It vastly overplays the prevalence and frequency of the use of violence on the parts of both criminals and law enforcers. Furthermore, it grossly exaggerates the ability of the police or the detective, properly equipped and deployed, to deal summarily with offenders. The criminal rarely gets away – the internal logic of the narrative requires that he be killed or captured and that, where

captured, guilt is already established. There is thus no need for the bothersome prevarication of a trial. Moreover, the nature and motivations of offenders (and their offences) is rigidly fixed. What arises from all this is a constant interplay between the cultivation of fear and the offering of reassurance. In the world of crime fiction, most crime is violence, but so also is most good policing. The unlucky citizen may be at risk from the inexplicable acts of violent men, but a more benign violence may be marshalled to his aid; a particular version of dangerousness and criminality invokes as appropriate an equal and opposite reaction.

2 It entails a certain image of authority. Most crime drama guarantees the restoration of the moral universe, but only after the personal and creative intervention of the hero. On the one hand, there is an impatience with bureaucratic structures and the tedium of procedure, but, on the other, no critique can be sustained because the hero intervenes to restore a precarious equilibrium.

3 Objections on the grounds of triviality are a distraction. What is interesting is how much violence we are able to tolerate because of the fact that most of our experience of crime and law enforcement is, precisely, trivial and vicarious. The simplicity of the moral economy of the crime drama entails both a stereotyping of the activities of criminals and law enforcers and a consequent justification of what might otherwise be taken to be themselves immoral, unethical or repressive acts.

There is, then, a preoccupation with authority, with violence, and with the necessity of the restoration of order. The relative secondariness of law to probity and strength as a source of justification, and the partial isolation of the hero from a power structure as one who, as Gitlin (1982) argues, may share the police's goals but disdains the standard rules, pinpoints what Graham Murdock (1982) calls the dilemma which liberal democracies face in 'balancing law *against* order'. Murdock argues that the stress placed by television, as a medium, on contemporaneity means that the visual iconography of television crime fiction must be seen as locking into 'current debates about the future of policing', which are likely to be interpreted in terms of key concepts which are presently salient for the viewer – principally the range of political ideas and incitements surrounding the talismanic words 'law and order'. Murdock is correct to remind us that a huge and complex investigation of audience reactions remains to be done before we are able to talk with confidence about the links between television presentations and popular conceptions. However, in terms of the preliminary task of mapping the range and inferential structure of television outputs, I believe that an argument can be advanced which suggests that the internal logic of television crime fiction presents law enforcement as pre-eminently a form of poetic justice in which order and retribution take priority over law.

Finally, and most generally, this raises questions about how we may participate in the processes by which our consciousness of ourselves, and our relations to the powers which govern our lives is constructed; a participation which the present structure of television inhibits. It is wise to observe caution before asserting any effect of television on popular consciousness. At the same time, however, it is clear that television re-iterates narratives which clearly prefer authoritarian solutions to the problems and enigmas which they posit. This is a reactionary posture: it does nothing to assist the development of our ways of thinking and speaking about crime and justice. To this extent, the constant presence of television in our homes must be accompanied by a similarly continual activity of critique, which subjects the blandishments of our entertainments to a sceptical and rigorous questioning.

Acknowledgements

I would like to acknowledge the help and encouragement of Colin Sumner, Graham McCann and Graham Murdock in the writing of this essay.

Notes

1 These arguments, and technical and methodological positions behind them, are developed more fully elsewhere (Sparks, 1984).
2 The 'elsewhere' in this case has been varied and widespread – it includes the activities of the research departments of television systems themselves (BBC, 1972, 1988; Gunter, 1985; Milavsky *et al.*, 1982), as well as reports by governmental and regulatory bodies (Surgeon General's Scientific Advisory Committee, 1972; HORS, 1977). It must also include the campaigns of various lobbying organizations and pressure groups, most famously in Britain Mary Whitehouse's National Viewers' and Listeners' Association, as well as millions of words of journalism. This subsidiary of the television industry deserves close study in its own right. This is not my purpose here, although much of what I have to say bears upon it (for a brief consideration of the ways in which television itself stimulates certain kinds of political activity, see Sparks, 1987).
3 The importance of this is beginning to be more widely recognized by students of communications, as well as in social theory more generally. For example, the treatments which are provided by Giddens (1984, 1987) of the role of seriality and routine in sustaining ontological security, can be fruitfully applied to the use of television in domestic leisure. Work by Morley (1974, 1980), Morley and Silverstone (1988) and Scannell (1986) demonstrates increasingly sensitive attention to the position of television and other domestic technologies in relation to social interaction and the division of daily time. Part of what this suggests is the inadequacy of older social psychological terms, such as attitude, to investigate or summarize properly the relation between the viewer and the medium.

Perhaps more powerful are, for example, Gouldner's notion of paleo-symbolism or Bourdieu's concept of the habitus, both of which seek to determine what underpins ideology, rather than simply examining the overt expression of ideas (Gouldner, 1976; Bourdieu, 1977).
4 A number of writers have noted the ways in which the 'obviousness' and 'triviality' or popular culture have been used as ways of deriding any attempt at popular culture studies (cf. Bigsby, 1976: 4, on the consequent defensiveness which students of these matters have tended to adopt). Jonathan Culler makes a similar point:

> The student of popular culture invariably finds himself charged with excessive ingenuity for offering elaborate explanations where none seems required. . . . But precisely because in this case there is lacking the initial experience of strangeness which, when we are dealing with spatially or temporally distant cultures convinces us of the existence of operative conventions, a strong theory is especially necessary if . . . we are to overcome the temptation of taking the meanings of our own culture for granted. (Culler, 1973: 29)

References

Altheide, D.L. (1984). Media hegemony: A failure of perspective. *Public Opinion Quarterly*, **48**, 476–90.
Anderson, D. and Sharrock, W.W. (1979). Biasing the news: Technical issues in media studies. *Sociology*, **13**(3), 367–85.
Auden, W.H. (1948). The guilty vicarage. In *The Dyer's Hand*. London: Faber.
BBC (1972). *Violence on Television: Programme Content and Viewer Reception*. London: BBC.
BBC (1988). *Violence and the Media*. London: BBC.
Belson, W. (1978). *Television Violence and the Adolescent Boy*. Westmead: Saxon House.
Bigsby, C.W.E. (ed.) (1976). *Approaches to Popular Culture*. London: Edward Arnold.
Bourdieu, P. (1971). Intellectual field and creative project. In *Knowledge and Control* (M.F.D. Young, ed.). London: Collier Macmillan.
Bourdieu, P. (1977). *Outline of a Theory of Practice*. Cambridge: Cambridge University Press.
Bourdieu, P. (1980). The production of belief. *Media, Culture and Society*, **2**(3).
Chaney, D. (1977). Fictions in mass entertainment. In *Mass Communication and Society* (J. Curran, M. Gurevitch and J. Woollacott, eds). London: Edward Arnold.
Conrad, P. (1982). *Television: The Medium and its Manners*. London: Routledge and Kegan Paul.
Corner, J. (1980). Codes and cultural analysis. *Media, Culture and Society*, **2**(2), 73–86.
Counihan, T.M. (1975). Reading television: Notes on the problem of media content. *Australian and New Zealand Journal of Sociology*, **11**(2), 31–6.

Csikszentmihalyi, M. and Kubey, R. (1981). Television and the rest of life. *Public Opinion Quarterly*, **45**(3), 317–28.
Culler, J. (1973). The linguistic basis of structuralism. In *Structuralism: An Introduction* (Robey, D. ed.). Oxford: Clarendon Press.
Debord, G. (1983). *La Societé du Spectacle* (Preface to the 3rd Italian edition, translated by M. Prigent and L. Forsyth). London: Chronos.
Eco, U. (1972). Towards a semiotic enquiry into the television message. *Working Papers in Cultural Studies*, **3**.
Eco, U. (1979). *The Role of the Reader*. London: Hutchinson.
Eysenck, H.J. and Nias, D.B.K. (1978). *Sex, Violence and the Media*. London: Temple Smith.
Fiske, J. and Hartley, J. (1978). *Reading Television*. London: Methuen.
Garnham, N. (1973). *Structures of Television*. London: BFI.
Gerbner, G. (1970). Cultural indicators: The case of violence in TV drama. *Annals of the American Academy*, **338**, 69–81.
Gerbner, G., Gross, L., Signorielli, N., Morgan, M. and Jackson-Beeck, M. (1980). The mainstreaming of America: Violence profile no. 11. *Journal of Communication*, **30**.
Gerbner, G., Gross, L., Morgan, M. and Signorielli, N., (1984). Political correlates of television viewing. *Public Opinion Quarterly*, **48**, 283–300.
Giddens, A. (1984). *The Constitution of Society*. Cambridge: Polity.
Giddens, A. (1987). *Social Theory and Modern Sociology*. Cambridge: Polity.
Gitlin, T. (1979). Prime-time ideology: The hegemonic process in television entertainment. *Social Problems*, **26**(3), 251–66.
Gitlin, T. (1982). Television's Screens. In *Cultural and Economic Reproduction in Education* (M. Apple, ed.). London: Routledge and Kegan Paul.
Gouldner, A. (1976). *The Dialectic of Ideology and Technology*. London: Macmillan.
Gunter, B. (1985). *Dimensions of Television Violence*. Aldershot: Gower.
Hall, S., Clarke, J., Critcher, C., Jefferson, T. and Roberts, B. (1978). *Policing the Crisis*. London: Macmillan.
Hirsch, P.M. (1976). The role of television and popular culture in contemporary society. In *Television: The Critical View* (H. Newcomb, ed.). Oxford: Oxford University Press.
HORS (1977). *Screen Violence and Film Censorship: HORS no. 40*. London: HMSO.
Knight, S. (1980). *Form and Ideology in Crime Fiction*. Bloomington, Ind.: Indiana University Press.
Kress, G. (1976). Structuralism and popular culture. In *Approaches to Popular Culture* (C.W.E. Bigsby, ed.). London: Edward Arnold.
Lévi-Strauss, C. (1970). *The Raw and the Cooked*. London: Jonathan Cape.
Marcuse, H. (1964). *One-dimensional Man*. London: Routledge.
Milavsky, J.R., Kessler, R., Stipp, H. and Rubens, W. (1982). *Television and Aggression*. London: Academic Press.
Morley, D. (1974). *Reconceptualising the Media Audience: Towards an Ethnography of Audiences*. Birmingham: CCCS occasional paper.
Morley, D. (1980). *The 'Nationwide' Audience*. London: BFI.
Morley, D. and Silverstone, R. (1988). Domestic communication. Conference paper, International Television Studies Conference, Institute of Education, London.

Murdock, G. (1975). The sociology of mass communications and sociological theory. *Australian and New Zealand Journal of Sociology*, **11**(2).

Murdock, G. (1982). Disorderly images. In *Crime, Justice and the Mass Media* (C.S. Sumner, ed.). Cambridge: Institute of Criminology.

Murdock, G. and Golding, P. (1977). Capitalism, communications and class relations. In *Mass Communication and Society* (J. Curran, M. Gurevitch and J. Woollacott, eds). London: Edward Arnold.

Scannell, P. (1986). Radio Times. Conference paper, International Television Studies Conference, Institute of Education, London.

Sohn, D. (1976). A nation of videots (interview with Jerzy Kosinski). In *Television: The Critical View* (H. Newcomb, ed.). Oxford: Oxford University Press.

Sparks, J.R. (1984). *Fictional representations of crime and law enforcement on television*. M.Phil dissertation. Institute of Criminology, Cambridge.

Sparks, J.R. (1987). Mary Whitehouse. *New Socialist*, April.

Surgeon General's Scientific Advisory Committee (1972). *Television and Growing Up: The Impact of Televised Violence*. Washington, D.C.: US Government Printing Office.

Williams, R. (1974a). *Television: Technology and Cultural Form*. London: Fontana.

Williams, R. (1974b). Communications as cultural science. *Journal of Communication*, **23**(4), 17–25.

Winn, M. (1977). *The Plug-in-Drug*. New York: Viking.

7 Strategies of censure and the suffragette movement

Alison Young

Introduction

This essay is about a group of women who campaigned for the enfranchisement of women in the early part of the twentieth century. It is also about the resistances to their demands and the means used to control their activities. The women involved in the militant group, the Women's Social and Political Union (WSPU), became the targets of a *censure* (see Sumner, 1983; Chapter 2, this volume), both individually and as an organization. Part of the essay will look at the details of the campaign, particularly between 1910 and 1914, and also at the specific responses to the WSPU's militant activities.

Because this work does not posit a purely 'repressive hypothesis' (see Foucault, 1978: 9–12), I will not only examine the various components of the censure, which have their roots in, for example, law or medicine or 'psy'-dominated theories, but also analyse their general foundations in a particular conceptualization of womanhood, an historically specific idealization which produced certain normative prescriptions about women's roles, natures and potentials. Within this idealized femininity, a woman's ultimate spiritual and physical achievement was to be a 'good wife and mother', to love her husband and bear his children:

> Woman is doomed to immorality, because for her to be moral would mean that she must incarnate a being of supernatural qualities: the 'virtuous woman' . . . the 'perfect mother', the 'honest woman' and so on. Let her but think, dream, sleep, desire, breathe,

without permission and she betrays the masculine ideal. (de Beauvoir, 1953: 492)

The dominant conception of femininity embodied ideal-typical norms which prescribed and proscribed the minutiae of everyday life. These lingered on from the Victorian era into the time of the 'votes for women' campaign. There was, therefore, a sort of 'general politics of truth' (Foucault, 1980: 131) made up of discourses, structures, ideologies and practices. It was through the existence of this that the demands of the suffragettes fell on deaf ears. If all women experienced the effects of this particular idealization of womanhood in a generalized and diffused manner, its effects were given *specificity* by the emergence of the suffragette with her demand for the vote. This essay will follow the stages of the militant campaign and the responses of the police, the courts, the press and the general public. The figure of the suffragette was highlighted at the intersections of certain discourses and their practices: discourse is therefore the crucial site for investigation and critique.

The members of the WSPU were unusual women in that they transgressed many social, legal and political norms and with a political end in mind. They had a name of their own: *suffragettes*. The construction of such a word seemed to link the notion of women's suffrage with its female advocates, according to Fowler, in his *Dictionary of Modern English Usage* (1977). Its use was primarily facetious he notes, and its essential significance lies in its connotation of *diminutiveness* (as a cigarette is a little cigar, so a suffragette is a little suffragist), even though 'many of the militant suffragettes were by no means diminutive' (Fowler, 1977: 603). The *Concise Oxford Dictionary* agrees with this, citing 'suffragette' as a compound example of the various meanings of the suffix '-ette', small, imitation and female.

Thus, the linking of the notion of female suffrage with its female proponents in the word suffragette was implicitly pejorative and derogatory, a neat coining that encapsulated its own unspoken but immediately recognizable censure. The word first came into common usage after its invention by the *Daily Mail* in January 1906, shortly after the first act of militancy by a WSPU member, Christabel Pankhurst.

The militant campaign

The franchise at this time was governed by the third Reform Act of 1884, whereby a male householder with unbroken occupation of a property for at least 12 weeks was entitled to vote. Under this Act, about 60 per cent of males were enfranchised, and about half a million had two or more votes. The demand of the WSPU was that the franchise be extended to women as well as men: 'Votes for Women' was to be shouted at demonstrations and painted on banners across the country over the next decade and more.

The main strategy employed by the WSPU in the campaign for women's enfranchisement was that of militant protest, particularly in the form of violence to property in the later years of the campaign. The writings and papers of the WSPU leaders show that they saw this as a vital tactic which could inexorably force the Government into a position where reform was inevitable. In the journal *The Suffragette*, on 13 December 1912, they wrote:

> The suffragists who have been burning . . . letters have been doing this for a very simple reason. They want to make the electors and the Government so uncomfortable that . . . they will give women the vote.

On 2 May 1913, in the same journal, they say:

> When militancy has done its work, then will come sweetness and cleanness, respect and trust, perfect equality and justice between men and women.

Although not systematic or widespread until 1910, militancy began in 1905, at a Liberal Party meeting in Manchester. Christabel Pankhurst and Annie Kenney attended, with the intention of disruption to gain publicity. They shouted the demand for the vote, unfurled a banner and were forcibly removed from the hall. Christabel spat at two policemen and struck one in the mouth, saying she wanted to assault a policeman. Both women were imprisoned for 3 days, having refused to pay their fines. The press in Manchester gave the story the most coverage, but by 16 October, even *The Times* was printing letters and articles of protest and outrage. At their trial, Christabel had said:

> . . . my conduct in the Free Trade Hall . . . was meant as a protest against the legal position of women today. We cannot make any orderly protest because we have not the means whereby citizens may do such a thing: we have not a vote, *and so long as we have not a vote we must be disorderly*. There is no other way whereby we can put forward our claims to political justice. (*The Manchester Guardian*, 16 October 1905; my emphasis)

Hannah Mitchell later wrote of the meeting held in honour of the release of the two women:

> The two girls who only a week before had been flung out of the hall like criminals were now the central figures on the platform, which was filled with sympathisers, while the vast audience in both the arena and gallery showed the interest evoked by the treatment meted

out to the women. . . . *Twenty years of peaceful propaganda had not produced such an effect.* (Cited in Rosen, 1974: 53; my emphasis)

So it was that militancy became the basic tenet of the WSPU. After Christabel's protest, arrest and release, it was demonstrated that new members could be persuaded to join the WSPU, swelling numbers and funds. Publicity was another result, drawing attention to the cause. Militant tactics, in the form of some pre-planned outrage followed by imprisonment, martyrdom and publicity, were seen as the obvious solution to the years of asking and always being refused. 'Deeds not words', announced the WSPU, and went on over the next decade to act out their conviction in the capacity of the combined force of public outrage and press publicity to turn women's suffrage into a political issue.

In 1910, the House of Commons was considering a Conciliation Bill which would enfranchise about 1 million women. It failed, as Asquith, the Prime Minister, moved that special facilities were needed for its Third Reading. In an attempt to win Conservative support, the Bill with its property qualification had moved too far from the interests of the Liberals, Labour and the Irish. A discrepancy was pointed to between the suffragist propaganda of 'all women have the *right* to vote' and the political reality of *'only if she is middle or upper class'*.

Asquith's announcement that the Conciliation Bill was abandoned was made on 18 November 1910, a day which was to become known as 'Black Friday'. As Asquith spoke before the House, a riot was in progress outside. Groups of 12 women at a time had marched to the House of Commons where they tried to rush the police lines. They were met with brutality and force unlike anything previously used against them. For 6 hours, the women were kicked and beaten, their arms were twisted, their noses punched and their breasts gripped and twisted. It is important to note the often specifically *sexual* nature of many of the injuries sustained, and also the allegations afterwards that the police took pleasure in inflicting these. One WSPU member later stated that:

One policeman . . . put his arm round me and seized my left breast, nipping it and wringing it very painfully, saying as he did so, 'You have been wanting this for a long time, haven't you?'. (Quoted in Brailsford and Murray, 1911: 9)

A total of 135 such statements were collected – almost all involved allegations of violence and 29 referred to assaults both violent and sexual. The large crowd of spectators who gathered to watch made no attempt to help; indeed, some seem to have joined in and most cheered on the police.

The campaign had been losing its news value, but 'Black Friday' changed that. Under the headlines 'Suffrage Raiders' and 'Disorderly

Scenes and Arrests at Westminster', *The Times* commented on the injuries sustained by the police in carrying out their duty, such as a kick on the ankle, a cut on one hand. Despite suffering the indignity of having their helmets knocked off, the police 'kept their tempers very well'. It admitted that their methods of repelling the 'raiders' were 'vigorous', but maintained that the police 'were at any rate kept warm by the exercise and so were the ladies who flung themselves about against the defending lines' (19 November 1910). This epitomizes the tenor of the press coverage of the demonstration. Only the *Manchester Guardian* criticized the actions of the police; the rest concentrated on the outrageousness of women who dared to take part in a political protest, and applauded the police – 'ever-courteous' approved the *Daily Express*.

Some of the press reports drew comparisons with situations under communist regimes. The *Daily Mail* quotes an 'eye-witness from the Privy Council' as saying that the scene of Black Friday was 'worse than anything . . . witnessed in St. Petersburg on Red Sunday'. *The Times* also hints at communistic threats ('militant comrades'). This practice suggests to the reader the possible political persuasions of the women and the potential consequences of giving into their demands: a loss of traditional political values and ideals.

The use of a war metaphor in the press reports is striking: the demonstration becomes a 'wild battle', the protesters transformed into 'raiders' and 'comrades-in-arms' who throw both 'missiles' and themselves 'against the locked lines of the police' in 'skirmishes on the battlefield' (*Daily Express*, 19 November 1910). The images here are of disorder, chaos and violence on the part of the women, whereas the police stand firm, a protection against these bizarre attackers: *their* violence is a justified measure to contain the threat and maintain order.[1] The effect of this type of press coverage is a *trivialization* of the purpose behind the demonstration: instead of being part of a militant political movement, it is reduced to a mode of exercise, a means of keeping warm. Thus decontextualized, it is abstracted and extracted from its political motivation and origin into a senseless, thoughtless disturbance of order.

Black Friday's demonstration was followed up, on 22 November, by a protest meeting outside 10 Downing Street, after Asquith's announcement that suffrage would not be considered until the next Parliament. The press reporting of this was similar in its decontextualization of the issue and its chosen mechanisms for defining the WSPU out of the political and into the more easily comprehensible realms of illness, madness and jocularity. 'A disgraceful scene', admonished the *Daily Express*:

> . . . women who so completely lost their heads in an orgy of hysterical excitement that 153 of them, including Mrs Pankhurst, had to be arrested. . . . Hundreds of hysterical women hurled themselves with

high-pitched cries and shouts on the police, knocking off their helmets and striking them with umbrellas . . .

The protesters here are portrayed as banshee-like creatures, who 'abandoned themselves to acts of violence' in an 'orgy of madness'. The images invoked by the language employed here are explicitly sexual, reinforcing the instinctive post-Victorian fear of sexuality. *The Times* takes a similar line, but uses the imagery of the mentally sick in need of treatment. The 'rioters had lost all control of themselves', it states, thus helping to legitimate the necessity for control to be provided for them by the forces of the state. 'Some shrieked, some laughed hysterically and all fought with dogged but aimless pertinacity': and of these some are but 'young girls who must have been victims of hysteria rather than serious conviction'. Who would seriously align themselves with these foolish women? Against these 'demented creatures' stand the police, who 'behaved with self control and good humour under the greatest provocation'. The threat posed to the state and to social order by the women is personified through a description of the Prime Minister's flight from 10 Downing Street into a waiting taxi-cab, surrounded by demonstrators, one of whom punches her fist through its window. By concentrating on the demonstrators, emphasizing both their numbers against the 'single line of police' and the apparent irrationality and perceived threat of their behaviour, the attention of the reader is shifted away both from the violence of the police and from the motivation behind the protest (the demand for the vote). The focus instead is on what is threatened, reinforcing and affirming taken-for-granted values and norms, through a highlighting of the abnormal and the dangerous.

Protest grows: Violence to property

Until the end of 1911 there was a cessation of militancy, a sort of truce while various franchise bills were debated and failed in Parliament. This was the time of the Conciliation Committee, which was attempting to draw up a suffrage Bill that would be acceptable to Parliament. Towards the end of 1911, a new strategy was adopted by the WSPU: window-breaking. On 21 November 1911, Mrs Pethick Lawrence led the suffragettes on a raid which smashed the windows of the Home Office, the War Office, the Foreign Office, the Treasury, the Board of Trade, the National Liberal Club, and many more. A total of 223 women were arrested, and 150 imprisoned for periods ranging from 5 days to 1 month. Asquith at this time became more openly opposed to women's suffrage. On 14 December 1911, he told the National League for Opposing Women's Suffrage that to 'grant votes for women would be a political mistake of the most disastrous kind'. For the WSPU in March 1912, window-breaking seemed to be seized on as the standard form for their protest. On 1 March, a marathon raid was organized, involving relays of women over a number of hours and causing thousands of pounds worth of damage.

The reaction in the press was one of unanimous, harsh criticism. The *Morning Post* represented the women as a threat to internal security and demanded their punishment through the enforcement of the criminal law.[2] The *Manchester Guardian* depicted the women as insane, under the headline 'The Madness of the Militants': as the insane cannot make political demands, this obviates any obligation to listen to their claim. While the *Morning Post* presented the window-breaking as the activity of 'deliberate vandals', that is, *rational* individuals, *The Times* pointed out to us the irrationality of the protest, dubbing the women insane and explicitly contrasting them with the 'rational observers' who looked on. The condemnation of the attack was strongest in this article:

> Mrs Pankhurst and her *maenads* have produced their answer to Wednesday's great meeting at the Albert Hall. It takes the now stereotyped form of broken glass. . . . None of its previous follies have been so thoroughly calculated to discredit the suffragist cause. . . . No-one can surely have imagined destruction on this scale in London as the work of a few unbalanced women whose *only grievance* lies in an insignificant point of Parliamentary procedure affecting a measure they have at heart. For whatever may be thought of the Suffragist agitation its immediate evidence is simply *infantile*. . . . An act of *wanton and hysterical self-advertisement* . . . (*The Times*, 3 March 1912; my emphasis)

One firm whose windows had been broken wrote on the same day of 'a cause that is apparently directly responsible for a dangerous form of hysterical mania'. After another attempted meeting in Parliament Square had been prevented by 'police precautions', 'further suffragist outrages' were perpetrated by 'bands of zealots' (*The Times*, 5 March 1912). These occurred at a demonstration in Parliament Square: anticipating much damage to property, the British Museum, galleries and shops nearby had been boarded up and 3000 police sent to the scene of the protest, but in vain, for hundreds of windows were shattered and most of the women escaped arrest. The 200 who were arrested received prison sentences ranging from 7 days to 8 months. Emmeline Pankhurst herself was sent to Holloway (where she went on hunger strike) for 'conspiring to incite to commit malicious damage to property'.

Letters which followed in the press spoke of the 'wantonness' of 'misguided and mad women'. *The Times* (5 March 1912) reported how 200 men marched to the premises of 'The Women's Press' and broke its windows amid cheering crowds, at the same time as the suffragettes were trying to hold their demonstration in Parliament Square. These men are seen as rational, understandable and *justified*; highlighting the sharp dichotomy between male protest about the perceived threat posed by the WSPU and the attempts made by these women to free themselves from their confining sphere of passivity and submission.

Throughout the rest of 1912 and on into 1913, the WSPU accelerated their strategy of violence against property. Once aggression and militancy have been settled on as the principal tactics in a campaign, in order to retain the eye of both the press and the public there must be a definite, irresistible increase in pressure, perhaps interspersed with periods of truce, but sufficient to achieve both publicity and the notoriety required to precipitate social change. The necessity of this acceleration of violence led the WSPU into the secret arson campaign of 1913, which was to cause hundreds of thousands of pounds worth of damage, and which was called *'burning to vote'*.

The first recorded arson attack was on 13 July 1913 at Nuneham House. At the same time, Sylvia Pankhurst was leading a campaign known as the 'Black Hand' in the press, where street lamps were broken, keyholes stopped with lead, flower beds wrecked, house numbers painted out, cushions in railway carriages slashed and bowling greens dug up. Thus there was widespread, continuous and small-scale destructiveness, interspersed with more ambitious attacks on property. After an attempt to bomb Lloyd George's house, the *Daily Express* dubbed the women 'The Bombazines'. Emmeline Pankhurst assumed responsibility for the attack and was imprisoned for 3 years.

Press reports in the spring of 1913 are full of accounts of the arson attacks: these 'new forms of suffragist activity' (*The Times*, 7 April 1913) 'which respect no property'. Public resentment manifested itself not only in angry letters to the press but also as suffragette meetings and demonstrations. At a meeting in Hyde Park at the beginning of March 1913, for example, Mrs Drummond (a leading member of the WSPU) and other speakers were pelted with turf and mud. The crowd often disrupted the speeches by singing loudly, trying to rush the platform, blowing trumpets, or jeering and calling out insults. Attendance at meetings frequently was for the purpose of satisfying curiosity (what one of the 'wild women' looked like), or ridicule (the crowd sang 'there's no place like home' at a march in Oxford on 8 January 1913), or disturbance (shouts of 'you ought to be tarred and feathered' or 'duck them!'). It became commonplace for the police to allow a meeting to proceed for a short time and then require the withdrawal of the speakers 'for their own safety'. Eventually, in the late spring of 1913, there was a blanket prohibition against *all* WSPU assemblies.[3]

Nevertheless, the campaign of property destruction increased in intensity, despite mounting press and public antipathy to damage which stood in excess of £500,000. Bombs were planted; many large country houses were gutted; churches, haystacks, racecourse stands burned down; golf courses burned with acid and various works of art mutilated. The act of destruction which inspired the most vehement and disbelieving press reaction was the mutilation of Velasquez' *Rokeby Venus*.[4] *The Times* described the painting for the reader with wistful lyricism:

> ... it represents Venus, a marvellously graceful female figure, lying on a couch, quite nude ... looking at herself in a small mirror. The picture ... is neither idealistic nor passionate, but absolutely natural and absolutely pure. *She is ... the embodiment of the perfection of Womanhood at the moment when it passes from the bud into the flower.* (*The Times*, 11 March 1914; my emphasis)

Here is all of the Victorian elegaic apotheosizing of woman summed up in one sentence. Woman is a flower to be plucked by man; that pure and graceful blossom, that perfect contrast to the disgraceful conduct of the unwomanly woman, the suffragette.

The judges of normality

Let us turn now to the forces against which the suffragettes were struggling, a shift of focus from the campaign itself to the exercise of control 'mechanisms' by both state and non-state agencies. Although not proposing a situation where one group dominates the others, I have tried to incorporate into this essay some awareness of a relative weighting of influences, which concentrates considerable degrees of the 'will to power' within the organization of the state. I am therefore seeking to reconcile an avoidance of a totally state-centred argument which reduces all sites where power is invested to state apparatuses, with an acceptance of some implied 'above' and 'below', a difference of potentials which invests more truth and more force in some social relations than others (see Foucault, 1980: 188 and 200–1).

Criminalizing militancy

There existed an anonymous and partially unspoken strategy of *criminalization* which formulated the issue in terms of its own law-and-order discourse, circling around notions of public order, morality, decency and respectability. Outside the boundaries mapped by this discourse lurked the criminals, the dangerous and the disruptive. The political motivation and signification of the suffragettes' militancy were sucked out and transformed into the predefined concepts of criminality, public disorder and illegal activity.

This can be well illustrated by McKenna's statement that he could see no political dimension to the WSPU's activities, which he defined as simple violations of the criminal law. It was an outrage to the WSPU leaders that Queenie Gerald, the owner of the Piccadilly Flat brothel, was sent to the second division to serve her sentence, while suffragette prisoners remained in the third with none of the privileges of the second.

When their militant action was packaged up in these terms of criminalization, there followed the operationalization of a law-and-order programme, which, in its inference of an ideal society, an inversion of the present which is both conflict- and crime-free, provides us with *a way of seeing*. This utopian vision, this imagining of a better-world-than-this, was at first disturbed by the political protests of the WSPU, but then it fastened on to them. Despite its utopian holism, the individualization of liberal democracy *produces* the criminal, the case history, the law-breaker, the lone suffragette.

These figures form the points of focus for technologies of power, especially those which operate in a regulatory or disciplinary manner. For the WSPU, those flowing from a law-and-order discourse in the early twentieth century, included sentences of hard labour, the tightening up of the laws of public assembly, the enactment of the 'Cat and Mouse' Act which lodged considerable legitimate and legal powers of re-arrest and detention with the authorities, and the rediscovery of old legislation which had fallen into disuse to be redeployed 'in the public interest' to ensure the maintenance of order and the upholding of the criminal law.

Perhaps resistance *is* implied in the operation of power (see Foucault, 1977, 1978). The WSPU certainly attempted to turn these sanctions to their advantage as much as possible. Women would appear in public on stretchers as invalids, fragile victims of a Liberal Government's oppression. Similar use was made of court appearances to both publicize the cause and to create disturbances (speeches were made from the dock and displays of violence occurred, such as throwing tomatoes). On 22 May 1914, 66 women in Bow Street magistrate's court shouted incessantly, refused to stand, turned their backs and threw various missiles at the judge.

The daily debates in the House of Commons (published in *The Times*) during the spring of 1913 were marked by heated discussions on how to respond to the threat to society's law and order posed by the militant women. On 18 March, this exchange took place, as reported by *The Times* (19 March 1913):

Lord Robert Cecil: These women should be deported from the country.
Mr W. Redmond: Where would you send them to? [Cries of 'Ireland!']
Lord Robert Cecil: These women were dangerous to the State, they were misguided, they were in the nature of insane women for they

were not normal, and they should be treated differently from other criminals.

Mr W. McKenna: We cannot minimise the gravity of the social condition in which a large number of women were acting in a fanatical manner . . .

A letter to *The Times* on 4 March 1912 asserted that:

> . . . orderly men and women will agree that it is quite time that sentimental dealings with these offenders should be dropped and that the law should be rigorously enforced. . . . It is time that they were stopped. One way is by harsher sentences which really mean business . . .

Lady Bathurst, the daughter of the proprietor of the *Morning Post* which was strongly anti-suffrage, suggested that the authorities should birch the women, shave their hair and deport them to Australia or New Zealand.

In Lord Robert Cecil's statement, we can see potential technologies of control arising out of strategies of *criminalization* (they were not like ordinary criminals, their law-breaking was more serious), and *medicalization* (they were insane and misguided, for normal women do not act like this). In Lady Bathurst's proposals we can detect the vestiges of colonialism (deport them) and the will to punish through physical pain (birching) combined with the disfiguring depersonalization of a shaven head; a stigma which would be felt all the more intensely by these women, firmly constrained by popular exhortations to stereotypical prettiness and 'femininity'.

It was the Prisoners' Temporary Discharge for Ill-Health Act of 1913 which the government enlisted as its main disciplinary technology. Hunger-striking had always been an important part of WSPU propaganda; the image of a lonely woman starving in prison or being forcibly fed by the Liberal Government was a strong one, redolent of martyrdom and self-sacrifice for a noble cause. In less than a month from the day that McKenna acknowledged the inadequacy of existing measures to deal with militant hunger-strikers, a Parliament which had often pleaded lack of time as a reason for not considering women's suffrage proposals had passed a statute, described in debate by Lord Atherley Jones as 'entirely contrary to the principle of criminal administration'. Under the 'Cat and Mouse' Act, as it was nicknamed, prisoners who went on hunger strike would be released to recover and then reimprisoned. Despite criticism of the Act as cruel, liable to cause abuse of the power of re-arrest and a supplement, not an alternative, to force-feeding, most saw it as a means of vindicating the criminal law and ensuring the implementation of the sentences imposed on the militants. Lord Atherley Jones, however, recognized what was implicit in this measure when he said:

When there is an undue strain of a temporary character upon the existing law there is always a cry for fresh legislation to strengthen the law and to do so at the expense of principles which governed the former law. (*The Times*, 2 April 1913)

This peculiar relationship between law and society, whereby law seems to be something *added to* society, a necessity to correct the defects of the social order, can be analysed by recourse to what Derrida calls the 'dangerous supplement': a 'terrifying menace, the supplement is also the first and surest protection against that very menace' (Derrida, 1976: 154). There *is* danger in the supplemental relationship of law to society; it gives some individuals the ability to impose oppressive requirements on others. Paradoxically, however, the only means that we can 'see' to limit and control this danger is through the law itself. The 'dangerous supplement' is here an integral part of the liberal dilemma involved in the questions of how to govern all without breaching the 'rights of the individual', and how to govern each individual without overlooking the duty to society as a whole. So militancy, perceived as a threat to the apparent stability of the social order, its to be dealt with by an augmentation of the power of the legal system, which ironically or cynically disregards the original danger implicated in the very existence of the law. Law and society are set up as a dualism, each defined in terms of the other, but with the potential social disruptions losing out to the repressive-and-affirmative role of the law. When militancy, the result of an oppression suffered by women through the *legal* discourse about their status both as individuals and as a class, is framed as such a potentially disruptive threat to order, *more law* is the answer. *The Times* (3 April 1913) commented:

Better late than never, but it ought to have been done long ago. . . . Our own impression is that a hunger strike on the proposed terms will lose most of its charms.

While the laws restricting public assemblies were being tightened up and more rigorously enforced, thus making it harder for the WSPU to publicize their cause and show the strength of their solidarity, the press often reported that the police would bring these infrequently achieved public meetings to an end 'for the women's protection' (press reports on 4 March 1912). When a meeting or demonstration had got under way, after a few minutes' heckling and jeering from the crowds, the police would break up the assembly, as instructed by the Home Office. In the months immediately preceding the advent of the First World War, Asquith was debating in Parliament how to introduce a measure that would enable the victims of WSPU arson and property attacks to sue its wealthiest subscribers for restitution or compensation. Further action involved attempts to seize the Union funds, hoping to cripple the movement financially, and temporary closure of its press offices in an effort to stop the women printing their propaganda posters and journals. As the WSPU was driven more and more underground, its activities inevitably grew more illegitimate: with all acceptable channels blocked, they *had* to be disorderly, to break the law and attempt to destroy preconceived ideals of womanhood.

The 'degradation of woman'

The militant 'suffragette' was engaged in *unwomanly* behaviour: her demands for the vote were shocking, but the fact that she dared to make them at all were enough to condemn her. To make speeches, to march in demonstrations, to break windows, to go on hunger strike and burn buildings – to do any or all of these meant that she was not a woman. Lucy Cavendish writes to *The Times* (5 March 1913):

> A few violent women's excesses are daily breaking the peace of the country, injuring innocent people, *and worst of all, degrading womanhood* . . . [my emphasis]

Once she had left the sphere of perfect ladyhood, she forfeited any claim to respect and chivalry: it is in this light that the violence of Black Friday, the derogatory press reports and the harsh legislation, must be understood. For the police, the press and others, these were not 'good wives and mothers', but dangerous, image-shattering inversions of this ideal.

As the women of the WSPU were attempting to break down the confining walls around the good wife and mother, they had to be redefined back into the dominant discourse in terms that rendered their actions more readily comprehensible while evading the question of the necessity of change. Discourses about sexuality at the turn of the century informed such contradictions as the *Daily Express* article of 23 November 1910, which called the WSPU both 'sexless creatures' and 'shameless women'. The militant woman was caught in a discursive double-bind: the effects of sexualization in language moved in two directions at once to trap her as both 'sexless' and 'oversexed'.

There was a thriving market in anti-suffrage propaganda postcards which capitalized on this dichotomy, emphasizing the physical unattractiveness of the suffragettes, depicting them as muscular and angular, with captions like: 'At the suffrage meetings you can hear some plain things – and see them too!' The women were also portrayed as lacking only a man in their lives for them to be content: 'It's not a *vote* you want – it's a bloke.' To counter these, WSPU posters were generally in the Pre-Raphaelite or Art Nouveau styles which romanticize a conceptualization of woman somewhere between a madonna and a divine goddess. How far can the wheel of discourse be said to have turned? From the Victorian angel to the WSPU's idol of the suffrage posters, woman is still trapped within the confines of a discourse of sexuality and the logic of its practice.

A medical model of militancy: The hysterical woman

On 16 March 1913, *The Times* took up the notion of the woman activist as irrational and hysterical, by publishing an article titled 'Insurgent Hysteria', which spoke of:

> ... the hysterical, the neurotic, the idle, the habitual imbibers of excitement. ... Some of them are out with their hammers and their bags full of stones because of dreary empty lives and high-strung over-excitable natures: they are regrettable by-products of our civilisation.

The process of sexualization, of the militant women met up with the strategy of medicalization, which is exemplified in the pronouncements of Sir Almroth Wright, prominent physician, first published as a letter to *The Times* and later as 'The Unexpurgated Case against Woman Suffrage' (1913). Wright started from the physiological differences between men and women, which meant that the behaviour of a woman is determined by her sexual organs and reproductive functions:

> ... these upsettings of her mental equilibrium are the things a woman has most cause to fear; and no doctor can ever lose sight of the fact that the mind of woman is always threatened with danger from the reverberations of her physiological emergencies. It is with such thoughts that the doctor's eyes rest upon the militant suffragist. ... There is mixed up with the women's movement much mental disorder ... (Wright, 1913: 79)

Wright's condemnation of the militants was part of a growing number of responses to the calls for 'scientific analyses' of many aspects of social life which began in the mid-nineteenth century. Many of the works in this new tradition made use of currently fashionable concepts of social Darwinism, atavism or biological determinism. Characteristics and traits were counted and related to their perceived origins in the nature–culture dichotomy. These positivist pronouncements had the air of inevitability of scientific knowledge linked to a consensual world view and were quick to dissolve any possibility of the existence of conflict or dissent. With their sincere appeals to 'objectivity' and 'truth', the positivist presentation of women was rooted in these notions of biological determinism and early psychoanalytic theory: the female was propelled through life by forces she cannot control, at the mercy of her sexual organs and reproductive functions.

Wright also outlined for us the several categories of female suffragist: we find 'sexually embittered women in whom everything has turned to gall ... and hatred of men'; 'the incomplete'; 'the woman who is poisoned by misplaced self esteem'; and 'troops of just grown girls' (Wright, 1913: 78). Wright's classification displays the terms generated by the growing discourses of medicalization and scientism which operate to censure something which cannot be slotted into the ideal notions of consensus politics and shared morality. The press often labelled the militants as 'insane' or 'mad'; others considered them to reflect the inherent instability of the female temperament. On 2 April 1911, the Women's Freedom League organized a boycott of the 10-yearly census. *Punch* commented wryly that 'these ladies must have taken leave of their census'. Other labels used included: 'the victims of hysteria rather than serious conviction'; 'a few unbalanced women'; and 'hysterical maniacs' fighting 'a mad struggle for a false equality' (*The Times*, 2 March 1912 and 7 March 1913).

The medicalization of militancy as 'abnormal' or 'unnatural', as the actions of 'mad' and 'weak-minded' women, is all the more insidious for its aura of scientific authority. Wright's letter was given considerable prominence in *The Times*, for it was written by an *expert*, a man of informed, privileged opinion.

The demands of the WSPU had been decontextualized, rendered symptomatic, while the women were depoliticized, set up as mad, hysterical creatures, unnatural women, or dangerous law-breakers. The unstable, undesirable 'suffragette' could be monitored and controlled within the interstices of these metaphorical lines of discourse, ideology and practice, while the Eternal Feminine, the wife and mother, continued to be revered and exalted as the pinnacle of womanliness.

The censure of the suffragettes

Many writers have proferred explanations for the existence of the WSPU which remain within the terms of the dominant discourses about women, their sexuality and psyches, with as much of an effect of trivialization and depoliticization of their activities as the articles in the press at the time of the campaign. Dangerfield (1961) insinuates lesbianism in the ranks of the WSPU. Mitchell (1977), prey to psychoanalytic preconceptions, hints that the suffragettes no doubt *wanted* to be assaulted by the police on Black Friday. Christabel Pankhurst, in Mitchell's (1977: 207) opinion, was a lesbian: '... lesbianism seems to have been rooted in incestuous feelings for a neurotic mother – an experience ... one feels was not unknown to Christabel'. The sexuality of these women should have been irrelevant to an assessment of their struggle. Yet, both at the time and in more recent accounts, speculations as to sexual predilections and peccadilloes provided the opening for wholesale condemnation of the women, while evading the necessity of evaluating their demand.

The analysis of the WSPU campaign by modern feminist writers has varied. Rowbotham (1977) took the socialist feminist viewpoint, which could not fail to see the WSPU and its leaders as reactionary, bourgeois, autocratic and élitist. The individual 'suffragette', however, is treated more sympathetically, presented as the victim of a patriarchal state in which she had no voice, tried and sentenced by men and under manmade laws.

Certain fundamental problems, however, underlie such an account as Rowbotham's. Employing a model that demands the overthrow of capitalism and its substitution with socialism, means a risk that anything whose objectives are less than this will be criticized for its bourgeois reinforcement of the social order. The failure of the WSPU to be a 'socialist' organization, even if that had been its intention at any time – which is doubtful – is but one perspective from which to examine the suffragette movement. It is necessarily incomplete, although this is obscured by its universal pretensions and its totalizing rhetoric, which desires to return always to the issue of class struggle.

Another perspective, another strand of the analysis, is provided by the feminist underpinnings of Rowbotham's account. The concept of patriarchy which underlies this is, however, a difficult tool for analysis. It predicates a universal system of political domination and subordination which functions within and in terms of sex relationships. It is this very universality with which I would take issue: such sweeping, pandemic generalizations deprive the theoretical tool of a cutting edge that will penetrate to the core of specific historical circumstances. That women were occupying a marginal position is undoubtedly a valid point to make, but to account for it by means of an all-encompassing patriarchal system results in a sociological reductionism which reifies the sex–gender confusion into an always–already given category founded on dominant notions of male–female relations.

I would advocate that to understand the significance of the suffragette movement and the responses to its 'disruptiveness', it is necessary to use some conceptual means that will set this in its widest context. As a starting point, the concept of social censure (see Sumner, 1983; Chapter 2, this volume) seems to offer the potential for an interesting analysis when extended to the press coverage of the WSPU: to what extent did the mobilisation of particular forces of control represent a social censuring of the fearful possibilities embodied in the 'suffragette'? She was, after all, a law-breaker, for she smashed windows and burned down houses; she was also a hysterical woman, suffering from some nervous or psychological disorder; and, finally, she was a lesbian or barren or wanton, any or all of these inversions of the sexual norm. Her existence could justify the repressive mechanisms such as the Cat and Mouse Act, and imprisonment in the third division with no political privileges.[5]

Cixous has looked at the application of one of these censures to women who disturb the accepted (masculine) notions about women's roles, natures and potentials. Questioning women, political and disorderly women, have often been labelled as hysterical. Cixous (1975) traces this to Freud's patient Dora who complained to him that she was an object of exchange for men. Dora's case history as Freud's 'hysterical woman' is Cixous' starting point for a consideration of the politically disruptive potential in such women. Dora is the name Cixous gives to a disturbing force which upsets the patriarchal merry-go-round. The hysteric makes permanent war on the dominant social order and leaves it no peace. So, the 'hysterical women' in the WSPU became targets for censure in these gender-specific terms because of the perceived threat they posed to relations of gender in society. Foucault (1978) considered the discursive practice and effect of what he called the 'hystericization of women's bodies'. For Cixous this would be a recognition of women's subversive potential: they shock, they disrupt, they change the order of things.[6]

I wish to take my analysis further than a focus on the movement's censure. The existence of a censure seems to me to provide, by implication, an affirmation of the 'desired way of life' itself. This dualistic process and double functioning must be the centre of any reading of a censure in discourse. The condemnation of the actions of the WSPU legitimates, through an appeal to contemporary moral and ideological principles, both the repression of those who are the censured targets and also their reabsorption back into a particular way of life. For example, the press coverage of the campaign is one practice which operates in the double movement of depoliticization on the one hand, and the reinforcement or reaffirmation of order on the other. The reaction of the WSPU was not just overtly repressive in the form of augmented policing powers or disapproving public opinion; it was also productive and affirmative, strengthening sexual and social norms threatened by the WSPU's actions. As these prescriptive norms were themselves constraining and limiting for women, the overt control of the WSPU was but the more visible tip of an iceberg of marginalization which operated to freeze out women in general.

It is also important to realize that the suffrage movement should not be imagined as a 'subversion' or 'moment of disruption' which offered a real threat to the established order. Although constituting resistance to certain structural, legal and ideological formations at that time, the suffragettes represented a sort of 'counter-power' or 'counter-society' which is an inversion of that which is opposed. The WSPU were a combination of Kristeva's (1981) two levels of feminism: first, the 'liberal feminism' of their demands for equality with men ('a false equalisation, however: to posit as equal men and women while still defining them in polarised, opposed terms is to subsume the weaker term [women] into the stronger. Women become not "women-equal-to-men" but "women-as-men"') and, secondly, the 'radical feminism' of their practice. Here there is a strong emphasis on femininity and separateness, with men often excluded from praxis: 'the logic of counter-power and counter-society', says Kristeva, 'necessarily generates, by its very structure, its essence as a simulacrum of the combated society or of power'. The struggle of the suffragettes remained entirely *within* the language and structures of the dominant social order, and never broke out of this spiral of power relations. Their very demand served to legitimate the processes of liberal democracy that were partially responsible for their oppression.

The actions of the WSPU, their objective and their own discourse, provided the nails on which to hang mechanisms of control both in the most visible sense (whereby the destruction of property asks to be punished by the deployment of the law) and in a more subtle manner: their concerns with remaining 'lady-like' at all times, and following the prescriptions for conventional attractiveness, meant that when ridiculed by the press and public as 'masculine', 'ugly' or 'unnatural', they must have suffered greatly. Arrest, imprisonment, insults and hunger-striking must have taken their toll on women still caught up in the treadmill of conforming to an ideal.

It is therefore clear that the repressive control mechanisms, such as the severe prison sentences or force-feeding, were the thin edge of a wedge of dispersed and diluted pinpricks of control and supervision which constrained and constructed 'Woman' in general. The censure of the suffragette, with its three main strands of criminalization, medicalization and sexualization, was one ideological formation within an overarching censure of women's activity independent from men. The 'suffragette' was marked out as deviant in particular ways and was then subject to certain sanctions; but *all* women, at this historical juncture in the patriarchal social order, were censured and sanctioned in some way.

All their failures to reach the normative standard of the Angel, the Perfect Victorian Lady, the Good Wife and Mother, are met with any or all of a multiplicity of censures and controls: from the Cat and Mouse Act, that overtly oppressive pole of a disciplinary continuum, to the frown of a husband, the whispered disapproval in a Victorian drawing-room.

Conclusions

Militancy and protest increased and accelerated as 1914 progressed. The immediate outcome of the WSPU's campaign can never be known, for circumstances were altered dramatically when the Great War of 1914–18 sank like a shroud upon all. The demand of the suffragettes was lost in the clarion that called the nation to war.

1918 brought peace to Europe and the vote to women. Their enfranchisement happened quietly, after so many years of fierce, impatient militancy and the long decades of campaigning before that. Women's suffrage crept in, almost unnoticed and unremarked. And the lives of so many women – were they radically altered? Christabel Pankhurst had looked forward to the day of perfect equality between men and women that would come with the granting of the vote, but it was not then, and has not now been, achieved. The campaign for the enfranchisement of women succeeded in getting them the ability to vote: an important achievement which should not be scorned from a less naïve, perhaps more disillusioned, perspective in the 1980s. The vote for women was a means of access, however limited, to the dominant political order of liberal democracy: it was also perhaps both the inspiration for the struggles for piecemeal reforms to take place over the next 70 years, and a starting-point for the increasing politicization of women in their fight to overturn the oppressive patriarchal system. The vote was, for women, a recognition of their political potential: one which has become stronger and more visible throughout the years.

The note of warning that I would add to this is that the WSPU campaign should not be regarded as achieving the ultimate answer to oppression, the end to the subordination of women that they themselves imagined would come with the enfranchisement of women. It was a success for women on one front, leaving many others where the struggle still had to carry on. In most areas of the law, in language and culture, the position of women remained an oppressed and marginal one. To see the vote as a 'be-all-and-end-all' is to forget that a formal recognition of the right to partake in the processes of liberal democracy ignores the informal encroachments of that which may occur, and the effect of the continuing oppression of women in the patriarchal order which exists independently of liberal democracy. This is the broad context in which I have attempted to locate the suffragette movement and its censure; the matter was an ideological mechanism operating to control a disruption of order while also reaffirming the values threatened by such a potential subversion. Within the interconnections of class, economics and gender, I have focused on the threat posed to dominant ideologies by the militant 'suffragette'. Superficial attention was directed to the issue of the vote, the ostensible crux of the matter; yet other suffrage agitators were not condemned in such a way as the members of the WSPU. It was the patriarchal order which was under fire from these women: liberal democracy relinquished the right to vote to a number of women in 1918 and in this sphere the WSPU campaign was a success. The general relations of power between men and women in a patriarchal system of gender imperatives were, however, challenged, although not overthrown, by the struggles of the suffragettes. Whether or not women should have a vote was not the fundamental issue, it was the future of a particular idealization of womanhood that was in question.

Acknowledgements

An earlier version of this essay appeared in 1988, in the *International Journal of Sociology of Law*, **16**, 279–93.

Notes

1 Other newspapers taking this line were the *Morning Post*, the *London Standard*, the *Daily Chronicle*, the *Daily Mirror* and *The Times*.
2 The *Morning Post* was fiercely anti-suffrage. On 23 November 1911, it demanded that suffragettes be dealt with as harshly as 'hooligans', 'drunkards' and 'lunatics'. (It is interesting to note here Geoff Pearson's work on 'respectable fears' in *Hooligan!*, 1983.)
3 Sir Edward Henry, Commissioner of Police, writes to *The Times* on 16 April 1913, a letter addressed to the WSPU, stating his intention to prohibit all WSPU meetings from that date onwards, due to the public disturbances they caused.
4 The offence to public sentiment seemed on a similar scale to that after Emily Wilding Davison's death on Derby Day in 1913. This time, however, the protagonist could speak, through the press coverage of her trial, and her words did nothing to appease the collective anger:

> I have tried to destroy the picture of the most beautiful woman in mythological history, as a protest against the Government destroying Mrs Pankhurst, who is the most beautiful woman in modern history . . .

5 It is important to note that the censure is an *ideological* formation and that there was no empirical basis for these labels, which functioned as a *displacement* of the fears about the suffragettes' potential subversion of patriarchal politics.
6 This potential challenge was felt or perceived in the patriarchal order.

References

de Beauvoir, S. (1953). *The Second Sex*. Harmondsworth: Penguin.
Brailsford, J.N. and Murray, J. (1911). *The Treatment of the Deputations of November 18th, 22nd and 23rd by the Police*. London: Home Office Conciliation Committee for Woman Suffrage.
Cixous, H. (1975). Sorties. From *La Jeune Nee*. Translated in *New French Feminisms* (E. Marks and I. de Courtivron, eds). Brighton: Harvester.
Dangerfield, G. (1961). *The Strange Death of Liberal England*. London: Capricorn.
Derrida, L. (1976). *Of Grammatology*. Baltimore: Johns Hopkins University Press.
Foucault, M. (1977). *Discipline and Punish*. Harmondsworth: Penguin.
Foucault, M. (1978). *The History of Sexuality*. Harmondsworth: Penguin.
Foucault, M. (1980). *Power/Knowledge* (C. Gordon, ed.). Brighton: Harvester.
Kristeva, J. (1981). Women's time. *Signs*, **7**(1), 13–35.

Mitchell, D. (1977). *Queen Christabel*. London: MacDonald and Jane.
Pearson, G. (1983). *Hooligan!* London: Macmillan.
Rosen, A. (1974). *Rise up, Women!* London: Routledge and Kegan Paul.
Rowbotham, S. (1977). *Hidden from History*. London: Pluto.
Strachey, R. (1978). *The Cause*. London: Virago.
Sumner, C. (1983). Rethinking deviance: Towards a sociology of censures. In *Research in Law, Deviance and Social Control*, Vol. 5 (S. Spitzer, ed.). Greenwich, Conn.: JAI Press.
Wright, Sir A.E. (1913). *The Unexpurgated Case Against Woman Suffrage*. London: Constable.

8 The press censure of 'dissident minorities': the ideology of parliamentary democracy, Thatcherism and *Policing the Crisis*

Colin Sumner and Simon Sandberg

Domination generates dissent and dissent is denounced. The hegemony of ruling groups is always grounded in, and supported by, a cocoon of interconnected ideologies and a monotony of ideological discourses. Domination is justified in these ideologies and all alternative politics denigrated. Usually the ideologies condense, focus and develop in the course of political conflict in the form of succinct terms of abuse or *social censures* (see Sumner, 1983). This essay centres upon an analysis of the social censure of political demonstrations in Britain in March/April 1973, as expressed in the discourse of the British national press. We will attempt primarily to do two things: first, to expose the ideological construction of this social censure and, secondly, to locate that construction within the dialectics of British politics at that time.

Our central thesis is that the ideology which gives a distinct pattern to the national press censure of political demonstrations in 1973 was very similar in content, tone and strength to that articulated by the governing Tory party, and that this ideology was directed towards a political, moral and constitutional reconstruction of the British state. In passing, we will dispute the view that the censure of the black mugger was the prime articulator of the hegemonic crisis at that time (cf. Hall *et al.*, 1978), arguing that the censure of 'dissident minorities' (Lord Hailsham's phrase) was a much greater, overarching concern, and one which paved the way for the reconstruction of the British state attempted by the radical right in the 1980s (see also Sumner, 1981a).

We see this essay as a small contribution to the developing analysis in the sociology of social censures. There is a real need to examine closely the detailed ideological composition of social censures and their precise structural roots and historical lineage. While not as precise or as deep as we would like, this work moves in that direction.

We doubt that there is any simple one-to-one relationship between social censures (often quite complex, composite ideological formations) and a generative social practice. Without particularly wishing to align ourselves with Foucault's whole project, we share the spirit of his methodological scepticism in the history of ideas and believe that social censures probably have multiple ideological inputs, and variable historical constitutions and roles (see the exegesis of Foucault's approach in Gordon, 1980 and Foucault, 1977). However, unlike Foucault, we assume that social censures in bourgeois societies do have a key determinant or crucial organizing matrix, and that is their contemporary relationship to the varying needs and hegemonic colourings of specific capitalist states. In that sense, our essay is also located within the sociology of law: it analyses an ideology which crucially colours the statutes, judgements and court hearings on the law relating to public order:

> The court implies, therefore, that these are categories which are common to the parties present (penal categories such as theft, fraud; moral categories such as honesty and dishonesty) and that the parties to the dispute agree to submit to them. Now, it is all this that the bourgeoisie wants to have believed in relation to justice, to its justice. (Foucault, in Gordon, 1980: 27)

The sociology of law must examine the ideological character and tone of these moral and penal censures, for that ideological composition will explain a great deal of what the police, courts and legislature do about 'deviants'. Therefore, we would argue that the British adoption of a paramilitary style of policing public order in the 1980s (see Fine and Millar, 1985; Lea and Young, 1982), targeted at groups like the miners, peace protesters and blacks, who had been openly, frequently and powerfully defined as 'the enemy within', is undoubtedly predicated upon, inspired and given precise form by the ideological censure of dissident minorities emerging and elaborated in the 1970s. This censure charged that the dissidents were a nuisance and a threat to democracy; it logically implied that their continued activity would make them enemies of the state. Therefore, this is a censure of considerable relevance to the regressive reformation of the contemporary British state in the 1980s.

The critique of ideology: Some methodological considerations

> Perhaps the main reason for studying ideology is its mirror-like quality, reflecting the moral and material aspects of our understanding. (Apter, 1964: 15)

Ideology is indeed a signpost to the character of a period. Its forms and messages tell many a tale. Perhaps more importantly, 'insofar as . . . actions reflect a mutual adjustment between ideology and social realities, an understanding of ideology becomes a necessary condition for an understanding of the action' (Inkeles, 1950: 21). Deciphering the social significance of the signs constituting a complex ideological formation is, however, no easy task. Especially since, as Apter (1964: 30) also points out, complex ideologies in modern advanced societies tend not to be programmatic dogmas but, we would say, incline towards being highly situated, pseudo-descriptive accounts which bury their fundamental political premises.

The difficulties of reading ideology have been analysed by Sumner (1979): we will not attempt to summarize that approach here. However, two things are especially pertinent to this essay from the conclusions of that text. First, the emphasis there on the basic Marxian thesis that ideologies are necessitated by specific social relations leads us to suppose that all kinds of social relations could generate ideologies. So, for example, political relations could generate specifically political ideologies. Therefore, we assume that in complex advanced capitalist societies, where there is often a joint articulation and overlapping of social divisions of age, gender, race, class, nationality and region, there will inevitably be some unholy mixtures of ideology in individual consciousness and institutional practice (e.g. socialism, male chauvinism, racism and parochialism). Consequently, there is no reason to expect a straightforward bourgeois economic ideology in media discourse; but there is every reason to expect a *condensation* of ideologies of differing parentage, reflecting not only the generalized economic and political relations, but also the 'structure of feelings' (Williams, 1977: 128), or the general mood, of the present conjuncture.

Secondly, concerning our methodological premises, the emphasis on the circularity of reading ideology and our permanent inability to move outside the hermeneutic circle (the dialectic between the ideologies read and the ideologies active in reading) led Sumner (1979: chs 6 and 7) to conclude that the only way forward was to burrow deeper into it, into our own premises, assumptions and evidence, while at the same time burrowing deeper into the intricacies of the object-text. An historical materialist semiology has to explicate the social structural roots of ideological formations before it can be truly persuasive and more than a superficial speculation. This follows Marx's observation that:

> It is, in reality, much easier to discover by analysis the earthly core of the misty creations of religion, than, conversely, it is to develop from the actual relations of life corresponding celestialised forms of these relations. The latter method is the only materialistic and therefore the only scientific one. (Marx, 1974: 352, n. 2)

But, as Sumner argued, Marx did not mean that we should *begin* with a pre-formed, historically abstracted model of social relations and read contemporary ideology off from that. Complex ideological formations, and equally complex historical-societal configurations, do not permit such a simplistic procedure. The task necessarily involves recognizing and activating a constant dialectical interplay between the theoretical concepts and historically specific, social knowledge of the reader, on the one hand, and the detailed characteristics of the text on the other. That is, we move in research through a series of approximations from first impressions to an adequate account of the relationship between the ideology under study and its generative social practices (Sumner, 1979: ch. 7); an account which can distinguish necessary components of the ideology from the merely contingent, residual or emergent elements.

Therefore, drawing on the in-depth research into the press coverage of political demonstrations in Britain in March 1973, which we have been doing over the last few years, what we will do here is to pick out some of the main 'findings' of that work and examine them in the light of contemporary theoretical and political developments. This is to say that we are a long way from a complete analysis and that this essay merely represents an early step in that research in moving beyond first impressions; but more importantly that, as theory and history move on, our 'findings' deepen, take on a new shape and acquire sharper/fresh tones. As history unfolds, the text permits a new reading: the critique of ideology is neverending and open, although never unprincipled and shapeless.

This present reading evidences two influences in particular. First, there is the paramilitary suppression of the 'riots' of Brixton and Toxteth in 1981, and of the miners' strike of 1984–5. In this way, the discourse of the press in 1973 is not just a mirror on history, but subsequent history is a mirror on that newspaper text. The text and its social history are forever engaged with each other; especially when one component of this dialectic, the British state, *makes* them collaborate. In as much as its self-justification involves an account of 'the rising tide of militancy and the threat to parliamentary democracy', that state invokes a history which supports the text and concretizes its 'truth' in police practice. The text is no longer a mere piece of 1973, and this is no essay about the past; both have been reconstituted, re-read, re-formed and refurbished for 1985 (the time of writing). Of necessity, we use our knowledge of 1985 to read the text, just as much as we need our political understanding of the text to read 1985: the contemporary emphasis on the past as a window on the present understates how much the present allows us a view of the past.

The second major influence on this reading of the press censure of political demonstrations is feminism. Changes in perspective, we are once again reminded, produce changes in what is visible. Aspects of our sample of press coverage were not so obvious in 1973, because of the historic limitations of conceptual vision. Today, the impact of feminism on our thinking enables us to recognize fully the substantial attention given in our sample to the political demonstrations of women and to the demonstrations arising from certain women's activities. It has forced upon us some reflections on the degree of sexist ideology inherent in the censure of political demonstrations. Once again, the circularity of hermeneutics is revealed: the empricist view of reading ideology does not deal with the fact that all such readings are heavily conceptualized and acculturated. The text is undoubtedly there to see, but do we ever see it in all its richness and depth?

March/April 1973 in the UK: The conjuncture

We would not claim that this particular period of one month was a watershed in British political history; it was simply the period in which our sample of newspaper cuttings was collected. We looked over everything the national press published on political demonstrations from 7 March up to 7 April of 1973. This was a time of intense political conflict; and at that time the press seemed to be able to cover demonstrations in such a way as to continually defuse their significance for the Left and for the working class in general.

Other writers, however, have claimed that the early 1970s was an extremely important period in modern British history:

> In 1972, the catchword 'crisis' no longer seems a mere journalistic hyperbole. Clearly, Britain is entering a major social, economic and political crisis. . . . The year is absolutely dominated from end to end by two simple abstract terms, linked in a single ideological couplet, and over-arching every single issue, controversy, conflict or problem . . . : 'violence' and 'the law' . . .
>
> . . . one of the deep structural shifts under way throughout the whole of our period [1970–2: C.S.], which is masked by the more immediate phenomenal forms of the 'crisis', is indeed the massive reconstruction of the position, role and character of the capitalist state in

general. This involved the progressive intervention of the state into spheres – the economic mechanisms of capital on one hand, the whole sphere of ideological relations and of social reproduction on the other – hitherto formally regarded as belonging to the independent spheres of 'civil society'. (Hall *et al.*, 1978: 299, 303)

As is now well known, Hall and his colleagues went on to argue that policing this crisis in 1972 became synonymous with policing the blacks, and in particular the urban, male, black mugger:

> ... *race* has come to provide the objective correlative of crisis – the arena in which complex fears, tensions and anxieties, generated by the impact of the totality of the crisis as a whole on the whole society, can be most conveniently and explicitly projected, and as the euphemistic phrase runs, 'worked through'. (Hall *et al.*, 1978: 333)

In short, there was, they claimed, a major social crisis in the early 1970s which precipitated a major reconstruction of the state by the Right, and which was sublimated first and foremost on to the black communities of Britain's inner cities. There are qualifications to this position we want to make, stemming from our own view of the historical conjuncture of March/April 1973, which we will now briefly sketch.

By 1973, the so-called 100-year decline of the British economy had bitten long and hard. A relatively low rate of growth, and a deteriorating trade position, throughout the 1950s and 1960s had begun to take their toll (Crouch, 1978: 191). Britain had become one of the weakest countries in Western Europe economically (Mandel, 1975; Blockaby, 1979; Rowthorn, 1980; Gamble, 1981), and capitalists were keen to identify wage-inflation in particular as the major threat to an already vulnerable economic base. In response, the labour movement blamed 'low and inefficient capital investment' (Crouch, 1978: 211). During the early 1960s, and more or less until 1979, 'capitalist planning' became the lietmotif, institutionalized in the National Economic Development Council, involving the participation or incorporation of the trade union movement, and resulting in a series of corporate attempts at pegging wage increases. The 'one-nation' possibility and the 'end of ideology' euphoria of the 1950s had given way to constant calls for workers' sacrifice for the 'national interest': the 'social contract' strategy finally epitomized and bankrupted in James Callaghan's incomes policies of 1974–9. Combined with constant cuts in the public service sector, this development effectively ended the phase of post-war welfarist, liberal consensus.

The failure of the collaboration between the trade union leadership and the Wilson administration (1964–70) to prevent unofficial strike action by a rank-and-file growing in militancy contributed to 'wage drift' and to the election of the Conservative government of 1970–4 under Ted Heath. By

1970, unemployment had increased to 4 per cent from a post-war average of 2 per cent, price inflation was at 7 per cent compared to the 3 per cent of the early 1960s, and (by 1971) working days lost to strikes had reached 13.5 million after hovering around 2–3 million since the war. Unhampered by any so-called 'special relationship' with the unions, the Heath administration, which was elected to cut prices 'at a stroke', set out to expand 'economic growth' and to curb the unions. By 1972, unemployment had reached 1 million and industrial militancy abounded; no doubt fired by the 1971 Industrial Relations Act (which restricted the unions' ability to strike and opened unofficial strikes up to liability for damages), by the pay freeze which hit the more vulnerable public-sector workers particularly hard, and by sharp rises in the prices of consumer goods. In 1972, a record of nearly 24 million working days were lost to industrial action: 'more strike days were lost in this year than in any since 1919' (Hall *et al.*, 1978: 294)

Things came to a head in 1972[1] when the Heath administration was forced to concede to a massive pay claim by the mineworkers, after a momentous confrontation between a large miners' picket and the police at Saltley Gate which saw the police backing down (unlike 1985 when enormous police manpower and a blatant disregard for the rule of law and civil liberties enabled Thatcher to break the miners' strike). Despite his initial *laissez-faire* approach to wage negotiations (which abandoned the existing corporate mechanisms), Heath chose to adopt a statutory incomes policy, which he pursued with vigour, and an ideological onslaught on all those workers who threatened to break it, defining them as a threat to the state and as enemies of the nation. By March 1973, this policy was well underway.

The rise in industrial militancy that occurred across most sectors of the working class in the late 1960s/early 1970s had been compounded in the 1960s by several other eruptions which were reaching a crescendo by the end of the decade. The 'end of ideology' and 'embourgeoisment' theses disintegrated as cultural matrices in the face of major social dislocations (see Hall *et al.*, 1978: ch. 8, for an important analysis of this). Increasing concentration and centralization of capital, naturally accompanied by the advance of technology and the need for 'modernization', had led to a considerable restructuring of the old working class. Deskilling, the decline of the old staple industries such as cotton and shipbuilding, the shift to light industry, the increased employment in the public sector, the growth of new towns and estates, and the rise of the new shopping markets were the foundations of a powerful, although uneven, process which was radically reconstructing the old working class. Many established communities were severely fractured, producing sharper distinctions between work and home, old work and new work, new towns and old, black and white, and North and South. These changes not only heightened industrial conflict, but generated a long series of highly stylized recalcitrant responses for a youth which now sat uneasily between the old and the new (see Cohen, 1972; Clarke *et al.*, 1979; Brake, 1980). These styles in turn re-ignited a long-running debate and panic about juvenile delinquency, the permissive generation and the decline of parental authority. This pattern was sharply compounded in the late 1960s by the rise of a radical student movement, following the expansion of the universities in the earlier part of the decade; a movement concerned with many issues but most prominently Vietnam and nuclear disarmament.

The 1950s and 1960s had also seen the substantial importation of labour from the Caribbean and a dramatic increase in the employment of women; in both cases, mostly in low-paid, low-status, labour-intensive jobs. When unemployment rose as the post-war 'boom' faded, these sections of the population were the hardest hit: first the blacks and then women. These developments, combined with continued racial discrimination, ghettoization, sexism and domestic exploitation, were the basis for increasingly confident rebellion and dissent by blacks and the women's movement. Finally, of course, the resistance of Catholics in Northern Ireland to the constant attacks upon them, and the persistent denial of their civil liberties, led to Wilson sending in the troops in 1970, resulting in an escalation of urban guerrilla warfare and the resurrection of an armed struggle by the IRA.

Together, all these 'winds of change' produced an enormous wave of extra-parliamentary politics by the end of the 1960s and the beginning of the 1970s. While commentators on the Right saw a bewildering array of challenges to the Establishment, and even many on the Left perceived it as an eclectic onslaught, we are struck in retrospect with the clear roots of this eruption in the working class as well as in the new petty-bourgeoisie. We respectfully differ with Hall (1974: 270), who argues that the political 'deviants' of the late 1960s are all marginal to 'productive class relations'. This is to use too narrow a definition of working class: there are sections of the class that do not produce surplus value directly or at all and they increased in size after the war with the growth of state intervention in the economy and of unemployment. Marx's understanding of the 'working class' in *Capital*, Vol. 1 clearly includes those marginally and sporadically employed in wage labour, unemployed citizens, children of workers, the disabled and the lumpenproletariat – and, quite arguably, poorly paid state employees like nurses, clerical officers and dustmen. It is important to stress the interconnections, overlaps and political convergences between sections of the working class, and between the 'new' working class and the 'new' petty bourgeoisie of Europe in the late 1970s. Too often the Left has operated with a concept of the working class which limits it to white, male, urban workers in steady jobs (for further comments on this and its implications for theories of rights struggles, see Sumner, 1981; and see Foucault (in Gordon, 1980: 16–18 and 23) for some interesting remarks on the way penal law and judicial practice work to divide the 'proletarianized' from the 'non-proletarianized' sectors of what Marx called the working class).

Hopes had been raised by the period of welfarism after 1945, and the continuity of relative deprivation, insufficient social provisions and undemocratic forms of organization resulted in waves of militancy, insubordination, recalcitrance and rebellion from many sectors of the working class. This did involve the traditionally Labourist, unionized male, manual sectors, but now included youth, blacks, women, public sector workers, and the nationalist movements in 'the Celtic fringe'. This dissent had hardly any unity, was discretely and unevently articulated, and often appeared at the time as a miasma of quite different political forces. However, what had happened was that substantial sections of the working class had mobilized, admittedly at the same time as vociferous sections of the new petty bourgeoisie, in a variety of ways, some more politically than others, but nevertheless *in dissent*.

We agree with the authors of *Policing the Crisis* that 1970 was an historic watershed; but their view that all the contradictions began to intersect at that time seems premature (see Hall *et al.*, 1978: 260). Certainly, however, there was now a major crisis in the political ethos of the post-war period. The value of the liberal philosophy of parliamentarism was now an issue: the social-democratic consensus had failed. However, the view that

> Britain in the 1970s is a country for whose crisis there was no viable capitalist solutions left, and where, as yet, there is no political base for an alternative socialist strategy. It is a nation locked in a deadly stalemate: a state of unstoppable capitalist decline. (Hall *et al.*, 1978: 309)

is clearly mistaken. There was a political crisis, but it gave birth to a new political strategy, which was a 'viable capitalist solution', namely Thatcherism.

The Conservative Party was elected to govern in 1970 after a campaign heavily influenced by the proclaimed 'need to restore law and order':

> The state itself had become mobilised – sensitised to the emergence of the 'enemy' in any of his[2] manifold disguises; the repressive response is at the ready, quick to move in, moving formally, through the law, the police, administrative regulation, public censure, and at a developing speed. This is what we mean by a slow 'shift to control', the move towards a kind of *closure* in the apparatuses of state control and repression. The decisive mechanisms in the management of hegemonic control are regularly and routinely based in the apparatuses of constraint. (Hall *et al.*, 1978: 278)

The Tories' electoral platform contained a clear denunciation of the rising tide of extra-parliamentary militancy. In the pre-election period, references were made to 'interference with the liberty of people going about their ordinary business by demonstrating minorities' (quoted in Hall *et al.*, 1978: 274). Journalists on the right linked political demonstrations with 'vandalism and the rise of organised crime' (*Sunday Times*, 8 February 1970). Reforms to public order law were threatened:'Demo clamp-down if Tories get back' boomed one *Sunday Express* front-page headline (1 February 1970). The Lord Chancellor, Lord Hailsham, declared that organized crime and violence 'cannot be separated from private dishonesty or public demonstration in defiance of law, (*Sunday Express*, 8 February 1970). Finally, the weekend before the election, Mr Enoch Powell, with his usual rhetorical skill and sense of timing, articulated the accumulated thoughts and fears of the Tory Party, and probably some of the members of the so-called 'silent (or moral) majority' when he warned:

> . . . of the 'invisible enemy within' – students 'destroying' universities and 'terrorising' cities, 'bringing down' governments; of the power of the 'modern form' of the mob – the demonstration – in making governments 'tremble'; the success of 'disorder, deliberately formented for its own sake' in the near-destruction of civil government in Northern Ireland; and the accumulation of 'combustible material' of 'another kind' (i.e. race) in this country, 'not without deliberate intention in some quarters'. (Hall *et al.*, 1978: 275, 276)

Powell proclaimed an enemy within, threatening the destruction of the nation-state: a many-headed hydra that was everywhere yet nowhere in particular.

This was indeed a Tory rhetoric that demanded a programme of penal law and a morally aggressive state. The first target in the ensuing months after electoral victory, say Hall and his colleagues (1978: 278), was what Mr Powell called the forces of 'organised disorder and anarchist brain-washing', as the Heath administration set out to defend the One Nation against the 'dissident minorities': the increasingly economically militant trade unions, the radical student movement, Northern Ireland Catholics, squatters, the women's movement, urban black youth, the revolutionary Left, the Welsh and Scottish national liberationists, the hippies and drop-outs of permissive society, the liberal literati and their 'obscene' books and plays, and the evergreen, stylized, sometimes delinquent cultures of adolescent youth.

Thus constructed within a political ideology of 'the need to restore authority', the censure of political demonstrations in the early 1970s is a highly targeted, politically textured feature of a very specific historical conjuncture. It does not centre upon race or black youth; it has many targets. Its immediate roots in the global 'threat to parliamentary democracy' ideology, dictate that focusing the attack on one tentacle of the many-headed hydra of revolt would have been politically naïve. Consequently, we disagree with the view in *Policing the Crisis* that policing the blacks became synonymous with policing the crisis (see also Sumner, 1981a). The policing that ensued, on the streets, in the factory and in ideology, was multifaceted with no single target: 'the enemy within' was seen everywhere and began to be disciplined at all points. All conflicts became a sign of the crisis in authority: even purely economic strikes became defined in the national press as political actions. Our period of press coverage suggests no particular concentration on mugging. There are far more news stories on political demonstrations than on muggings (689 demo cuttings in 1 month of 1973 compared with Hall *et al.*'s 202 mugging cuttings in 12 months of 1972–3). Quantity, of course, is not definitive of meaning or significance, but it is one indicator or symptom.

Nor would our account of the conjuncture lead us to concur with the view that the British state was undergoing a 'massive reconstruction' (Hall *et al.*, 1978: 303). That was attempted later during the Thatcher regime. In our view, March 1973 is part of a period when the British state began to move on to a full-scale offensive against its many oppositions: against a militant pluralism of dissent which conservative ideologies saw as a threat to the whole system of parliamentary democracy. This offensive involved a shift within repression: an increased rigidity in the apparatuses and processes of power and an expansion of the technology of policing. But there was also a closure of ranks within dominant ideology: a movement in the discourse of power. We saw a gradual move away from the old imperial, 'philanthropic', patriarchal conservatism, geared to producing a consensual nationalism, towards an aggressive, strident reassertion of bourgeois fundamentalism, in classically philistine and heartless fashion geared to securing capital accumulation and the pacification of the dissident sections of the population. As the saying goes, we were 'getting down to brass tacks'.[3] The ruling class were making secure the infrastructure of the bourgeois nation-state. What some writers portray as 'the security state' (e.g. Gleizal, 1981) is really no more than the political drive to secure the essentials of capital accumulation – Free Trade, gunboats and penal law.

None of this, of course, was unopposed. A strong labour movement and a Labour Party only recently in power were soon able to mobilize powerful counterforces. So the process was uneven and gradual. March 1973 is a moment within this struggle of contradictory forces. Consequently, political demonstrations and their press coverage are a good index or expression of the issues at state: they offer an excellent view of the most dramatic movement in British politics since the Second World War. This is a period of intense conflict involving two sides: *Policing the Crisis* overstresses the moves made by the state. Wielding legal sticks does not amount to a 'massive reconstruction' of the state: that was attempted later under Thatcher's administration.

What is happening in 1973 is not simply a shift in gear within the hegemonic mechanism towards repression and away from ideology, rather it is a shift in the nature of the hegemonic ideology itself. The ideological component of the strategy of hegemony persists in the 1970s, but it changes substantially, although gradually, from the persuasion of welfarism and technocratic reason to the shrill commands of a Victorian bourgeoisie committed to monetarism and militarism. Moreover, its class targets change: the new hegemony evolves around a smaller, well-heeled class bloc and is little concerned with winning over the whole working class. Indeed, it is a hegemonic strategy that, in our view, requires the firm political subjugation and policing of all socialist and dissident elements (for further details of the strategy, see Jessop *et al.*, 1984, 1985; Hall, 1980, 1983, 1985; Gamble, 1984, 1985; Leys, 1983, 1985). Thus the Keynesian-welfarist hegemonic strategy as a whole declines. In 1973, Thatcher is only the Minister of Education and there was still some consensus to protect; but who better in 1979 to follow the philanthropic patriarch Heath than the authoritarian Iron Lady? The century-old imperial programme of English nationalism had declined to a low point and in the 1970s was gradually replaced with a revived blueprint for a more narrowly bourgeois political domination of the territory (and of our neo-colonies overseas). Such a programme gives a lesser role to the winning of national or total consent. How could it do otherwise when it implicitly specifies the resumption of class warfare? The task undertaken in the early 1970s was the revival of British capital: the infrastructure of the British nation-state. Yet, paradoxically, this is a fundamentally anti-nationalist programme, at least for all those members of the working class who lose wages, benefits, services and jobs because of the export of capital: its directive interest is the restoration of untrammelled, international capital accumulation and circulation. Nationalist programmes require a hegemonic strategy with a strong, consensual ideological component; anti-nationalist defences of sectional interest here, as in South Africa or the Philippines under Marcos, do not, they depend primarily on force. The coincident occurrence of the 1985 'riots' in British and South African cities was not much of a coincidence: the change in the character of the hegemonic strategy in Britain had by then considerably narrowed the difference between them.

For these reasons, while race was indeed a rich metaphor for the key political tensions since the war, its continuity and vigour should not blind us to its different political meanings and functions during the period. Discriminatory immigration controls in a nationalist welfare state are quite different from hysterical campaigns against young black muggers in a period of high conflict, change and redirection, and are quite different again from the militaristic suppression of urban uprisings by black, brown and white people in a period of class war. They all reflect the institutional racism of the English state of course. The censure of colour is continuous. But the new sociology of social censures should constantly attend to the shifting meaning and role of a censure, its relative position in different discourses of policing, and its relative importance in the catalogue of social censures used by the state. Police harassment of blacks was certainly part of policing the crisis of the early 1970s, but only one of several assaults on the panoply of 'dissident minorities'. *Policing the Crisis* drifts towards a theory of blacks as scapegoats for the crisis in bourgeois hegemony. However, this was not the case; instead we should attend to the fact that a whole range of groups were censured, harassed and penalized in the early 1970s.

This was a time when the system of parliamentary democracy was under heavy criticism and often ignored by oppositional groups. The political system itself was at stake, and the traditional political party of the bourgeois classes was undertaking the task of restoring the authority of the capitalist state. March 1973 is thus a moment in a period where the dominant class bloc were beginning to re-examine their historic economic and political interest in parliamentarism. Their view was perfectly expressed in a speech by the Lord Chancellor, Lord Hailsham – who better in a period of increasing use of law in crisis-management than the nation's senior law officer to articulate the dominant political ideology of March 1973? Here is an excerpt from the report in *The Times* (12 March 1973, p. 2):

LORD HAILSHAM SEES FRUSTRATION OF GOVERNMENT BY DISSIDENT MINORITIES AS A THREAT TO DEMOCRACY

Mr Harold Macmillan's famous phrase 'the wind of change' might be replaced by a 'change of wind' in the struggle between individual freedom and the power of the state or the multitude, Lord Hailsham . . . said . . .

The Conservative Party should consider events of recent months and years to decide whether the principal enemy of civilization was dictatorship or anarchy, he said . . .

Lord Hailsham recalled that after the general election he compared Britain with the Weimar Republic, with the French Third and Fourth republics and other democratic societies 'which one way or another have gone down before the blast of dictatorship'. He had warned this country to administer to itself a strong dose of self-discipline.

Democracies had not failed through giving too much power to their governments but because governments and parliaments had counted for too little. He said:

'No democracy has been defeated by a dictatorship from inside or from out because it has been itself too disciplined.

It has been destroyed in the end by force or fraud. It is not strength but weakness which kills democracy. It has been overthrown or it has been taken over. It has not been eroded or undermined: it is not decisiveness but dither which undermines the prestige and its will to resist. It is not inaction but inability to act that destroys the authority of democratic institutions. It is no use masking anarchy or indecisiveness under the bland names of liberalism or permissiveness'.

Lord Hailsham called for liberty under law, and suggested that frustration of government by 'dissident minorities' rather than excessive authority was the greater threat to democracy.

'Is there not something rather false about those who condemn exploitation of economic strength when it is committed by a speculator, or an employer, or a buyer of property, but wish to defend it when it takes place at the instance of a union or a group of militants who have the sick in hospital, or the jobs of workers in another industry, or the old and cold shivering in their apartments within their grasp some February or March in the winter of 1973?'

Lord Hailsham said he believed many Britons longed to move towards the unselfishness of patriotism, respect for law and obedience to Parliament and the courts.[4]

As he also said later on in the year:

The symptoms of our malaise may be economic, and show themselves in price rises, shortages and industrial disputes. But underlying the symptoms is a disease which has destroyed democracies in the past, and the causes of that disease are not economic. They are moral and political and constitutional, and in order to cure it we must recognise them as such. (*The Times*, 3 December 1973; quoted in Solomos *et al.*, 1982: 19)

Our contention is that the political ideology giving a distinct pattern to the press coverage of demonstrations in 1973 was one which would logically produce an attempted political, moral and constitutional transformation of the British state. This was ideological work which helped to pave the way for the emergence of the radical Right of the late 1970s and early 1980s; a radical Right that is now carrying out a concrete programme of reconstruction of the British economy and state.

The press coverage of political demonstrations in March/April 1973

> Put bluntly, the media generally strive to be impartial and objective, but *not* about the rule of law and the maintenance of democratic society ... (Alan Protheroe, then assistant director of news and current affairs programmes at the BBC, quoted in Sumner, 1982: 53)

> ... a governing class which can assure the people that a political demonstration will end in a mob riot against life and property has a good deal going for it – including popular support for 'tough measures'. Hence the 'criminalisation' of political and economic conflicts is a central aspect of the exercise of social control. (Hall *et al.*, 1978: 189, 190).

The tone for the whole month was set by Mr Barber, the then Chancellor, on the night of 6 March, in a television budget broadcast. He declared that the government would not give way to any industrial action by workers. Strikes, he said, would only make the workers and the nation poorer. He called for those who believed in 'moderation' and 'common sense' to stand up for themselves and defeat the 'small minority of militant trouble-makers' (*Daily Telegraph*, 7 March 1973, p. 10). In the month of demonstrations that followed, the national press duly censured those they identified as 'militant' (and decided to report), while giving quite positive coverage to those of the 'moderate silent majority'. We would argue that there was a sustained, double-pronged ideological movement towards the restoration of moral authority and the constitutional denunciation of dissident, extra-parliamentary politics.

Previous studies have merely illustrated the general denunciation of 'militant' demonstrations; mainly because they focused on single cases (e.g. Halloran *et al.*, 1970; Murdock, 1974), or because they did not use total samples, merely selected examples (e.g. Hall, 1974). To be fair, none of these works pretend to be systematic investigations of the portrayal of political demonstrations. Our analysis is based on a sample of *everything* published (i.e. not just stories, but also cartoons, features, etc.) on political demonstrations in the English national press from 7 March to 7 April 1973. This involved nine daily and seven Sunday newspapers, and resulted in 689 cuttings: the subject was certainly in the news that month. In this particular essay, however, we will only deal with the news stories of UK demonstrations, of which there were 110. Our intent was never just to illustrate, but was always to be receptive to the full range of the coverage.

Previous studies have also established that news is not simply descriptive (see Rock, 1973; Glasgow Media Group, 1976, 1980; Chibnall, 1977; Hall *et al.*, 1978; Murdock, 1980). What we want to emphasize here, however, is that while the economics of capitalist news production demands an overreliance on certain news values (e.g. personalities, negativities, abnormalities and conflicts), the content and form adopted by news values in specific instances are determined by the ideological understanding of the newsworthy event. It is that ideological overdetermination of the economic which concerns us here now. Violence and conflict may sell newspapers, but the news event has to be seen and captured in those terms before it can be packaged and sold. This vision is a matter of political ideology, however unconscious or routine that ideology may be to the journalists.

Perhaps the single most striking finding of our analysis is that three of the four newspapers with the highest proportion of working-class readers (*Daily Mail*, *Daily Mirror* and *Sun*) carried few news stories about demonstrations during the month. These popular papers each had half as many 'demo' stories as the *Daily Express*, *Guardian* and *The Times* (on average 8 as opposed to 16) and only about one-seventh of the *Morning Star*'s coverage (55 demo stories). Working-class readers, with no other direct experience of it, could be forgiven for thinking that little political conflict existed in the country.

From previous researches (Hall, 1974; Murdock, 1974) we expected demonstrations to be characterized as the 'demos' of an irrational militant minority, and indeed that was true in abundance. Of our sample of 110 demo stories, 55 per cent were portrayed through what we called the militancy paradigm, but this was less than we expected. These reports portrayed 'the demonstrators' as angry, politically organized crowds whose ultimate goal or effect is anarchy. It is often implied that they are only interested in confrontation, disruption and violence. Such news stories often carry headlines such as 'Blackmailed say Hospitals' (*News of the World*, 25 March) or 'Picket case demo brings Mersey docks to halt' (*Daily Telegraph*, 16 March).

But the denunciation of so-called militant dissent is not the whole story. One of our major findings is that a large minority of demo stories (31 per cent of this sub-sample) covered demonstrations quite favourably. This is something that has not emerged from previous researches, possibly because of their selective sampling, but possibly because of the differing political circumstances of our period. It clearly means that extra-parliamentary politics is not *ipso facto* censured. The censure of political demonstrations in 1973 is, like many other censures, a *selective* affair. This is a selectivity that rather betrays the universalist principles drawn upon in the censure. Let us now look more closely at the two distinct types of coverage.

The censure of militancy

While a small percentage (about 7 per cent) of our news stories were not easily classifiable and some others were weak in identifiable ideological content, the systematic reading of the news stories strongly impressed upon us the logical and frequent association of certain signifiers, amounting to a paradigm of militancy. Often we were tempted to draw more from the cuttings, but we remained cautious, on the assumption that the more subtle nuances would be revealed explicitly in the editorials, cartoons and features – and they were. The most frequent cluster of connotations was the ideological paradigm (or formation) of militancy. Its key elements were as follows:

1 Violence
2 Anger
3 Staging

1 *Violence* The press focused on the violence occurring during the demonstration and neglected the grievances motivating the protestors. This double tendency works to suggest that the violent effects were a prime but mysterious motive: thus generating the fear that arises from the possibility of random violence. So, in one story, 'WOMEN'S LIB CLASH AT UNIVERSITY' (*Daily Telegraph*, 19 March, p. 19), 'Women's Liberation supporters stormed a dinner' at a Cambridge college and 'clashed with porters'. 'They tried to sit at the High Table with the dons and scuffles broke out when half a dozen porters moved in to resist them.' No reason is given for their action and the whole cutting focuses on their disruption of the tranquillity of college life: they are the active subjects who produce violent effects. Even worse, by giving them a political label, 'Women's Liberation supporters', and not even gendering the undoubtedly male dons, the subtle impression is given of a politically motivated group disrupting an innocent dinner. The point is even clearer when one realizes that the report could have begun as follows: 'Supporters of an antiquated, male supremacist, élitist academic ritual, strangely dressed in long flowing black gowns, were joined for dinner last night by an uninvited group of young female students, but they asked the porters to throw the women out . . .' A few changes in the words and a story about feminist violence could be converted into one about strange old men in black gowns.

What follows from this theme is that the police are portrayed as being forced to turn out to restore peace and harmony to the scene. The police are thus presented as a passive force, just doing their job, often receiving painful injuries for their trouble. From a report of another feminist demonstration, we hear: 'Helmets flew. Some police officers writhed in agony . . . some policemen had scratched faces and policewomen laddered tights' (*Sunday Mirror*, 11 March, p. 2). That story was headlined 'Women's libbers get stuck in' (ibid.), and 'Fights end Women's Lib sit-in' (*Sunday Telegraph*, p. 3).

The overall effect of this theme is to suggest an image of a violent political challenge to an otherwise peaceful and always rational apolitical order.

2 *Anger*   People on militant demonstrations are frequently described as angry.[5] Thus, 'STEELWORKERS ANGRY AT ATTITUDE TO CUTS. . . . About 400 demonstrators went to Sheffield to demonstrate anger' (*The Guardian*, 8 March, p. 6), 'Glass in hand, striking hospital worker . . . angrily confronts Health Minister' (*Daily Express*, 29 March, p. 2), 'DEMO GIRLS RIP IT UP IN COURTROOM' (*Sun*, 8 March, p. 4) were classic lines. This emphasis on angry demonstration, rather than on rational self-expression, conveys a strong picture of the unreason of dissent, and the old notion of the hysterical crowd. The contagious emotion of the crowd is a disease metaphor which powerfully dehumanizes the actions of the dissidents. At a minimum, it converts difference into deviance; at its worst, deviance is transformed into irresponsible criminality.

It is worth reflecting that emotion is not the only symbol of unreason. The notion of pestilence, the plague of locusts, is activated subtly in the phrase 'protestors descended' as 'POLICE SEAL OFF TOWN' (a headline suggesting a state of quarantine: *Daily Express*, 16 March, p. 6). The notion of childishness also carries the sense of unreason: 'the fourth-form antics of a few trouble-makers' (*Daily Mirror*, 9 March, p. 15). And, as our references have already indicated, the coverage of feminist demonstrations implies a wild, cat-like fury. From our study, feminism, childishness, foreigners, emotions, animals and pests seem to be major symbols of unreason, seemingly aimed at connoting a world beyond rational action; yet revealing that the portrait of militancy in the British press is saturated with the specific culture of rational action belonging to the old imperialist patriarchy. This is the world of Peter Tinniswood's (1981: 9; 1982) comic brigadier whose disdain for 'the lady wife' and her 'vile and detestable' activities links up with the honour he found, 'in the name of freedom and natural justice to slaughter and maim men (and women) of countless creeds and races'.

3 *Staging*   Militant demonstrations are frequently described as having been staged. It seems unthinkable (on this notion, see Bourdieu, 1971) that large numbers of people can voluntarily and rationally rally on the streets to air grievances against established authorities. Such a thing, of course, clearly implies a failure in the formal process of parliamentary democracy. So the press gave much attention to the groups organizing the demonstrations: 'The National Union of Students which had ordered

the boycott...' (*Daily Telegraph*, 15 March, p. 2), and another demo against 'the lump' was said to be '... organized by the communist-dominated Building Workers Charter Group.... Moderates in the industry claim, however, that the Charter Group is using "the lump" only as a pretext to call stoppages in support of its 40 claim' (*The Times*, 29 March, p. 22).

When the unthinkable is eminently unignorable (e.g. 'TEN THOUSAND TEACHERS STOP LONDON'S TRAFFIC': (*Financial Times*, 22 March, p. 14), it seems that the strategy is to divide it up to produce a much smaller unthinkable and a new thinkable possibility. If that is not enough, then a further sub-division can be made and the unthinkable reduced even further. So, in the *Financial Times* story headlined above, the unthinkable is first reduced by the observation that this was only 10,000 out of 36,000 NUT members in Greater London and that the NUT had hoped for 20,000. What at first seemed like an awful lot of responsible people demonstrating is thus reduced to a minority. It is still a lot of teachers, though, so in later paragraphs we find that they are marked off from 'militant teachers' who 'have shown anger at union meetings'. 'This anger, however, was not reflected by yesterday's 10,000 marchers.' What was thus initially quite unthinkable turned out to be merely a group of teachers who like going for a stroll together in central London.

The staging theme, then, works to deny the spontaneity of political demonstrations, and usually to suggest the notion of militants or extremists working behind the scenes. Demonstrators are thus the dupes of political plotters with ulterior motives: plotters who never seem to be able to turn out the size of support they hope for.

There are many more things that could be said about the ideology in the news stories of 'demos'. For example, generally, MPs are seen as having the difficult job of properly representing their constituencies, and thereby 'heading off' the rise of militant, extra-parliamentary politics, so that the police have the unhappy task of dealing with their failures. This involves an interesting colour scheme. The police are seen as the thin blue line between the red peril of dissent and the black abyss of anarchy. They simply respond, it is implied, to the threat of criminal disorder and, therefore, act in a politically neutral role. Thus the militant paradigm works to depoliticize police action and to criminalize that of the demonstrators.[6] In short, the bulk of the news stories seemed to carry an approach to 'dissident minorities' strikingly correspondent to that of the Tory Government and its leading ideologues.

The approval of the uprising of moderation

The demonstrations reported favourably, in what we called the paradigm of moderation, are an interesting collection. There are 34 such demo stories: 7 were reports of a big anti-abortion march, 5 were of anti-Soviet protests, 4 concerned a protest by so-called 'strike victims' and 1 celebrated a housewives' protest against the effects of union militancy. These 17 are all clearly about pro-establishment causes; they concern the rise of the silent majority in contemporary politics. Of the rest, three were moderate accounts of student demonstrations, nine concerned industrial action and the remainder were 'human interest' protests usually involving a highly salacious element. These 12 stories approving particular student and worker demonstrations (compared with 41 that censured such protests) were contained in three newspapers: the *Guardian* (6), *Daily Mirror* (2) and *Financial Times* (4).

These figures show that we must be careful with our conclusions; apart from the obvious fact that they are small numbers. Clearly 17 to 12 means that it is not sufficient to say that there was a clear attempt to support the rising extra-parliamentary activism of the so-called 'silent, moderate majority'. It is also evident that there is a section of the British national press that does not always censure anti-establishment protests. This must lend a little support to the contention that there is some pluralism still left in the British press (see Murdock, 1980; Schlesinger *et al.*, 1983). But, 10 of these 12 demo stories are contained in quality newspapers with relatively low circulations and business-professional class readerships, and therefore this support is *very* limited and does *not* sustain the thesis that working-class readers are presented with a range of political opinion.

The paradigm of moderation involved headlines such as 'NUS claims huge response to strike call' (*Guardian*, 15 March, p. 6), 'Pin-striped muggers'. 'Abortion doctors are as bad as street thugs, rally is told' (*Daily Mail*, 26 March, p. 11) and 'Tough-line wives get gas back' (*Daily Express*, 15 March, p. 6). This paradigm, or ideological formation, does not seem to be simply a polemical inversion of the militancy paradigm. It seems to have its own self-sustaining components. The connections between the two ideological formations seem to be rooted in the logic and content of a much broader ideology and in the hegemony-constructing political practice containing that ideology.

The main themes of the paradigm of moderation were as follows:

1 *Peaceful protest* There is never any suggestion of violence from moderates. The police are untroubled, except by militant counter-demonstrators. Everyone is very good-humoured and good-natured in these reports, as if people on 'militant' demonstrations are bad-tempered and miserable. Motorists seem to be quite happy to be held up in long traffic jams if these are caused by anti-abortionists, and rarely is loss of production mentioned: 'The atmosphere was almost carnival' (*Guardian*, 28 March, p. 5) and 'the demonstration . . . was as

quiet as the old Whit walks' (*Guardian*, 26 March, p. 22). These demonstrations have silver bands, beautiful banners, funny slogans, explicit and complex symbols, pageants and sunshine. The sun suffuses the stories with a warmth lacking in the militants' sombre affairs.

2 *Spontaneous rallying* The organization of these demonstrations always seems successful. Organizers are frequently given a say: 'I think we've had a visible and vocal demonstration, but with dignity' says a hospital shop steward on one story (*Guardian*, 28 March, p. 5). 'It has been one of the biggest and best rallies ever held in this country' said 'one of the organisers' of the anti-abortion march (*Daily Telegraph*, 26 March, p. 6), and 'a fantastic success' another one said (*Daily Mirror*, 26 March, p. 5). There is little gulf between leaders and led here. What we have is a united, spontaneously expressive mass: phrases like 'a vast crowd', 'fellow feeling' and 'massive support' abound. Large quantities of people perhaps inevitably move through animal verbs, but 'flocked' (*Daily Telegraph*, 26 March, p. 6) has distinctly more gentle and religious overtones than the militant 'swarmed' and 'descended'. It is true that sheep are symbols of mindless obedience as well as of religious devotion, but there is nothing positive you can say about a plague of locusts. The sheep 'flocking' to the anti-abortion march were not presented with agitative, hysterical propaganda from angry militants; rather they were addressed by named and titled dignitaries, like MPs, and were represented at the head of the march by 'patrons', not power-crazy demagogues. This imagery is not deterred by any maniacal bigotry in the speeches of their ideological shepherds, which, incidentally, are often quoted at length in the press and often provide the headlines.

3 *Good causes* Moderate demonstrations are rational: they have a just cause. This cause is often outlined properly in the news report. In one story of the anti-abortion march, there is a marvellously evocative photograph of a section of the crowd. At the centre of the picture, surrounded by the earnest, calm, silent, thoughtful 'faces' of moderation, the subject of its loving mother's gentle gaze, a tiny child, dressed in a fluffy white jump suit, stares innocently at the goings-on, blissfully unaware of the ideological use to which it is being put in the campaign to deprive women like its mother of their basic rights (*Guardian*, 26 March, p. 22). 'Could you kill that?' screams the photograph, as the speakers rant on about abortion as psychopathic murder and about the 'carnage' in our surgeries.

A sure sign that the cause is just is that 'wives' and children are in attendance: as if 'militant' demonstrations are not family affairs.[7] A clear distinction is apparent in the press usage of 'women' as opposed to 'wives' and 'mothers'. 'Women' often appear in those stories where the demonstrators are presented as angry, violent, mindless 'Women's Libbers'; 'wives' and 'mothers' usually appear when the demonstration has a 'good' cause. Not one strong militant story contains 'wives' or 'mothers', but there are several where militant women are described as 'girls'. The logic of these representations is surely that militancy is immature, and that the mature, moderate woman is married with children and cares only about protecting her nest. The patriarchal ideology of the woman's place joins forces here with the dominant class political ideology to effect the legitimation of some demonstrations and the censure of others. A typical example here is the *Daily Mirror*'s (21 March, p. 7) story 'WIVES JOIN DOLE ROBBERY DEMO', where the essence of the tale is that 'Laid-off workers turned up at a demonstration yesterday . . . with their families. For their wives decided to join them . . . some with small children' (21 March, p. 7).

In short, the paradigm of moderation is largely employed to celebrate the extra-parliamentary activism of the silent majority, that ideologically constructed group of real individuals, of conservative persuasion, who never complain but who were beginning to get restless in the mid-1970s, after the raging torrent of militancy of the previous decade. But, occasionally, in some newspapers, it serves to legitimize some of the protests of the workers and students who Lord Hailsham wanted to stay at home.

The social censure of 'dissident minorities'

The social censure of political demonstrations studied in this essay is revealed as a complex, composite ideology with definite, quite predictable targets: striking workers, feminists and radical students. It is not an abstract principle applied equally to all. Nor is it simply a negative, disapproving expression, but a positive force affirming certain specific premises and values.

The censure, as expected, denounced most extra-parliamentary demonstrations as militant. But much more than that was involved:

1 Not all extra-parliamentary demonstrations were denounced as militant. Those demonstrations in favour of approved, pro-establishment causes were hailed as welcome rallies of the moderate voice. It is not extra-parliamentary political action as such that is censured, but that of disapproved or enemy groups.
2 Militancy and moderation were not terms used in any scientific way to describe actions. Instead, they were held constant as classifying markers to distinguish approval from disapproval. That is, they are not, in any sensible way, empirical terms; rather they are terms of moral-political judgement, belonging to a quite conservative political ideology, which are used to evaluate empirical reality. Thus militancy is always bad and to the Left, whereas moderation is always good and

to the Right. Try imagining it otherwise, it is difficult; that is, the power of ideology when deeply embedded in words.
3 The censure of militant demonstrations did not just specify and attack their pointlessness, dangerousness and damage, it also reminded workers that their job is to labour, women that their place is in the home, and all citizens that the police are an apolitical force successfully maintaining the order of reason and progress articulated in parliament. In short, the censure was positive in reaffirming desired practices and values, as well as negative in denouncing 'dissidence'.
4 It is clear from the above that the censure has no unifying rational principle which can be defended on logical grounds. It was internally contradictory. The value of parliamentarism was affirmed in one breath while, in another, the silent majority were encouraged to take to the streets. *The unifying element of the censure, therefore, is not an abstract principle but a political strategy, a practice.* From our analysis of the historical-political conjuncture of this expression of the censure, that unifying strategy would seem to be that articulated by the Lord Chancellor: the moral, political and constitutional restoration of 'democracy', or, in reality (i.e. our terms), the emergent hegemonic strategy specifying the resurrection of classical bourgeois politics and values and the regulation of the dissenting classes.

The social censure of political demonstrations in the UK of 1973 was, therefore, a highly targeted ideology. Essentially, it was the social censure of 'dissident minorities'. Its precise shape was an historically specific reflection of the configuration and balance of power in its generative field of social practice, the field of political relations. While that balance of power is no doubt causally shaped by, and shot through with, the phase of capitalist development, the needs of contemporary capital, and the state of the class struggle, none of these explain the details of the censure and its conjunctural shape. This social censure is essentially generated in conflictual political practice; its territory is the field of contemporary politics; its purposes are political; and its concepts are most definitely political. In March 1973, the censure of 'dissident minorities', targeted mainly at striking workers, feminists and radical students, was part of an attempt to restore political authority and traditional values. The balance of power in the late 1960s and early 1970s had shifted: the capitalist state was now responding to the multiform challenge to parliamentarism coming from below. The ideology of the militant demo in the news stories of 1973 frequently exudes the need for greater state repression articulated by Lord Hailsham; and the ideology of the moderate rally suggests that the dominant class bloc no longer felt compelled to play politics solely in parliament, or to enforce law through 'due process'. The emergent new hegemonic strategy consummated in

Thatcherism, gives less value to parliament and other elected bodies than prior post-war strategies.

Hailsham had argued that democracy would not be lost if the state became more dictatorial. This feeling was very fully articulated in the editorials and feature stories of the period. There are many worth quoting, but just to take one feature article by a leading conservative commentator, Peregrine Worsthorne:

> How much inconvenience, anxiety and danger will most people accept resignedly before concluding that they would be better off under an authoritarian system of government which put an end to such troubles? How many more bomb explosions in Central London, railway disruptions throughout the land, hospital breakdowns, gas stoppages, mugging epidemics, student sit-ins – to mention only the troubles that currently plague us – before society is more trouble than it is worth? (*Sunday Telegraph*, 11 March, p. 20)

The ideologues of British Conservatism were undoubtedly baying for a sharp move to the right. They did not achieve it at that time because the Heath administration was not prepared to authorize the changes in administration and policing required to smash the miners' strike of 1974.

Under Thatcherism, 'society' clearly became defined as 'more trouble than it is worth'. The new drivers of the transcontinental express train of capital accumulation uncoupled the useless, unprofitable coaches (those containing the unemployed, blacks, pensioners, youth, etc.), and shunted them into the sidings, where their occupants could rot or rebel, subject to the constant gaze of the police. Thatcher had the economic stratgegy, the political will and the electoral mandate to sideline the 'dissident minorities' for a long time to come. When they resisted in Brixton, Toxteth, Belfast, Greenham, Grunwick and Orgreave, they were brutally pacified with paramilitary police attacks, conveyor-belt court processing, and a whole range of abuses of the rule of law characteristic of authoritarian states. But the ideological work, marking out and defining 'the enemy within', had begun much earlier. The censure of the 'dissident minorities' played an important part in the ideological construction of the Thatcherite hegemonic strategy. It defined a criminal-political element in the society, and portrayed its purposes as subversive. It criminalized dissent of all kinds, declaring all critics to be enemies of the state. Throughout the 1970s and 1980s, the anger and anxieties of the hegemonic bloc were channelled against these elements. This ideological targeting, the social censure of the 'dissident minorities', was one of the conditions that created the electoral support for the divisive and oppressive Thatcherite economics of the 1980s. It has always been the case that if a ruling class can persuade its population to see all its critics as enemies or alien forces, then it can legitimate the use of the tactics of war to suppress them.

The censure of 'dissident minorities' was therefore one of the preconditions and justifications for the increasing paramilitarism of the British state in the 1970s and 1980s. It played a vital part in the emergence of the new 'principles of domination' (Leys, 1984) characterizing the contemporary period. This role was not achieved, we would suggest, through any supposed blanket effect on all press readerships, but rather through the appeal of this censure to a specific configuration of social classes and class fractions, composing and supporting the hegemonic power bloc of British society. It is beyond the scope of this essay to articulate this receptive class bloc precisely, but it certainly seemed to include sections of the traditional working class. The censure of the 'dissident minorities' articulated the fears and anxieties of these receptive classes and channelled their prejudices against the monstrous regiment of strikers, students, feminists, blacks and other 'subversive' elements. It encouraged, reinforced, incited; and, at a minimum, neutralized any conscience these classes may have had about the repression that followed.

Social censures, hegemony and Thatcherism

Stuart Hall (1974: 290), following Gramsci, once argued that dominant ideologies are 'one of the principal mechanisms which expand and amplify the dominance of certain class interests into a hegemonic formation'. This is an importation formulation which we want to develop briefly here. In our view, dominant ideologies are not best described as mechanisms, but rather as raw materials which are creatively deployed in the context of specific political conjunctures. Therefore, our general conclusion is that our study illustrates the view that most social censures become embedded within dominant ideologies, and are important features of the process whereby a dominant class bloc reconstructs its hegemony within the nation-state. In an older sociological language, the categories of deviance are not simply instruments of crime control, but play an important role in the construction and reconstruction of state power. They are not just the effects of state power but also part of its constitution; a latent and meaningful ideological sub-text behind the constitution of the state.

Containing both positive and negative elements, these social censures are 'educative' forces (in Gramsci's sense) in the historically specific, political struggles for class hegemony, and the regimes of gender, ethnicity, regional development and general domination which that hegemony entails. In this case, the censure of 'dissident minorities' publicized certain political interests, those of finance capital and the New Right, and it did this while at the same time expressing a whole world view of comprehensive dominant ideology, that of the white imperialist patriarchy whose values include tough government, free enterprise,

English chauvinism, hard masculinity and racism. Social censures are rarely simple class instruments expressing undiluted economic ideology. Class domination in Western societies is usually also the domination of white, male nationalists. Therefore, dominant class ideology does not just entail the censure of subordinate classes, but also of blacks, women, devolutionists, and all kinds of dissidents. Consequently, we should expect social censures, especially those most involved in hegemonic struggles, to condemn a wide range of dissent and to contain a wide range of prejudicial assumptions. Thus, they usually appear as composite denunciations, unified by their focus on specific targets and their hegemonic purpose in authorizing the state against alternative claimants to power.

It is not, however, just a matter of basic principle. The specific historical context in which this censure of 'dissident minorities' arose and flourished in Britain also determined its form and importance. As Jessop and his colleagues (1984) have argued, the Keynesian welfare state and the corporatism of the post-war years involved a reduction in the power of parliament, and thus in the potency of the ideology of parliamentarism. We have already mentioned the challenge to parliamentarism from below (from the dissenting classes of the late 1960s and early 1970s). Therefore, 1973 is part of a period when parliamentarism was in crisis: it had to be redefined. Lord Hailsham's speeches directly address this question, and make a plea for constitutional reform (to the right). For the white, masculine imperialists of the hegemonic class bloc, the ideology of parliamentarism is a pivotal legitimation of their domination. It is a key belief in the imperialist catechism, specifying what they think distinguishes their rule from that of fascists and barbarians. Its erosion down to a state of ambiguity, in itself, amounted to a legitimation problem of considerable proportions.

The continued extra-parliamentary action of dissenting groups in the early 1970s, highlighted in the defeat of the Heath administration at Saltley Gate in 1972, forced a re-examination of liberal parliamentarism. Therefore, we believe that the social censure of 'dissident minorities' in 1973 can be seen as part of the practical re-establishment of the political centrality of an effective parliamentarism between 1970 and the present; a parliamentarism of a much less liberal kind. The censure justifies a more repressive, more pro-active and more combative criminal justice system: to deal with the 'subversive' elements of society, and thereby to restore the state to centre-stage. Through the appeals to 'the rule of law' and 'the need for order', the censure promotes ideological and technical rearmament at the top and the criminalization of dissent from below. Criminal justice, in the process, becomes more overtly an ideological and practical force used by the directors of society to restore and restructure their hegemony. Indirectly and ironically, therefore, the extra parliamentary militancy from below became a political justification for the further disinvestment of power in Parliament, under Thatcher, and for its redeployment in more authoritarian procedures of administration and policing.

The defeat of the Heath administration in the 1974 election, precipitated by another defeat from the miners, and the ultimate failure of the following Labour administration to incorporate dissent (culminating in the famous 'winter of discontent' of 1979), saw the emergence of Thatcherism: a form of administration of a considerably more authoritarian kind. Whether one should characterize this form of domination as new, or as authoritarian statism, or as authoritarian populism, is not our concern here. Our main purpose is to show that the ideological developments of 1973 were an important precursor of what was to follow. Thatcherism has been fruitfully portrayed as a 'Two-Nations project':

> Increasingly Tory populism is taking the form of a unification of a privileged nation of 'good citizens' and 'hard workers' against a contained and subordinate nation which extends beyond the inner cities and their ethnic minorities to include much of the non-skilled working class outside the South-East. (Jessop *et al.*, 1984: 50)

Whether Thatcherism has actually mobilized people, or even attempted to in any systematic way, is a matter of some debate; however, we would otherwise agree with Jessop and his colleagues when they claim that:

> ... the twin failure of parliamentarism and corporatism to secure the institutional and social bases for a legitimate representative state helps us to understand why Thatcherism should seek to address and mobilise the people through the mass media and ideological discourse rather than through party-political organization and corporatist channels. (Jessop *et al.*, 1985: 95)

Also, we would substantially agree with the argument of Poulantzas, summarized by the same authors as follows:

> ... the rise of authoritarian statism involves a significant restructuring of the dominant ideology as well as new forms of open and/or symbolic violence ... the channels which elaborate and diffuse the dominant ideology have been restructured. The mass media have taken over from the school, university and publishing house; and, within the state system itself, the administration has assumed the legitimation functions traditionally performed by political parties. Furthermore, the mass media typically draw both their agenda and their symbolism from the administration, falling under its growing and multiform control. (Jessop *et al.*, 1985: 89)

Our main difference from this view, however, is that this 'significant restructuring of the dominant ideology' was a causal antecedent condition of the rise of the authoritarianism of the Thatcherite state, not just its concomitant. This, of course, has been the view of Stuart Hall all along. He has constantly stressed the important, active part played by ideology in the hegemonic struggles of the 1970s and 1980s. He believes that Poulantzas' position neglects:

> ... the one dimension which, above all others, has defeated the left, politically, and Marxist analysis theoretically, in every advanced capitalist democracy since the First World War: namely, the ways in which popular consent can be so constructed by a historical bloc seeking hegemony, as to harness to its support some populist discontents, neutralize the opposing forces, disaggregate the opposition and really incorporate *some* strategic elements of popular opinion into its own hegemonic project. (Hall, 1985: 117–18)

How successful Thatcher's directive class bloc has been in constructing a popular consent for its hegemony is a matter for careful consideration which is beyond our scope here; however, we are convinced that the press coverage of political demonstrations in 1973 expresses an ideology which is logically linked to, and clearly active today in, the divisive Thatcherite strategy which has done so much damage, in many people's eyes, to the economic, political and moral fabric of British society. Winning a more popular legitimacy for the struggles of the oppressed is an important counter-hegemonic task, and one that should not be impossible given the growing unpopularity of Thatcherism. But clearly we do have to move beyond the fragments ...

Social censures and criminal justice practices can in this way be seen as centrally implicated in the major political movements (or trends) in our society. They are not just instruments for defining 'deviance' and catching 'criminals', but are more incisively conceived of as important ideological resources in the practical business of hegemonic politics. The definition of deviance and the organization of crime control are, fundamentally and profoundly, political questions. Deviance, criminality and policing, in the times and societies we know, have never ever escaped their basic ideological role in the everyday, practical politics of domination by one class, gender and race over others. The professional ideology of police, social workers, judges and lawyers that suppression is necessary 'social control', a neutral, technical exercise free from politics, has never achieved the slightest shred of truth. One of the major tasks of the critical analysis of social systems must be the constant exposure of the fraudulent claims of that ideology.

Notes

1 '1972 is by any reckoning an extraordinary year: a year of sustained and open class conflict of a kind unparalleled since the end of the war ... the year in

which the working class, virtually without leadership of any strategic kind, at the high point of sheer trade-union resistance, took on, defeated and overturned the whole Heath confrontation strategy, leaving it in ruins . . .' (Hall *et al.*, 1978: 293).
2 And hers. The press censure of feminist demonstrations is severe and vituperative in our sample period, as it has been since and before (see Young, this volume).
3 The television programme of that name (*Brass Tacks*) in the late 1970s and 1980s offered us the perfect image of the new (but old) order in the character of Bradley Hardacre, the dour, mean, ruthless capitalist.
4 The *Daily Express* headline for its report on the same speech read 'REBEL THREAT HAMMERED BY HAILSHAM': the language of Star Wars as the Empire strikes back.
5 No doubt they often are too. But so they are on moderate demos also, yet that is not rendered significant in the coverage. The point is that, like all censures, the censure of militant demonstrations has a selective, variable and contingent relationship to the reality it portrays. It may capture and emphasize elements of the reality of demonstrations; but it may not. The censure is certainly not 'caused' by the reality; indeed, 'reality' is sometimes partly caused by the censure, in that it is taken as the official account, or in that censure can undoubtedly amplify 'deviant' practices.
6 A police manual of 1977 warned new recruits to watch out for people who:

> . . . although not dishonest in the ordinary sense, may, owing to extreme political views, intend to harm the community you have sworn to protect. . . . Whilst there are subtle differences between these types of extremists and thieves, it is difficult to put one's finger on material distinctions. (Quoted in Kettle, 1983: 228)

7 There is almost a presumption that militants do not have families. This became much more clear in the portrayal of the Greenham Women nearly a decade later. In 1973, it remained implicit; although there was the fundamental myth of militants' sexual deviance, well illustrated in the popular novel *Demo* (Allen, 1971).

References

Allen, R. (1971). *Demo*. London: New English Library.
Apter, D.E. (1964). Introduction. *Ideology and Discontent*. (D.E. Apter, ed.). New York: Free Press.
Blackaby, F. (ed.) (1979). *De-industrialisation*. London: Heinemann.
Brake, M. (1980). *Sociology of Youth Culture and Youth Subcultures*. London: Routledge.
Bourdieu, P. (1971). The thinkable and the unthinkable. *Times Literary Supplement*. 15 October.
Chibnall, S. (1977). *Law-and-Order News*. London: Tavistock.
Clarke, J. Critcher, C. and Johnson, R. (eds) (1979). *Working Class Culture*. London: Hutchinson.

Cohen, P. (1972). Subcultural conflict and working-class community. *Working Papers in Cultural Studies*, **2**, 5–52.

Crouch, C. (1978). The intensification of industrial conflict in the UK. In *The Resurgence of Class Conflict in Western Europe since 1968* (C. Crouch and A. Pizzorno, eds). London: Macmillan.

Fine, B. and Millar, R. (eds) (1985). *Policing the Miners' Strike*. London: Lawrence and Wishart.

Foucault, M. (1977). Nietzche, genealogy, history. In *Language, Counter-memory, Practice* (D.F. Bouchard, ed.). Ithaca: Cornell University Press.

Gamble, A. (1981). *Britain in Decline*. London: Macmillan.

Gamble, A. (1984). *The British Party System and Economic Policy 1945–83*. Oxford: Clarendon.

Gamble, A. (1985). Smashing the state: Thatcher's radical crusade. *Marxism Today*, **29**(6), 21–6.

Glasgow Media Group (1976). *Bad News*. London: Routledge.

Glasgow Media Group (1980). *More Bad News*. London: Routledge.

Gleizal, J.-J. (1981). Police, law, and security in France. *International Journal of Sociology of Law*, **9**, 361–82.

Gordon, C. (ed.) (1980). *Power/Knowledge*. New York: Pantheon.

Hall, S. (1974). Deviance, politics and the media. In *Deviance and Social Control* (P. Rock and M. McIntosh, eds). London: Tavistock.

Hall, S. (1980). Popular-Democratic versus Authoritarian Populism. In *Marxism and Democracy* (A. Hunt, ed.). London: Lawrence and Wishart.

Hall, S. (1983). The great moving right show. In *The Politics of Thatcherism* (S. Hall and M. Jacques, eds) London: Lawrence and Wishart.

Hall, S. (1985). Authoritarian populism: a reply. *New Left Review*, **151**, 115–24.

Hall, S., Critcher, C., Jefferson, T., Clarke, J. and Roberts, B. (1978). *Policing the Crisis*. London: Macmillan.

Halloran, J.D., Elliott, P. and Murdock, G. (1970). *Demonstrations and Communications*. Harmondsworth: Penguin.

Inkeles, A. (1950). *Public Opinion in Soviet Russia*. Cambridge, Mass.: Harvard University Press.

Jessop, B., Bonnet, K., Bromley, S. and Ling, T. (1984). Authoritarian populism, two nations and Thatcherism. *New Left Review*, **147**, 32–60.

Jessop, B., Bonnet, K., Bromley, S. and Ling, T. (1985). Thatcherism and the politics of hegemony: a reply to Stuart Hall. *New Left Review*, **153**, 87–101.

Kettle, M. (1983). The drift to law and order. In *The Politics of Thatcherism* (S. Hall and M. Jacques, eds). London: Lawrence and Wishart.

Lea, J. and Young, J. (1982). The riots in Britain 1981. In *Policing the Riots* (D. Cowell, T. Jones and J. Young, eds). London: Junction.

Leys, C. (1983). *Politics in Britain*. London: Heinemann.

Leys, C. (1985). Thatcherism and British manufacturing. *New Left Review*, **151**, 5–25.

Mandel, E. (1975). *Late Capitalism*. London: New Left Books.

Marx, K. (1974). *Capital*, Vol. 1. London: Lawrence and Wishart.

Murdock, G. (1974). The press coverage of militant political demonstrations. In *Deviance and Social Control* (P. Rock and M. McIntosh, eds). London: Tavistock.

Murdock, G. (1980). Misrepresenting media sociology. *Sociology*, **14**, 457–68.

Rock, P. (1973). *Deviant Behaviour*. London: Hutchinson.
Rowthorn, R. (1980). *Capitalism, Conflict and Inflation*. London: Lawrence and Wishart.
Schlesinger, P., Murdock, G. and Elliott, P. (1983). *Televising Terrorism*. London: Comedia.
Solomos, J., Findlay, B., Jones, S. and Gilroy, P. (1982). The organic crisis of British capitalism and race. In *The Empire Strikes Back* (Centre for Contemporary Cultural Studies, ed.). London: Hutchinson.
Sumner, C.S. (1979). *Reading Ideologies*. London: Academic Press.
Sumner, C.S. (1981a). Race, crime and hegemony. *Contemporary Crises*, **5**(3), 277–91.
Sumner, C.S. (1981b). The rule of law and civil rights in contemporary Marxist theory. *Kapitalistate*, **9**, 63–91.
Sumner, C.S. (1982). *Crime, Justice and the Mass Media*. Cambridge: Institute of Criminology, Cropwood Series no. 14.
Sumner, C.S. (1983). Rethinking deviance. In *Research in Law, Deviance and Social Control*, Vol. 5. (S. Spitzer, ed.). Greenwich, Conn.: JAI Press.
Tinniswood, P. (1981). *Tales from a Long Room*. London: Arrow.
Tinniswood, P. (1982). *More Tales from a Long Room*. London: Arrow.
Williams, R. (1977). *Marxism and Literature*. Oxford: Oxford University Press.

Index

age, 30, 36, 46, 169–70, 172, 174, 183
anarchism, 1, 23, 181
archetypes, 26, 37n
Australia, 152
authoritarianism, 9–10, 42, 96, 138, 174–6, 186, 189

behaviourism, 18–20

capitalism, 28, 30, 33–4, 44–6, 49, 54, 61, 107, 111–13, 118n, 157, 165, 167–76, 178, 185–91
censure, 3, 4, 6–10, 15–40, 46–50, 93, 102–5, 108–11, 115–8, 142, 156–61, 163–4, 171, 175, 177–191
China, 2
Christianity, 34, 48, 106, 166, 183
class, 2–3, 6–7, 25–7, 30–4, 36, 43, 45–7, 50–1, 53–4, 59–64, 70–7, 82–4, 86, 98–102, 105, 111–13, 118n, 145, 157, 160, 165, 167–76, 178, 184, 187–9
colonialism, 33–4, 45, 48–9, 54, 108, 152
communism, 8, 9, 93, 107, 146, 181
conflict theory, 23

Conservative Party, 7, 51–2, 64–70, 145, 163, 168–77, 186–90
content analysis, 124–6
Costa Rica, 37n
criminal justice system, 2, 4, 5, 6–9, 27–8, 34, 41–56, 59–92, 94–7, 105, 117, 123, 128, 136–8, 186, 190
criminology,
  administrative, xi, 3, 6
  Cambridge Institute, 1, 5–6, 7, 81
  feminist, 36
  general, 1–5, 7, 8–10, 19–21, 37n, 48–9, 80–1
  radical, 1, 23–4
  socialist, 1–12, 16, 25, 36, 48–9, 81
culture, 18, 26–8, 30, 42, 101, 105, 125–7, 132, 139n, 155, 160

democracy, xii, 2–4, 7, 17, 19, 29, 52, 54, 59–92, 108, 151, 159–60, 163–5, 172–7, 184–7
development, 6, 24, 29, 41, 43, 53, 111, 113
deviance, 15–41, 49–50, 180, 187, 190
discipline, 19, 35–6, 52, 151–3

discourse, 5, 8, 27, 35, 52, 61, 111, 116, 125–7, 136, 143, 150, 153–6, 158–9, 163, 166–7
dissidents, 10, 19, 26–8, 34–5, 42, 45–6, 49, 53–4, 72–3, 105–18, 143–56, 158–60, 163–93
domination, 17, 35, 45, 94, 157, 163, 187
doxa, 135–6
drama, 42, 47–9, 123–41

ecology, 37n, 54, 130
economism, 23–5, 41, 44, 54, 98–100, 165, 176
emergency powers, 4, 45, 54, 115, 117
environment, xi, 4, 36, 37n, 46, 125
epistemology, 3, 5, 15–16, 49
ethnomethodology, 35
Europe, xi, xii, 2, 16, 160, 168

fear, 28, 123, 127, 137
female deviance, 9, 143, 154–6, 159, 179–80, 191n
feminism, 1, 30–33, 36, 142, 156–60, 167, 172, 179–80, 184–5, 187, 191n
France, 38n, 175

gender, xi, 25, 27, 30–5, 36, 45, 46, 47, 51, 100, 132–5, 155–60, 165, 170–1, 179–80, 182–4, 187, 190–1
geography, 60–2, 86, 127–8
Germany, 7, 175

hegemony, 2, 9, 26–8, 38n, 45–54, 61–2, 77, 101–3, 105, 109, 111–13, 117, 163–5, 171, 174–5, 182, 185–90
historical materialism, 5, 31, 166
history, 15, 26–8, 31, 38n, 98, 100, 102, 104, 164, 166–7, 172
Hungary, 7

ideology, xi, 3–5, 10, 16, 19, 22–31, 38n, 46–9, 52–3, 61, 79, 94, 98, 100, 104, 112–3, 115, 123–4, 126–7, 136, 139n, 143, 156, 159–61, 163–7, 172–9, 182–91
imperialism, 33–4, 42, 49–54, 173–4, 180, 187–8
instrumentalism, 18, 23, 41, 95

internationalization, xi, 6, 44, 49–54, 62
Ireland, 45, 65, 170, 172, 186

jurisprudence, 36
justice, 9, 21, 36, 59, 72, 107, 114, 135, 180

labelling theory, 22–3, 25, 29, 35
Labour Party, 3, 7, 51, 66–86, 145, 171, 173, 189
language, 8, 30–1, 42, 110, 154, 159, 160, 179–85
law, 2, 4, 8, 10, 16, 23–4, 26, 30–1, 33–6, 41–54, 81, 85, 94–7, 108, 113, 125, 134–7, 142, 150–3, 160, 167, 171–3, 175–6, 185–6, 188
Liberal party, 64–73, 145, 147, 151
literary sources, 31, 50, 126–7, 134, 172
local state, 54, 59–92

madness, 9, 146–8, 155–7, 180, 183
magistrates,
    appointment of, 65–86
    association, 77–83
    general, 16–7, 47, 50, 59–92, 151
    political allegiances, 67–86
Marxism, 15–16, 23, 25, 29–30, 36, 38n, 41, 60, 97, 110, 116–17, 118n, 157, 165–6, 170, 190
masculinity, 9, 27, 28, 42, 47, 132–5, 158–9, 165, 188
media, 4, 8–10, 23, 27, 35, 42, 47–9, 50–1, 94, 110, 123–41, 143–50, 154, 157, 161n, 163, 172–89
medicalization, 155–6, 159, 180
men, 27, 42, 47, 49, 83, 132–3, 144, 155–6, 159, 179, 188
modernity, 9, 42–8, 49, 50–4, 72, 169–70
morality, 3–5, 6, 7, 10, 17, 18, 19, 23–9, 31, 34, 36, 42, 46, 49–53, 96, 128–30, 132–8, 150, 163–5, 175–7, 184–6

narrative, 8–9, 37, 96, 123, 125, 129–38
nationality/nationalism, 30–1, 42, 45, 49–54, 159, 165, 173–6, 187–9
New Zealand, 152
norm, 18–19, 116, 147, 150–9

patriarchy, 45, 52, 157–61, 173, 180, 184, 187
Philippines, 174
pluralism, 10, 22, 60–1, 136, 173, 182
policing, 19, 27, 33–5, 46, 47–8, 50, 51–5, 102, 105, 109, 129–38, 143–9, 163–4, 169–75, 179–81, 186, 188, 190, 191n
political crime, 94–7, 102–3
politics, xi–xii, 2–4, 7–9, 15–17, 21, 27, 36, 41–54, 60–86, 93–120, 124, 134, 146, 150–6, 163–5, 167–91
positivism, xii, 5, 15–16, 124, 155
power, 22–3, 24, 27, 28–9, 38n, 42, 43, 60–2, 64–5, 98, 102, 123, 150, 159
professionalism, 78–85
prostitution, 31–3
psychoanalysis, 26, 156
punishment, 28, 35, 42–3, 50, 123, 131, 135, 144, 148, 151–3, 159, 175

race, 25, 27, 30, 34–5, 36, 49–54, 83, 85, 100, 106–18, 163–5, 168, 170–5, 186–8
realism, xi, 4–5, 16, 48–9, 110
relativism, 5
Russia, 2

schools, 34, 71, 189
science, xii, 3, 16, 18–21, 26, 30, 48–9, 52, 80–2, 155–6, 166
Scotland, 172
sexuality, 9, 24, 42, 131–4, 145, 147, 154–9, 191
social policy, 3, 16, 18, 21, 26, 44, 49
social psychology, 18, 19, 26, 28, 37n, 50, 125, 131, 138n, 142
social regulation, 19, 31, 35–6, 42, 44, 50–2, 53–4
social relations, 10, 18, 23–4, 28–31, 45, 47, 98–9, 104, 150, 165–6
socialism, 2–3, 11, 36, 44, 52, 70–7, 157, 171, 174, 190

sociology,
general, 4–5, 15–16, 26, 28–9, 36, 157
of censures, 10, 15–41, 50–1, 164, 175
of deviance, 15–26, 35–7, 102, 130, 187
of language, 31
of law, xii, 2
South Africa, xii, 4, 7–8, 45, 93–120, 174
state, the, xi, 6–8, 10, 24, 27, 42, 47, 49–54, 59–63, 71, 83–6, 95–105, 108–18, 150–1, 163–5, 167–76, 185–90
structuration, 26–7, 38n
suffragettes, 142–62

Tanzania, 44, 53
targeting, 30–1, 45, 108, 116, 142, 172–3, 186–9
television, 8–9, 35, 47, 123–41
Thatcherism, 10, 19, 24, 36, 54, 163–5, 171, 174, 186–90
theory, xi, 6, 10, 15–16, 157
treason, 93, 105–18
trial, 7–8, 27, 43, 47, 50, 59–92, 93–120, 151, 161n, 164

underdeveloped societies, 6, 21, 33–4, 37n, 44, 54
USA, 15, 17, 19, 22, 37n, 124
USSR, 2

Vietnam, 170

Wales, 59, 63, 68, 80, 84, 172
wartime, 51, 54, 75–7, 153, 159–60, 173–4
welfare state/welfarism, 17–19, 47, 54, 168–76
Whigs, 64–5
women, 9, 31–3, 45, 47, 49, 50, 83, 133–4, 142–62, 167, 170–1, 179–80, 182–5, 191n

Zimbabwe, 33–4